CAMBRIDGE STUDIES IN PHILOSOPHY

Natural agency

CAMBRIDGE STUDIES IN PHILOSOPHY

General editor SYDNEY SHOEMAKER

Advisory editors J. E. J. ALTHAM, SIMON BLACKBURN,
GILBERT HARMAN, MARTIN HOLLIS, FRANK JACKSON,
JONATHAN LEAR, WILLIAM LYCAN, JOHN PERRY, BARRY STROUD

Natural agency

AN ESSAY ON THE CAUSAL
THEORY OF ACTION

John Bishop

The University of Auckland, New Zealand

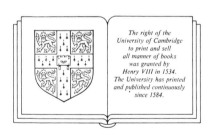

*The right of the
University of Cambridge
to print and sell
all manner of books
was granted by
Henry VIII in 1534.
The University has printed
and published continuously
since 1584.*

Cambridge University Press

Cambridge

New York   Port Chester   Melbourne   Sydney

Published by the Press Syndicate of the University of Cambridge
The Pitt Building, Trumpington Street, Cambridge CB2 1RP
40 West 20th Street, New York, NY 10011, USA
10 Stamford Road, Oakleigh, Melbourne 3166, Australia

First published 1989

Printed in Canada

Library of Congress Cataloging-in-Publication Data
Bishop, John (John Christopher)
Natural agency: an essay on the causal theory of action / John Bishop.
p.   cm. – (Cambridge studies in philosophy)
Includes bibliographies.
ISBN 0-521-37430-8 (hard covers)
1. Act (Philosophy)   2. Causation.   3. Agent (Philosophy)
I. Title.   II. Series.
B105.A35B54   1990
128' .4–dc20   89-33231
                              CIP

British Library Cataloguing in Publication Data
Bishop, John
Natural agency: an essay on the causal theory of
action. – (Cambridge studies in philosophy)
1. Man. Actions. Causes – Philosophical perspectives
I. Title
128' .4
ISBN 0-521-37430-8 hard covers

Contents

Acknowledgments

In parts of Chapters 4 and 5 of this book, I have recast (and, occasionally, directly reused) material previously published in my articles, "Is Agent-Causality a Conceptual Primitive?" *Synthèse,* 67 (1986): 225–47; and "Sensitive and Insensitive Responses to Deviant Action," *Australasian Journal of Philosophy,* 65 (1987): 452–69. The copyright over the first of these articles is held by D. Reidel Publishing Company: I am grateful to Kluwer Academic Publishers, Dordrecht, Holland, for permission to reuse material from this article. For permission to reprint material from the second article, I am grateful to the copyright holders, the Australasian Association of Philosophy.

My work on this book was assisted by a period of study leave granted by the Council of the University of Auckland, and spent partly in the Department of Philosophy at the University of Calgary and partly at Darwin College, Cambridge. I thank the Council for granting me leave and my kind hosts at both Calgary and Cambridge for helping me to make productive use of it. I am grateful to Alastair Anderson for his assistance in compiling the index.

Auckland   John Bishop
October, 1989

Introduction

Human persons are natural organisms. They are also morally responsible agents. They have, within limits, power to change themselves and their surroundings, and they may sometimes rightly be held responsible for the way they exercise this power. Some parts of nature (human beings) are thus literally the authors of, and responsible for, the state of other parts of nature (human deeds and artifacts). This, surely, is a fact – yet it has an air of paradox, and there is a major philosophical problem about understanding how it can be a fact. The idea of a responsible agent, with the "originative" ability to initiate events in the natural world, does not sit easily with the idea of a natural organism, whose behavior conforms to biological and physical laws under the conditions set by its natural environment and constitution. Our scientific understanding of human behavior seems to be in tension with a presupposition of the ethical stance we adopt toward it: How can something ever be genuinely responsible for what it does, when "what it does" is only an episode in impersonal natural history?

The point of metaphysical tension between natural scientific and ethical perspectives on human behavior has often been identified as the problem of an apparent incompatibility between freedom (or "free will") and determinism. Responsible behavior must be freely chosen and performed – yet how can it be so if it is causally "determined" by antecedent conditions in accordance with natural laws? I believe, however, that this standard identification is a mistake. As I shall seek to establish in Chapter 1, the perennial and exhausting debate about whether free will is or is not compatible with determinism does have, at its core, an entirely serious basis for doubting whether our ethical self-image coheres with a naturalistic view of ourselves. But as I shall claim, this serious basis for skepticism *has nothing essentially to do either with freedom or with determinism*.

1

Rather, it has to do with the possibility of accommodating *actions* within the natural universe. Persons can be morally responsible only for what occurs through their actions, where an action is here understood (in a semitechnical sense) as an exercise by the agent of his or her powers of control over what occurs. Actions thus seem to involve something foreign to the ontology of natural science: "agent-causation" – the determination of what happens *by agents* rather than by antecedent events. Thus, the nub of the skeptical problem is that a necessary condition for moral responsibility – the existence of actions understood as episodes of agent-control – appears not to be satisfiable within the causal order as natural science understands it.

This "problem of natural agency," as I shall call it, would be resolved if it could be shown that the existence of actions (as our ethical perspective understands them) does not, after all, entail the existence of episodes of a special kind of agent-causation. There is a philosophical theory of action (or more properly, a family of theories) that has precisely this consequence. According to the *Causal Theory of Action,* actions consist in behavior that is caused by appropriate mental states – mental states that make it reasonable for the agent to perform behavior of just that kind. What we think of as *agents* doing things, it is suggested, is actually a matter of *certain of their mental states* causing those things to occur. Thus, for example, the theory would maintain that my raising my arm consists in my arm going up as a causal consequence of, say, my intention to raise my arm. On this theory, agent-causation is (in a certain sense) reducible to "ordinary" causation by mental events, and so it fits unproblematically into the ontology of scientific naturalism – provided, of course, that mental events may themselves be understood as consisting in natural, physical occurrences (presumably, of a neurophysiological kind).

The validity of this reduction, however, is far from obvious. In fact, our initial intuitions are strongly to the contrary: Being caused to behave by one's mental states seems quite different from – and indeed, exclusive of – the kind of action that functions as a necessary condition for moral responsibility. My central project in this essay is to consider whether, despite this initial intuition, a version of the Causal Theory of Action may nevertheless be defended as resolving the problem of natural agency. Is it possible to show that scientific naturalism presents no obstacle to the existence of actions by establishing that action consists in behavior with appropriate causes of a kind unproblematically admissible within our natural scientific worldview?

My conclusion will be that it is: There *is* a correct version of the Causal Theory of Action, and the problem of natural agency is thereby solved. The main body of this essay is therefore devoted to developing a causal analysis of action that will survive the various challenges that can be raised against it. I shall seek to blunt, and gradually to erode, the initial intuition that sharply contrasts mentally caused behavior with the kind of genuine action for which the agent might properly be held responsible. In doing so, I shall not, of course, be starting from scratch. Contemporary interest in the Causal Theory of Action stems mainly from Donald Davidson's defense of reasons as causes of actions in his famous paper, "Actions, Reasons and Causes,"[1] and I shall take as my point of departure a causal analysis of a kind this paper suggests.

My procedure will be to seek successive refinements of this analysis in order, step by step, to overcome the obstacles that the Causal Theory faces. I largely follow Davidson in my view of what these obstacles are: First, there is the challenge posed by the possibility of "weak-willed" *(akratic)* intentional actions (which I discuss in Chapter 3); and second, there is the more serious problem of *causal deviance* (which I treat in Chapters 4 and 5). In a word, the problem is to specify the right kind of way in which the agent's reasons have to cause the appropriate behavior if he or she is to perform a genuine intentional action. Davidson's own responses to these problems are, of course, of great interest. I shall, in effect, endorse his way of coping with akrasia, although I want to present it in a new way, which draws proper attention to the need to accept intentions as a sui generis class of mental states that can serve as the constitutive causes of action. By way of contrast, I shall repudiate Davidson's pessimism in the face of the problem of causal deviance: I shall maintain that unless a deviance-excluding causal analysis of action can be produced, there can be no hope of using the Causal Theory to rebut skepticism about natural agency. By critically examining the work of other philosophers sympathetic to the Causal Theory (especially David Lewis and Christopher Peacocke), I seek to develop a causal analysis of action that is immune to deviant counterexamples, and so to support the core ontological claim of the Causal Theory: Actions consist in behavior with suitable mental causes.

Let me now make some more general remarks about the nature, structure, and motivation of my project. First, to avoid a serious (if unlikely) misunderstanding, I should stress that this essay is not a contribution to *empirical* theories of natural agency. The reader will not find in these pages explanatory hypotheses about how it is that natural organisms put their decisions and intentions into action, nor suggestions about how machines might be constructed to do the same. Such empirical theories belong to neurophysiology, cybernetics, robotics, and cognitive science generally. This essay is, rather, a philosophical prolegomenon to the whole enterprise of developing natural scientific theories of action. It has point only because there are serious grounds for skepticism about the very possibility of a natural organism that is also a genuine agent. If these skeptical arguments are correct, agency will simply fail to be a proper object of natural scientific inquiry. Dealing with these skeptical arguments thus presents a characteristically philosophical task, and it is this task to which my essay contributes.

Although it would be foolish to treat science as irrelevant to philosophical theorizing, the fact remains that there are distinctively philosophical questions. Many of these (perhaps all?) are generated by skeptical reflection on commonsense beliefs and the presuppositions of scientific inquiry – reflection that usually has a relatively a priori character. To put it in concrete terms for the present case, doubts about the existence of genuine agency are doubts about whether actions could exist in the natural causal order as science understands it, not doubts about whether there are any natural actions *as a matter of fact*. Skepticism here rests on the claim that there is something in the nature of action, as we understand it, that logically precludes its realization in the natural universe – also as we understand it. We may expect to deal with such skepticism, then, only by undertaking an inquiry into our understanding both of agency and of nature. And this inquiry is essentially a *conceptual* one. It will not be settled by facts about actions in the world – for of course, any such facts will be contested by the skeptic, who doubts whether there can be such facts. If there are facts relevant to settling it, they are not, strictly, facts about actions but rather facts about *what we take action to involve,* given the way we employ the concept within our ethical perspective on human behavior.

4

Yet the inquiry cannot be a purely factual one, even granted that the facts sought would have to be facts about our own understanding of action. Although the aim is, of course, to articulate an understanding that already exists among those who use the concept of action (and in the light of that articulation, to judge the force of the skeptical arguments), it is possible that philosophical inquiry will yield some proposals for a refined theoretical understanding of what agency is, and thus serve partly to *create* the facts about how agency is understood. Our unarticulated commonsense notion of the kind of agency necessary for moral responsibility may well be vague or confused. On examination, skepticism about natural agency might be at least partly traceable to such vaguenesses or confusions – and some conceptual revision may be required to deal with it. Where this proves so, I shall maintain that the intuitions about agency that need revision are neither central nor uncontested.

Second, to remark on the way I have structured my inquiry – on how I understand the burden of proof to fall and why I think a positive defense of the possibility of natural agency is required. My initial stance is *reconciliatory naturalism:* I start by assuming that the presuppositions of our ethical and natural scientific perspectives are, in fact, mutually consistent. It is tempting to hail this assumption as straightforward common sense. But I suspect that it actually rests finally on a value judgment: that, somehow, it is *better* for reconciliatory naturalism to be true than for it to turn out either that our belief in agency is mistaken or that, as agents, we belong mysteriously beyond the natural universe that is open to scientific inquiry. (In my own case the roots of this value judgment, I realize with a shock of surprise, lie in attitudes best described as religious.) The skeptical arguments, of course, challenge this stance. To maintain rational belief in reconciliatory naturalism, a reply will be needed to each argument that suggests that systems subject to the laws of nature cannot be originative, morally responsible agents. Each skeptical argument, as it comes up, places the onus on the reconciliatory naturalist – the believer in natural agency – to defend that stance.

None of the skeptical arguments, I believe, is decisive. Nevertheless, some of them have considerable plausibility. They call up antinaturalist intuitions about agency, which, I shall claim, can be dismissed only in the light of a *positive* case for natural agency – a theory of agency that decisively shows that actions have a place in our natural ontology and, therefore, that skepticism about natural agency must be misplaced. I believe that it is the Causal Theory of Action that offers the best prospects for a positive case of this kind, and in Chapter 2, I seek to establish its superiority over alternative approaches. I reject any attempt (such as made recently by Daniel Dennett[2]) to reconcile the ethical with the natural perspective "on the cheap" by adopting an antirealist account of action. And I am also suspicious of libertarians, such as Peter van Inwagen,[3] who hold that the reconciliation can be achieved – but only because the natural universe is not a deterministic system. I shall argue that a successful Causal Theory of Action will be enough to vindicate the natural possibility of action, whether the universe is deterministic or not.

Finally, a comment on my motives: Recent philosophical literature is rich in discussions of agency, and in particular, of the merits or otherwise of the Causal Theory of Action. There is some virtue, I believe, in attempting a unified critical account of the current state of these discussions. To a degree, my motivation in this essay is to make a modest attempt along these lines (especially with respect to the state of the art on the causal deviance problem[4]). But more important, I wish to situate some of the increasingly abstruse topics beloved of "action theorists" in a context that reveals their full significance.

Many philosophers proceed as if the topic of agency were somehow sui generis – an intrinsically given item on the philosophical agenda. Adequate explanations of what is really philosophically problematic about agency are surprisingly rare. In this essay, I seek to provide such an explanation by relating theories of agency to the problem of freedom and determinism. As I have said, it is my view that this problem is, at root, a problem about the very possibility of agency in the natural causal order – a problem that can be solved by successfully defending the Causal Theory of Action. Although recent debate on freedom and determinism has been extensive and vigorous, the significance for it of the correctness or otherwise of the Causal Theory of Action has not been properly emphasized. I aim to repair that omission. I hope to show that what keeps the old freedom and determinism debate alive (in the face, especially, of scientific rejection of the deterministic hypothesis) is its relation to the problem of natural agency – and *that* is the context which gives philosophical discussion of agency (and especially of the Causal Theory) its central point.

Davidson, whose work on the Causal Theory of Action has been the greatest single philosophical influence on this essay, has explicitly recognized the significance of the Theory for the problem of natural agency. He claims that the Causal Theory "is enough . . . to explain the possibility of autonomous action in a world of causality."[5] Yet Davidson does little to explain why this should be so and shows no patience for debating with incompatibilists (who hold free action to be impossible under determinism).[6] Furthermore, he finds himself, because of the causal deviance problem, unable to provide a causal analysis of action that would positively prove the truth of a Causal Theory capable of playing this vital philosophical role. I hope to repair these unfortunate gaps in Davidson's position. I want to establish that a Causal Theory of Action is just what we need to defend the possibility of natural agency (though, as I shall mention shortly, autonomy may be another matter). And I want to show that a Davidson-inspired causal analysis can, despite its inspirer's pessimism, be brought to proper completion. It should thus be clear that the detailed consideration I shall give to the problem of causal deviance is no isolated academic game. As I see it, dealing with causal deviance is actually at the cutting edge of the attempt to rebut a historically and currently influential source of skepticism about the place of persons in nature.

That said, however, I should make it clear that I do not profess to be dealing here with the whole philosophical problem of how it is that persons can exist in the natural world as conceived by science. My concern focuses on one aspect of personal existence: the fact that persons are agents, in the sense that they exercise their own control over outcomes. I acknowledge that skepticism about making intelligible the place of the person in nature might be based on other features of personhood besides this one. There seem to be, in fact, two other aspects of personhood that might present difficulty for the naturalist – one, so to speak, on either side of the problem of natural agency.

There is a problem prior to the problem of natural agency – namely, the problem of how conscious minds can be part of the natural order. Surely we may understand how agency is naturally possible only if we first understand how *mentality* may be part of nature? That this is so is entirely clear if a Causal Theory of Action is to provide the solution to the problem of natural agency because this theory holds that action consists in behavior caused by relevant *mental* states. And there is a problem posterior to the problem of natural agency – namely, the problem of explaining how *those extra properties beyond agency as such* that are required for personal moral responsibility can themselves be realized within a natural scientific ontology. Although capacity for agency is (as I have been stressing) a necessary condition for moral responsibility, it is only a necessary and not also a sufficient condition for it since there can be beings who can exercise their control in action, yet who cannot appropriately be held morally responsible for the way they do so. Young children and some nonhuman animals provide cases in point.

So there could in theory be three grades of skepticism about the possibility of making intelligible the place of persons in nature as science understands it. First, there is skepticism about understanding how minds (or, better, beings capable of mental states and functions) can be part of nature. This, of course, is the mind/body problem. Second, there is the skepticism that accepts the natural possibility of minds, but doubts the possibility of a coherent naturalist account of agency, understood as the capacity to exercise one's own control over outcomes. This is the problem of natural agency. Third, and finally, someone who has solutions to both the mind/body problem and to the problem of natural agency might still persist in doubt because he or she believes that those extra properties required for an agent to be a *moral* agent cannot be understood as realizable within our natural ontology. Without wishing to be precise about what these extra properties are, I shall simply dub this the problem of natural moral autonomy. Thus, to vindicate reconciliatory naturalism completely – to show that our ethical perspective coheres with scientific naturalism – one would need to rebut skepticism at each of these points.

In this essay, I do not attempt a complete vindication of reconciliatory naturalism. I seek to deal only with the second of the three skeptical problems just outlined. I simply assume that the first problem can be solved – that a naturalist account can be provided of mental states and how they can function as causes. Under that assumption, I then consider whether the existence of agency poses any further problem for a naturalistic viewpoint. As to the third problem, the problem of natural moral autonomy, my view is that it is far less serious than the other two. Those who have doubted whether moral agency can be realized in the natural order have, I believe, been puzzled essentially about how nature as science understands it could accommodate systems with a genuinely originative power of control, giving them the capacity to act for reasons of their own in shaping the course of natural events. And this, of course, is just the problem of natural agency. Once you grant the natural possibility of agency, I believe that all you then need for full moral autonomy are certain extra mental capacities whose natural possibility does not present any new category of metaphysical problem. I believe, then, that resolving skepticism about natural agency does remove the metaphysical doubts we have about whether we really can see ourselves the way we want to – as morally responsible persons who belong, entire and complete, to the order of nature as our science understands it. As I shall explain in Chapter 6, however, this position is not equivalent to a full naturalist justification of the rationality of our ethical practice in assigning responsibility.

NOTES

1 Reprinted (in revised form) in Donald Davidson, *Essays on Actions and Events* (Oxford, England: Clarendon Press, 1980).
2 Daniel Dennett, *Elbow Room: The Varieties of Free Will Worth Wanting* (Oxford, England: Clarendon Press, 1984).
3 Peter van Inwagen, *An Essay on Free Will* (Oxford, England: Clarendon Press, 1983).
4 I hope to draw together (and at certain points, correct) some of the arguments I have already published on agent-causation and the problem of causal deviance for a causal analysis of action. See my "Agent-Causation," *Mind,* **92** (1983), 61–79; 'Is Agent-Causality a Conceptual Primitive?" *Synthèse,* **67** (1986), 225–47; and "Sensitive and Insensitive Responses to Deviant Action," *Australasian Journal of Philosophy,* **65** (1987), 452–69.
5 Davidson, *Essays on Actions and Events,* p. 88.
6 See ibid., p. 63.

1

The problem of natural agency

I. A THEORY IN SEARCH OF ITS PROBLEM

This essay is an inquiry into a philosophical theory of agency that claims that actions are events with a special type of causal history. To put it briefly, according to this Causal Theory of Action, to act is to be caused to behave by mental states of one's own – mental states that make the behavior reasonable in the circumstances. But what is the point of such a theory, and why is it worthwhile to conduct an inquiry into its truth? These are the questions I shall address in this chapter. As with all philosophical theories, the point of the Causal Theory of Action may be understood only in relation to the philosophical problem it professes to solve. What, then, is the problem that the Theory claims to resolve, and why is it philosophically important? Starting from my dissatisfaction with a standard answer to this question, I shall argue that the Causal Theory of Action offers an answer to one of the major perennial metaphysical problems – the problem of "freedom and determinism." The quotation marks are used advisedly because, as I shall argue, the problem essentially concerns neither freedom nor determinism, but is rather about making intelligible the possibility of agency within the natural order. And this problem is one that must be solved by anyone who seeks to defend a fundamentally naturalistic account of human personhood. Thus, this chapter will present the case for taking the Causal Theory of Action seriously on the grounds that if it is true, it resolves what I shall call the problem of natural agency, and thus advances the naturalistic program for understanding the place of human persons in the universe.

The Standard Answer: Accounting for the Action/Behavior Distinction

The standard answer to the question of the importance of the Causal Theory of Action begins by claiming the need for a philosophical theory of action to account for the distinction we draw, in our ordinary usage, between actions and other forms of behavior. What is the basis of this distinction? Why, for example, does my shouting (usually) count as an action, in contrast, say, with my sneezing or my breathing? Furthermore – and more intriguingly – the very same type of behavior may sometimes count as action and sometimes not. When my arm goes up, it may be that I am raising it. Alternatively, it may be that *I* am doing nothing at all: Perhaps my limb is paralyzed and someone else is lifting it up. Something about the context, then, must make the difference between action and mere behavior in a case like this, and we need to explain what. Wittgenstein's question has become an action theorist's cliché: "What is left over if I subtract the fact that my arm goes up from the fact that I raise my arm?"[1] To answer these questions, so the story goes, we need a philosophical theory that tells us *what it is* for behavior to count as action. And the Causal Theory is just such a theory – *that* is why it is important. According to the Causal Theory, subtracting my arm's movement from the fact that I raise it will leave a residue of rational mental causes. In other words, my arm's going up counts as my raising it if, and only if, its elevation is a causal consequence of mental states that make it reasonable for me to raise my arm – for example, my intention to vote for the motion and my belief that raising my arm was the way to signal my vote.

Given the question, the Causal Theory has the makings of a sensible answer – a promising initial hypothesis, at least. But why are we "given" the question? Is it enough to hold that the question of what an action is "just simply arises" once we reflect on our ordinary usage? I think not – and that is the source of my dissatisfaction with the usual way of setting the context for the Causal Theory of Action, or indeed, for any philosophical theory of action. For one thing, the fact that common sense draws a distinction does not automatically warrant the need for a philosophical theory of its basis: To provide motivation for such a theory we need to find a source of genuine philosophical puzzlement in the wider context in which the distinction functions. Moreover, the distinction between the actions and the mere behavior of humans and other animals is hardly a "commonsense" distinction at all. In fact, the term *action,* as applied to persons, animals (and perhaps, some machines), is, along with the related terms *agent* and *agency,* something of a philosopher's technical term. People do not, ordinarily, use these terms much – and hardly ever in the intended sense. One might talk of the wind's action in eroding soil or of the fast action of a new pain-killing drug, but obviously no reference is here intended to personal or animal agency in the philosopher's sense. Closer to the mark, people do speak of "*taking* action" or of "a time for determined action" and so on – but ordinary discussion of what the philosopher calls *action* rarely makes use of the term. Rather, people speak of *doing* things, *letting things happen, meaning* or *not meaning* to do things, and so on.

So although it is perfectly true that the Causal Theory of Action matters because it offers an account of what distinguishes action from mere behavior, this by itself gives insufficient motivation for the Theory. To provide adequate motivation, we need to set the semitechnical notion of an action in its context and to explain what is philosophically puzzling about our use of it.

Locating Agency in Context: Our Ethical Perspective

There is no great difficulty in locating the context in which the philosopher's concept of agency has its central use. It is the role it plays in our moral point of view that gives the distinction between an action and mere behavior its main significance. Briefly, that role may be explained as follows: Our ethical perspective on the world has at its core the practice of making moral evaluations. We make moral evaluations of many types of things (situations, persons, institutions, properties of persons or institutions, etc.). But primarily, moral evaluations are made of events or states of affairs – let us call them *outcomes* – for which agents are morally responsible. Outcomes are not open to moral assessment unless there is someone who is morally responsible for them. And moral judgments of agents are appropriate only if made in relation to outcomes for which those agents are morally responsible. Assignments of moral responsibility, in turn, are justifiable only if certain factual conditions are satisfied, and it is here that the concept of an action (as opposed to mere behavior) plays its role. We hold an agent morally responsible for a given outcome only if it came about or persisted *through that person's own action*. Thus, even if an agent's *behavior* contributed to a certain outcome, the agent would not be morally responsible for it unless the behavior involved the agent's own action.

Let me note that the claims I have just made hold true only if we understand *action* in a broad sense to include what might strictly be better described as *inaction*. Agents may, of course, sometimes be morally responsible for an outcome by failing to act to prevent it. So, for example, if I sit and do nothing while the kettle boils dry, I may still be morally responsible for the damage – but only if my behavior is genuinely my own (in)action rather than a result of paralysis or being in a cataleptic trance or the like. To put it somewhat paradoxically: Not doing something may be something I do, rather than something that merely befalls me. There are, then, two distinctions that cut across one another: The first we might describe as the distinction between active and passive behavior (between making movements and staying still – in the relevant respects); and the second is the distinction between behavior that is genuinely my own – and through which my moral responsibility can, *ceteris paribus,* be transmitted – and mere behavior that just happens to me and that blocks my responsibility. I shall follow a widespread – but of course, technical – usage by taking the contrast between an agent's action and his or her mere behavior to amount to the second of these distinctions. In this sense, then, even an agent who remains stock still may yet be "performing an action," and a welter of activity may amount to the "action" of failing to do something else.

So if our ethical perspective really does apply to the world, there are some outcomes for which agents are morally responsible. And if agents are morally responsible for some of what happens (or fails to happen), then actions must be a feature of the world. The real application of our ethical perspective, then, has as a necessary condition the existence of actions.[2] Their existence is, however, *only* a necessary condition. It is not also sufficient. There could be a world containing actions in which no agent was ever morally responsible for any outcome, and to which, therefore, our full ethical perspective would fail to apply. The possibility of agency without moral responsibility is illustrated both by young children and by some nonhuman animals.[3] Neither young children nor animals can be morally responsible for any outcome, yet some of their behavior surely counts as action rather than as mere behavior. If this is correct, then our ethical perspective is not the sole context in which the notion of action plays a role. There is what might be called a subethical perspective, which employs the concept of action without that of *moral* responsibility – although the idea of an agent's being responsible *(tout court)* for an outcome might still be retained. There are interesting questions here: What conditions must an agent satisfy to be capable of moral responsibility? What is needed for a being to count as an agent *at all,* rather than just as a mere behaver? I suspect that beings count as agents only if they are capable of certain kinds of interaction with us – linguistic interaction if they are to be moral agents, and less complex forms of interaction (involving the capacity for learned response, for example) for agents *tout court.* But I shall not pursue these questions, as my immediate aim is only to provide a context that indicates the, admittedly somewhat technical, notion of action of which the Causal Theory offers an account. The notion of action with which we are concerned is the sort of action whose performance must contribute to an outcome if the agent is to be morally responsible for it. Of course, there is more to be said about this concept of agency – and some of it will emerge as we start to consider why there should be anything philosophically problematic about agency of this kind.

What Is Philosophically Puzzling About Agency?
The Natural Perspective on Action

The next stage in providing motivation for the Causal Theory is to explain why there is a philosophical puzzle about the sort of action required for moral responsibility and how the Causal Theory (if successful) would resolve it. It is not sufficient just to observe that there is a need to analyze what it is that distinguishes actions from mere behavior. This observation may suggest that all we have here is an academic puzzle, of interest only to those whose hobby it is to analyze conceptual distinctions. Such an impression is, I believe, quite misleading. In fact, the philosophical problem that a successful Causal Theory of Action would resolve is among the most profound of all philosophical problems – namely, the problem of

14

understanding how it can be that a complex natural organism can also be the bearer of moral responsibility. The problem that gives the Causal Theory of Action its significance is that of explaining how morally responsible agents can be part of the natural order as our natural scientific worldview conceives of it. My task in the remainder of this chapter is to examine various ways in which this problem has been expressed, and to argue that the difficulty focuses on the notion of an action that we have just identified in terms of its role within our ethical perspective. I shall then, finally, briefly explain how the difficulty about action *(the problem of natural agency)* would be resolved by a successful Causal Theory of Action.

If our ethical perspective applies to the world – if, that is, the world is one in which people are sometimes morally responsible – it contains some items that count as an agent's actions. Such actions, however, are (or at least, necessarily involve) physical events or states of affairs – concerning, in the simplest cases, the movement of human bodies. These physical states and events, of course, are open to explanation by one or more of the natural sciences and are, therefore, intelligible from within the theoretical perspective of those sciences. People are natural organisms, and so the "natural" perspective applies to all their behavior, including their morally responsible actions.

Thus, for our ethical perspective to apply to the world, actions must have a place in the natural order of things. But there is a philosophical puzzle about how this can be so. Typically, philosophical puzzles arise from skepticism – from coming to take doubt seriously, at least from a theoretical point of view. This one is no exception. Doubts can be raised about whether it is possible for items that belong clearly to our natural ontology (the world as natural science conceives it) also to constitute the actions of a morally responsible agent. We seem committed to two perspectives on human behavior – the ethical and the natural – yet the two can be put in tension with one another, so seriously in tension, in fact, as to convince some philosophers either that the acting person is not part of the natural order open to scientific inquiry or that morally responsible natural agency is an illusion. The task, then, is to examine doubts about the place of agency in nature to determine whether or not there is any real inconsistency in coapplying the ethical and the natural perspectives on behavior –

15

and if there is, to decide which perspective must give way before the other.

Why, then, has the possibility of natural agency been doubted? Certainly, the notion of action at its most general contains nothing inimical to the natural scientific view of the world. We can speak, for example, of the corrosive action of acid on a metal, or the action of the heart in pumping blood, without any hint of a problem about explaining these actions as straightforward natural phenomena. That something "does" things (as well as have things happen to it) does not, as such, create any difficulty for a naturalistic understanding of it. But of course, as we have been at some pains to show, it is not this highly general notion of action with which we are concerned. What is supposed to create difficulty is something special about the notion of action *as it features as a necessary condition for moral responsibility*. And this difficulty has generally been expressed by arguing that the kind of action required as a necessary condition for moral responsibility is *free* action, and that it is this *freedom* of action whose place in the natural order gives rise to doubt.

Skepticism About Natural Agency: A First Statement

Skepticism about natural agency is traditionally expressed by questioning whether events in the natural order (assumed to be "in the grip of" the determinism of natural causal laws) can attain to the "freedom" required for them to constitute the sort of actions necessary for moral responsibility. As a first statement, the skeptical case for taking the ethical and natural perspectives on behavior to be incompatible with one another may be put as follows:

1.   If the ethical perspective (with its notion of moral responsibility) applies to the world, then there are some events that constitute the freely performed action of an agent.
2.   If the natural perspective applies to the world, then all events are causally determined.

But,

3.   No event can both constitute the freely performed action of an agent and also be causally determined.

16

If each of these premises is true, it follows that our ethical and naturalistic perspectives cannot both apply to the world.

The skeptical case, so understood, turns on establishing the truth of each of these premises, of which the most contentious appears to be premise 3, the traditional *thesis of incompatibilism.* This thesis may be argued for as follows: If an event is causally determined, it could not but have happened given the past and the laws of nature. However, if an event is a free action, the agent could have done otherwise and so could have avoided its occurrence. Therefore, if an event were both a free action and causally determined, it would have to be true of it both that the agent could have avoided it and that, given the past and the laws of nature, it could not but have happened. But this is evidently impossible; hence no event can be both a free action and causally determined.[4]

This kind of argument for incompatibilism is persuasive but problematic. (Does it, for example, rest on a fallacious inference from the necessitation of an event by its causal antecedents to the necessity of its occurrence beyond any agent's control?) It is important to recognize, however, that even if a fully worked argument along these lines does survive objections, its success would not immediately establish the skeptical result that the ethical and the natural perspectives cannot both apply to the world. For, this conclusion follows only if we accept the truth of premises 1 and 2 – and, furthermore, only if we accept their truth *on the interpretations relevant to* the given argument for incompatibilism. (Incompatibilists who affirm the existence of actions – commonly known as libertarians – are, of course, well aware of this, and reject premise 2 by taking the view that the natural perspective does not entail that *all* events are subject to a kind of causal determination that, according to their argument, excludes the possibility of freedom. Thus, traditional incompatibilism is not the same as skepticism about the coapplicability of the ethical and natural perspectives: All I wish to suggest is that it is a necessary component of a standard case for such skepticism.)

It may, then, seriously be questioned whether the ethical and the natural perspectives do indeed have the implications that premises 1 and 2 state them to have. Thus, before debating whether free acts can be causally determined, it is profitable to consider whether, and in what sense, the moral perspective really does presuppose freedom of action; and whether, and in what sense, the natural perspective really does presuppose that all events are causally determined. These two questions, then, set our immediate agenda. I shall argue that a proper understanding of the ethical and the natural perspectives on action does show them to be in tension, but that the focus of this tension is not adequately expressed by the traditional argument for the incompatibility of free will with determinism. There is a real problem of natural agency, but it is not to be identified with the problem of establishing traditional compatibilism between freedom of action and determinism.

Is Skepticism About Action Out of Date?

Our first statement of the skeptical case may at once seem flawed by an anachronistic assumption about what a natural scientific perspective on action really requires. According to premise 2, scientific naturalism requires that all events be causally determined in a sense that entails that, given the context, they could not but have happened. In this sense of causal determination, to say that an event, e, is causally determined is to say that e's occurrence is a deductive consequence of a set of true statements about relevant laws of nature and prior states and events. Yet natural science no longer adheres to determinism – the thesis that all events are causally determined in this given sense.[5] Some scientific theories admit events that literally have no causes at all or that are caused according to probabilistic rather than deterministic laws. Thus, some natural explanations of an event's occurrence show only that, given the past and the laws of nature, an event of that type had a certain probability of occurrence. Accordingly, since the natural perspective is not committed to determinism, its coapplication with the ethical perspective need not confront us with the apparent paradox that there are free acts that could not but have happened given the past and the laws of nature. So even were it true that free action is incompatible with causal determinism, this fact would not support skepticism about the very possibility of free action in the natural order.

In fact, the matter is not so straightforward. It might be argued, for instance, that natural science admits indeterminism only at the submicroscopic level and that, therefore, the natural perspective on macroscopic behavior does treat it as 100 percent causally determined – in which case, the truth of traditional incompatibilism would yield the skeptical conclusion. We may, however, postpone further reflection on the implications of indeterminism in the natural sciences until after we have examined the commitments of the ethical perspective. For, some have argued that the ethical perspective does not require actions to be free in the sense (whatever it may come to) that the agent could have done otherwise.[6] If they are correct, it may be beside the point to debate whether the natural perspective on behavior is deterministic or not because the condition that is supposed to be unsatisfiable in a deterministic universe may turn out not to be required by the ethical perspective after all.

II. COMMITMENTS OF THE ETHICAL PERSPECTIVE

What Kind of Freedom of Action Does Moral Responsibility Entail?

Is it true, as premise 1 claims, that the world must contain some free actions if the ethical perspective is to apply? And if so, is there even an apparent conflict between freedom of action in the relevant sense and the causal determination that (as we shall for the moment assume) the natural perspective requires?

I have already claimed that the existence of actions is entailed if our ethical perspective is to apply to the world, on the grounds that agents can be morally responsible for outcomes only if those outcomes occur through their own actions. But what precisely are we supposed to be adding by describing such actions as free? The force of *free* here, presumably, is to emphasize that the actions must be genuinely the agents' *own* if they are to transmit moral responsibility for outcomes. And it has often been argued that once we properly understand what freedom in this sense really amounts to, all appearances of incompatibility between freedom and causal determination are removed. First, it is claimed that to perform one's own free action (in the required sense) is just to act *without any relevant constraint* (and a list of what would be a relevant constraint has then to be provided: being physically restrained, being under hypnosis, being under the influence of an incapacitating drug, being unable to know what one is really doing, etc.). Then it is argued that an action's being causally determined does not as such introduce any element of relevant constraint – that mere causal determination is not on the list of conditions that defeat freedom of action.

It is, of course, true that in learning our paradigms of free (i.e., unconstrained) action, we do not treat causal determination per se as a form of constraint that defeats the freedom required for moral responsibility. But appealing to this fact is not enough to answer the skeptic. The skeptic is well aware that in practice the question of whether an agent's action was causally determined is assumed to be quite irrelevant to the question of whether it can transmit moral responsibility for an outcome. What the skeptic doubts is the *justification* for this assumption. From the standpoint of theoretical reflection, the skeptic poses the question of whether we could be globally mistaken in our unreflective assumption that causal determination is consistent with freedom of action. The way to answer this question is to review the familiar list of constraints that defeat freedom and responsibility and to consider *on what general principles* this list is constructed. What do these various conditions that defeat moral responsibility have in common that justifies the inclusion of each on the list? This question answered, the skeptic's concern may then be addressed by asking whether, on those general principles, it is consistent to allow that causal determination per se does not defeat the freedom of action needed for moral responsibility.

Freedom as Satisfaction of the "Could Have Done Otherwise" Condition

It is clear that the concept of free action that is required for moral responsibility is not readily equatable with any broadly inclusive notion of unconstrained action. Agents can act under severe constraint, by any ordinary standard, and still rightly be held morally responsible. For example, the bank teller who opens the safe at the point of a gun acts under constraint but does not therefore forfeit moral responsibility: Indeed, in so acting the teller discharges a duty to the bank, whose staff are instructed to comply when so threatened. When people act under the constraint of coercion, otherwise untoward behavior is usually excusable – but is not therefore beyond the scope of moral responsibility.[7]

Perhaps, then, what is needed for free action is that agents not be *totally* constrained so that no alternative whatsoever is open to them. (This condition is satisfied in our bank teller case.) Arguably, what the various freedom-defeating conditions have in common is that under each of them, the agents *could not have done otherwise* than behave as they did. This suggestion yields a standard account: Persons are morally responsible for their behavior only if they acted freely in the sense that they could have done otherwise. I will follow Daniel Dennett's usage[8] and call this *the CDO principle,* and the condition of freedom it expresses, *the CDO condition.*

The Frankfurt Counterexamples

It is, of course, a presupposition of the skeptical case as we have initially formulated it that the CDO condition is necessary for moral responsibility: It is this condition that the skeptic claims to be unsatisfied by behavior that is causally determined. There is room for debate about how the CDO condition should be interpreted: Does it mean that the agent could have done otherwise, even given the very same circumstances; or does it mean only that the agent could have done otherwise had circumstances differed appropriately? The soundness of the argument for incompatibilism may well depend on whether a categorical or a conditional construal of the CDO condition is adopted. Indeed, it is a standard compatibilist move, whose merits we shall review in Chapter 2, Section V, to insist on a conditional analysis of the CDO condition. This question of interpretation, however, may seem to have been preempted by the radical claim that the CDO condition (however interpreted) is *not* necessary for moral responsibility. If this claim is correct, then the skeptical case based on the argument for incompatibilism fails, even if that argument is sound.

To establish that an agent who could not have done otherwise might still be morally responsible, Harry Frankfurt argues, in effect, as follows: Consider an agent (Jones) who exhibits *a*-ing behavior under those conditions (whatever they are) required for him to be morally responsible for doing *a*. Now, suppose that Jones's performance takes place under the further condition that had he decided to perform any alternative to action *a*, another agent (Black) would have successfully intervened to ensure that Jones exhibited *a*-ing behavior. Intuitively, this addition does not cancel our judgment that Jones is morally responsible for doing *a*, even though it apparently entails that Jones could not have done other than *a*.[9]

Frankfurt's example does establish that an agent may be morally responsible for doing *a* when the agent could not have done otherwise on what we may call the *alternative outcome* construal, according to which to say that *M* could have done other than *a* in circumstances *C* is to say that, given *C*, there could have been an outcome alternative to *M*'s doing *a*. And so, if there might be an incompatibility between causal determination of behavior and its satisfaction of the CDO condition only on this alternative outcome construal, such an incompatibility would not show the ethical and the natural perspectives to be in conflict. Yet there may be a different construal of the CDO condition, on which,

(i)   CDO's satisfaction is necessary for moral responsibility (and hence CDO is met in the Frankfurt-style counterfactual intervener cases),

and

(ii) it is problematic whether causally determined behavior can satisfy CDO.

Or alternatively, there may be some other "freedom" condition, not intelligible as a construal of CDO at all, which meets (i) and (ii). In either case, a skeptical problem about the possibility of natural agency may remain.[10]

It is notable that in Frankfurt's example, Jones's doing *a* counts as an action of his even though there could, in the circumstances, have been no other outcome. Had Black intervened, of course, Jones's *a*-ing behavior would presumably not have constituted an action of Jones's (although it might have of Black's), and Jones would then not have been morally responsible for *a*-ing. So it may be that what is necessary for moral responsibility is not the CDO condition on the alternative outcome construal but what Thomas Nagel has called *the condition of control*. Nagel sketches this condition thus:

People cannot be morally assessed for what is not their fault, or what is due to factors beyond their control . . . the appropriateness of moral assessment is easily undermined by the discovery that the act or attribute, no matter how good or bad, is not under the agent's control.[11]

Moral Luck and the Condition of Control

Admittedly, we are inclined to agree with remarks like those just quoted from Nagel, but do we really believe that people cannot rightly be held responsible for "what is due to factors beyond their control"? Apparently not, for in practice we often accept that agents are responsible for outcomes influenced greatly by factors outside their control. For example, if a person kills a child while driving a vehicle he knows to have faulty brakes, his moral responsibility is not mitigated by the fact that it was not under his control whether he would need to brake suddenly. (We meet here the problem of *moral luck:* Should we carry the intuition that lack of control cancels responsibility to its extreme by maintaining that people are responsible only for what is *entirely* under their control? Or may we find a way of systematically justifying our actual practice of holding people responsible for much of what is, to an extent, just their good or bad luck?)

What is necessary for an agent to be morally responsible for an outcome is just that the outcome should have been produced *through an exercise of the agent's control,* or in other words, through the agent's action. It is not necessary that the outcome shouldn't have been in any way subject to causal influences beyond the agent's control. One may exercise control without having total control over what happens. So the negligent driver does meet the necessary condition for moral responsibility for running over the child because although the outcome was affected by luck, it was partly caused through the driver's exercise of control – through his failure to refrain from driving a vehicle he knew to be seriously faulty.[12]

The Condition of Control as a CDO Condition

It is easy to see why philosophers have supposed that a CDO condition was the right way to express the condition of control that is a necessary condition for moral responsibility. Actions, or exercises of control, constitute the use of a *power* that the agent possesses, and an agent possesses a power, surely, only if he or she can exercise that power in more than one way. Hence, if an agent exercises control in doing *a,* that agent employs a power that *could have been otherwise employed.* Therefore, if we require, for an agent to be morally responsible for an outcome, that it come about through the agent's action, it seems that we are requiring that some CDO condition should apply.

The condition of control may, then, entail some version of a

CDO condition – but it certainly does not entail CDO on the alternative outcome construal. If, in context C, Jones performs action a, in doing so Jones exercises a power that could have been otherwise exercised. But this is not equivalent to the alternative outcome CDO condition, according to which it could have happened, given C, that Jones did not do a. The logical forms of the two conditions are importantly different. The alternative outcome CDO condition uses "could have" as a modal operator on a complex proposition, so that "In context C, Jones does a and could have done otherwise" is to be expressed as

C & Jones does a & Could Happen [C & Not-(Jones does a)].

But in the condition of control, "could have" is embedded in a description of an attribute possessed by the agent and is not a propositional operator at all. The logical form here may be given thus:

C & Jones does a & Jones-could-have-refrained-from-doing-a.[13]

That the condition of control does not entail CDO on the alternative outcome construal is established by reflection on Frankfurt's counterfactual intervener examples. These examples show that an agent can have a power of action under circumstances in which, if he or she decides or tries to exercise it in any way but one, that decision or attempt suffices to deprive the agent of the power. Nevertheless, if the decision is made to exercise the power in the one way that will not trigger its loss, the agent's behavior counts as a genuine exercise of control – as the use of a power that, *had it been retained,* could have been used otherwise. Of course, agents so situated will be subject to a severe constraint and, if they do exercise power in the one way that permits their action, will do so most unfreely (even though they need not know this themselves). Thus, it is a condition of *freely* exercising a given power that with respect to a suitably large set of alternative ways of employing it, it would have been retained no matter which of these the agent might have chosen or attempted. But this condition of freedom is not necessary for moral responsibility; what is necessary is the condition of control, and the condition of control does not *entail* that in the circumstances there is some outcome other than the actual that could have occurred.

24

What have we discovered, then, about what must be true of the world if the ethical perspective is to apply to it? For it to be the case that agents are sometimes morally responsible for certain outcomes, what we have just been referring to as "the condition of control" must sometimes be satisfied. That is, it must sometimes happen that agents exercise their own powers of control – that what happens comes about through an exercise of agent-control. So a world to which our ethical perspective applies must be one in which there are exercises of agent-control – which is just to say that it must be one in which there are *actions,* if by an action we mean simply the controlled exercise of an agent's own power. To be morally responsible for an outcome, then, an agent must contribute to it through his or her own exercise of agent-control – through his or her own *action.*

Is there any point in using a notion of any kind of freedom to express this necessary condition for moral responsibility? A very weak sense of freedom is perhaps essential to the present notion of an action, for as we have seen, an action is an exercise of a power that could have been otherwise exercised had it been retained, and such exercises might therefore he described as free. But since all actions will be free in this weak sense (including, counterintuitively, the actions of those beset by counterfactual interveners), it seems preferable not to adopt this usage and to reserve the notion (or notions) of free action for conditions of autonomy and unconstraint, which not all actions meet. Of course, I do not deny that the satisfaction of some of these latter conditions, which are usefully characterized as conditions of freedom, is also necessary for moral responsibility – my point is just that the condition of control (as a construal of the CDO condition) is a necessary condition for moral responsibility that is not usefully expressed by using the notion of freedom. And it is the satisfaction of this necessary condition for moral responsibility – of the condition of control – that according to the skeptic creates a special difficulty for a naturalistic understanding of morally responsible behavior.

But how exactly is the difficulty created? How does construing the CDO principle as the requirement that agents can be responsible only for what occurs through an exercise of their own control affect the skeptic's case? Now that we have separated the condition of control from the CDO condition on its alternative outcome construal, does anything remain of the original skeptical case? Do we still have apparent reason to believe that actions (exercises of control) cannot be causally determined, even after we recognize that an agent can exercise control to yield an outcome to which, in the circumstances, there could have been no alternative? The following restatement of the argument for incompatibilism suggests that we do, since it avoids reliance on the CDO principle under its alternative outcome construal:

If an event that constitutes an agent's action is causally determined, it occurs as a deductive consequence of relevant laws of nature and prior states and events. But neither of these determining factors is under the agent's control. Still, to count as the agent's own action, what happens must be an exercise of *the agent's* control. Therefore, the very same event must both occur under the agent's control and also be determined by factors that are beyond the agent's control. But this is impossible. Hence, no action can also be causally determined.[14]

It appears, then, that the skeptic can accommodate the discovery that CDO (on the alternative outcome construal) is not necessary for moral responsibility and still maintain initially plausible grounds for doubting the possibility of action in a causally deterministic universe. The source of skepticism is now seen to be, not simply that every outcome under determinism is necessary relative to antecedent events and the laws of nature, but also that these conditions are themselves beyond the agent's control. The merits of this case for incompatibilism remain to be considered (see Chapter 2, Section II); but we have at least shown that a consideration of the commitments of the ethical perspective does not yield the conclusion that skepticism about how it may cohere with the natural perspective is straightforwardly misguided. The ethical perspective requires as necessary for moral responsibility that persons sometimes perform actions in which they exercise their own control – yet it is puzzling how the causal determination of a person's behavior can leave room for such control.

III. COMMITMENTS OF THE NATURAL PERSPECTIVE

But why is it puzzling how causally determined behavior can be an exercise of an agent's power of control? If the restated argument for incompatibilism is supposed to express the grounds for this puzzlement, there is a problem only if the natural perspective is committed to determinism. And as we have already noted, modern natural science makes no such commitment. We need, then, to reconsider the charge that the problem of natural agency has been of purely antiquarian interest ever since natural science rejected the thesis of universal determinism.

The "Containment of Indeterminism" Response

As already acknowledged, any such swift dismissal of the skeptic's case might be resisted by claiming that science has admitted exceptions to universal determinism only for certain submicroscopic events. Thus, the kinds of macroscopic changes that come about through action are still to be regarded, from a natural scientific perspective, as, let us say, 100 percent causally determined. (I use this expression to label the sense of causal determination defined earlier.) Thus the effects of admitting probabilistic determinism or indeterminism may be contained so as to leave the skeptic's argument intact: The natural scientific perspective does require 100 percent causal determination of the kind of behavior involved in actions.

This response is not altogether convincing. Of course, it is true that the rejection of universal determinism does not entail that scientific explanations of behavior be indeterministic. The physics and physiology of the behavior of animals might be a deterministic science even if quantum mechanics is not. But this concession is not enough to warrant the view that the natural scientific admission of indeterminism is irrelevant to skepticism about the natural possibility of action. Once the scientific naturalist breaches the bastion of determinism in one place, at least the possibility of further breaches must be acknowledged. Thus, if the argument for incompatibilism did turn out to be sound, it would then be reasonable to maintain a common-sense commitment to coapplying the ethical and the natural perspectives by allowing that macroscopic behavior (as well as subatomic events) can sometimes fail to be 100 percent causally determined. Unless some a priori argument is available that shows that causal indeterminism is necessarily restricted to subatomic events, it would seem adequate to respond to skepticism about the natural possibility of action by admitting incompatibilist intuitions

27

and using them as part of an argument for extending indeterminism to the causation of behavior.

On the other hand, it would be premature to use the indeterminism of modern physics as grounds for consigning the traditional debate about incompatibilism to the rubbish heap of outmoded metaphysics. It is at least possible that scientific fashion in physics might shift back in favor of universal determinism or that physiology or even psychology might be deterministic sciences – and in either of those cases, one would have to defeat traditional incompatibilism to maintain rational belief in the natural possibility of action. Although not completely outmoded, however, the traditional debate no longer deserves center stage: Once we regard it as a real possibility that natural science need not treat actions as 100 percent causally determined, resolving the problem of natural agency can no longer simply be reduced to deciding who wins in the old debate between compatibilists and incompatibilists. If there is something truly puzzling about fitting actions into a naturalistic view of the world, then the puzzle is likely to be deeper than the traditional problem of defending the possibility of (free) agency under determinism.

Restating the Problem of Natural Agency
as Independent of Determinism

Some indication of what that deeper puzzle may be is offered by a more radical response to the attempt to defeat skepticism about natural agency by rejecting the claim of premise 2 that the natural perspective is committed to universal determinism. This is the "irrelevance of determinism" response, which holds that the fundamental problem of understanding the natural possibility of action is independent of the truth of determinism. Even though determinism may be false, there is still some tension between counting behavior as the agent's action and regarding it from a natural scientific perspective.

One way to articulate this irrelevance of determinism response is to hold that the problem of natural agency should properly be expressed as a *dilemma,* of which the traditional freedom and determinism problem is only one horn. A well-known recent revival of this formulation is given by Roderick Chisholm.[15]

The "Dilemma" Formulation of the Problem
of Natural Agency

Chisholm's formulation may be put like this: Any behavioral sequence is either (100 percent) causally determined or it is not. If it
is, then, by the argument for incompatibilism, it cannot be an
agent's action. However, if it is not, then it cannot be an action
either because events that are not causally determined are "fortuitous or capricious,"[16] and events that are fortuitous or capricious
cannot count as actions. On this formulation, a puzzle about the
mutual consistency of the ethical and the natural perspectives remains, whether or not the thesis of determinism is true.

Some philosophers (C. D. Broad, for example) have supposed
that this dilemma (with the required argumentation suitably filled
out) actually constitutes a proof of skepticism about natural agency
– a proof that what we understand by a responsible action is not
realizable in the natural order.[17] But the consensus is that the
dilemma may be avoided and a defense given of the natural
possibility of action. Commonly, it is assumed that there are two
ways of mounting such a defense. First, there is *libertarianism,*
which accepts incompatibilism (the argument of the first horn),
infers the falsity of determinism in order to affirm the existence
of action in the natural order, and is therefore committed to denying the argument of the second horn by showing how events
that are not 100 percent causally determined can constitute actions.
Second, there is a corresponding position that accepts the argument of the second horn, infers the truth of determinism in order
to affirm the existence of action, and is thus committed to denying the incompatibilist argument of the first horn. (This second position incorporates but is not identical with what has traditionally been called *soft determinism;* however, it goes beyond soft
determinism by claiming not just that the universe is a deterministic causal order within which action is possible but also that action is impossible without determinism.) But there is a further
option.[18]

Why should it be assumed that the existence of action must either
be incompatible with determinism or incompatible with indeterminism? It could, surely, turn out to be compatible with
both?[19] The soft determinist, who believes that the universe is
deterministic and that this does not exclude the possibility of action, may concede that action would still have been a possibility

even if the universe had not been deterministic. Similarly, the compatibility of action with 100 percent causal determination might consistently be acknowledged by a philosopher who believes that this is in fact an indeterministic universe in which actions sometimes occur. There is, then, viable ground on which a stand might be made between libertarianism and the view that the existence of action positively requires determinism.

I shall not now assess the arguments that are alleged to constitute the dilemma; neither, therefore, shall I seek to decide the respective merits of libertarianism, "strengthened" soft determinism, or the intermediate view allowing that action is compatible both with determinism and indeterminism. My purpose is just to emphasize that if Chisholm's version of it is correct, the problem of natural agency is not limited to the traditional debate about the compatibility of action with (100 percent) causal determinism. If determinism is true, there is a puzzle about how action is possible, namely, to explain away the initial plausibility of the argument for incompatibilism. But if determinism is false, there may still be a puzzle about how agency is possible, though this time a different one.

But is this different puzzle about the natural possibility of actions that are not 100 percent causally determined really a serious one? If to say that an event is fortuitous is to say that there is literally no explanation for its occurrence, then, indeed, it is highly plausible to deny the status of action to any behavior that occurs fortuitously. As we saw at the close of Section II, actions are exercises of an agent's control, and this surely implies that behavior must at least have an explanation if it is to count as action, even if no explanation for it is actually known. However, the fact that behavior is not 100 percent causally determined does not entail that its occurrence is *altogether* inexplicable. There may be, for instance, a probabilistic causal explanation of it, or even (if such a thing is possible) a noncausal explanation. Thus, this argument imposes a false dichotomy in assuming that events are either explicable as 100 percent causally determined or else fortuitous in the sense of being totally inexplicable. Accordingly, there seems to be no danger whatsoever of becoming impaled on the second horn of the dilemma.[20]

Nevertheless, there may be better grounds for puzzlement about the possibility of actions that lack 100 percent causal determination. To the extent that an event's occurrence is to some degree a matter of chance, so we seem less inclined to class it as an action. This intuition may be vague – but it is widespread and well entrenched. There seems to be something obviously correct about remarks like Norbert Wiener's to the effect that "the chance of the quantum-theoretician is not the ethical freedom of the Augustinian, and Tyche is as relentless a mistress as Ananke."[21] What accounts for this intuition, I think, is that we tend to assume that chance undermines control, and so we conclude that since agency requires the exercise of control, "chancey" events cannot count as actions. The question is, of course, whether this assumption is correct: Does any element of chance totally exclude control, or can control over behavior persist when its occurrence is merely made probable by its antecedents – and if so, what degree of probability is then required? It is puzzlement over the answer to these questions that should replace the inadequate argument of the second horn of Chisholm's dilemma. Thus, just as the compatibilist has to explain how *only some* 100 percent causally determined events can be actions, so the libertarian has to explain how *only some* merely "probabilified" events can have this status. And neither the compatibilist nor the libertarian can expect an easy time of it in providing these explanations: Skepticism about natural agency seems to have at least some serious basis whether or not the universe is deterministic.

A Radical Separation of the Problem of Natural Agency from the Question of Determinism

On our account so far, the attempt to rebut skepticism about action in the natural order will be unable to ignore the question of determinism because its truth or falsity will determine *what form the skeptical case will take*. For, on the present formulation, what poses the problem in fitting responsible action into the natural order varies, depending on whether or not the natural order is deterministic. Some philosophers, however, regard the question of determinism as totally irrelevant to the skeptical problem of action. As Dennett has put it,

> We are afraid that science has shown . . . that we can't be what we want to be. The threat is not determinism – if it were, we could all relax, since physicists now seem to agree that our world is fundamentally indeterministic – but science itself, or the "naturalism" that is its enabling world view.[22]

This way of stating the problem suggests that it may be radically reformulated to show that whether determinism is true or false, there is still the same fundamental reason for doubt about the natural possibility of action. But what could such a fundamental reason be? What is the naturalism to which Dennett refers and how does it threaten the application of our notion of agency?

The "Clash of Explanation-Types" Formulation

A standard expression of this more radical view is to construe "naturalism" as the assumption that all occurrences have some kind of natural scientific explanation (whether deterministic or otherwise) and to claim that actions cannot consistently be regarded as open to such explanation. Dennett himself posed the problem this way in earlier work:

> It seems that whenever a particular bit of human motion can be given an entirely mechanistic explanation – with or without the invocation of "random" interveners – any non-mechanistic, rational, purposive explanation of the same motions is otiose.[23]

This way of formulating the problem rests on accepting that, as has been repeatedly argued,[24] behavior counts as action only if it is explicable in a special kind of way, namely, in terms of the agent's *reasons* for performing the behavior explained. I shall call explanations of this kind *intentional explanations,* following Dennett's usage.[25] Intentional explanations are apparently different from natural scientific explanations in several ways,[26] of which the most basic is that an intentional explanation confers intelligibility by *showing the point or meaning* of what happens, rather than by exhibiting the explanandum as probable to a stated degree, given the past and the laws of nature. For the immediately ensuing discussion I shall grant the assumption that it is definitive of actions that they have intentional explanations – although later it will be necessary to consider the objection that this property belongs only to *intentional* actions – and that accordingly there could be genuine actions that are not done "for reasons."

Granted that assumption, the natural possibility of action amounts, on the present formulation, to the possibility that intentional explanations should correctly explain the occurrence of some sequences of natural events. And skepticism about action may then be construed as a doubt about the possibility that both an intentional explanation and a natural scientific explanation might apply to the same behavior. The skeptic's argument may then be expressed thus:

32

1'. If the ethical perspective (with its notion of moral responsibility) applies to the world, then there are some events whose correct explanation is an intentional explanation.

2'. If the natural perspective applies to the world, then all events have a correct natural scientific explanation (whether it be deterministic or probabilistic).

3'. No event can be such that its correct explanation is an intentional explanation and it also has a correct natural scientific (deterministic or probabilistic) causal explanation.

Given these premises, it follows straightforwardly that the ethical and the natural perspective cannot both apply to the world.

Assessment of the Clash of Explanation-Types
Formulation

Premise 1' is straightforward. It would, I think be acceptable even if we were not operating under the assumption that having an intentional explanation is definitive of action. Even if there can be actions that are not intentional, it is surely clear that a world to which our ethical perspective applied would have to contain some full-fledged intentional actions. The wider conditions for moral responsibility would not be satisfied if no one ever acted for a reason.

Premise 2' claims to express a central commitment of naturalism. It might be suggested that as it stands, premise 2' states this commitment in too strong a form. Perhaps all that naturalism requires is that natural events, if they are explicable at all, should have a deterministic or probabilistic causal explanation. In other words, it might be quite consistent with the natural perspective to admit that some events should have no natural explanation and yet still count unambiguously as natural events. Well, how would this weakening of premise 2' affect the skeptic's case? Coapplicability of intentional and natural explanations (which premise 3' claims to be impossible) would be avoided if all natural events that have intentional explanations were inexplicable from the natural perspective. But it is just highly implausible to suppose that this is so: The implication that human bodily movements (the paradigm case of the type of events open to intentional explanation) literally have no natural scientific explanation (deterministic or otherwise) is clearly unacceptable since it would require us to believe that neurophysiological explanations of behavior are wholly false! Besides, it is a moot point whether the spirit rather than just the letter of reconciliatory naturalism would have been achieved if the reconciliation between the ethical and the natural perspective depended on accepting that those events that are constitutive of actions (even if these are not bodily movements, but brain events) necessarily are beyond scientific explanation. It is hard to see what could be meant by describing an event as "natural" if it could not have any natural scientific explanation of its occurrence. So weakening premise 2' does not by itself lead to a satisfactory reply to the skeptic. I shall thus leave it as it stands, noting that even if naturalism isn't committed to the existence of a natural scientific explanation for *all* natural events, it is committed to the view that the sort of events that constitute actions (i.e., have intentional explanations) are open to natural explanation.

Thus, the skeptic's case on this formulation turns on premise 3': What reasons may be given for accepting that events cannot have at the same time both an intentional and a natural explanation for their occurrence? The first step will be to show that an intentional explanation of an agent's behavior is indeed distinct from any natural scientific explanation of it. If intentional explanations were, despite appearances, just alternative ways of expressing say physiological explanations of the same behavior, skepticism of the present variety would be groundless. However, it seems unlikely that this should turn out to be the case; certainly many philosophers (including some committed to physicalism) have offered impressive reasons for believing that intentional explanations do form a logically distinct category of explanation from natural scientific explanation, especially if the latter is rightly understood as requiring subsumption under strict laws.[27]

We may thus more profitably focus our assessment of the skeptic's case for premise 3' on considering what reasons could be advanced for the claim that *assuming intentional explanations are indeed distinct,* it then follows that they cannot coapply with any natural scientific explanation. What could be problematic about accepting that the same behavior might have both an intentional and a physiological explanation? Perhaps it will be claimed that in general two genuinely distinct explanations cannot both apply to the one explanandum – if, that is, they are both offered as *true* explanations of the explanandum's occurrence. (Evidently enough, there would be no conflict if at least one of the competing explanations were construed purely instrumentally or in some other non-realist fashion.) It might be urged, in support of this claim, that a given explanation cannot be adequate if it omits anything that explains why the explanandum occurred; hence, two distinct accounts must be in competition if each claims to provide an adequate explanation for the same explanandum's occurrence.

But this argument is unconvincing. A description may be a true description even though it (necessarily) omits some features of what is described; surely, then, an explanation might equally be a true and adequate explanation for an explanandum that may also be differently explained. This possibility suggests that a natural scientific explanation for behavior need not exclude its having a distinct intentional explanation as well. In which case, a full understanding of an agent's behavior would, of course, require both explanations; but either explanation alone might nevertheless provide a satisfactory answer to the question why the behavior had occurred.

The Dennett–MacKay Complementarity Thesis

There seems, then, to be no a priori reason for excluding in general the possibility that the same explanandum may have more than one distinct explanation. But is there perhaps some specific reason for ruling out the coapplication of an intentional explanation with a natural scientific (say, a physiological) explanation of behavior? Donald MacKay offers an analogy from communication engineering to persuade us that there is not. The behavior of a computer, he observes, can be understood in two complementary ways: as "determined as to its energetics by a certain pattern of energy flow, and as to its form by a certain pattern of information flow."[28] Similarly, intentional explanations account for behavior at the level of informational analysis, without conflicting at all with quite distinct explanations at the level of physical analysis. This powerful idea has been developed by Dennett, who distinguishes three different stances that may be adopted in predicting the behavior of a system – the physical stance, which explains relative to knowledge of the system's physical state and the laws of nature; the design stance, which explains relative to some hypothesis about the functional design of the system; and the intentional stance, which explains on the assumption that the system is behaving rationally relative to its goals and beliefs. Dennett calls a system an *intentional system* "when one can successfully adopt the intentional stance toward it."[29]

Dennett clearly establishes that it is possible (and, depending on context, sensible) to apply each of these three stances to one and the same physical system. In particular, explaining a system's behavior from the intentional stance does not preclude its explicability from the physical stance also. The fact that the physical stance explains a system's behavior without presupposing rationality does not entail that the system is not in fact a rational agent, whose behavior is open to intentional explanation: "the absence of a presupposition of rationality is not the same as a presupposition of non-rationality."[30] May we take it, then, that the skeptical problem of natural agency is solved by the Dennett–MacKay *complementarity thesis,* which affirms, in effect, that a system can be at once a physical, a teleological, and an intentional system?

Limitations of the Complementarity Thesis

There are two features of this complementarity thesis that prevent it from solving the skeptical problem of natural agency. First, as Dennett emphasizes, "the success of [the intentional] stance [as applied to a given system] is of course a matter settled pragmatically, without reference to whether the object *really* has beliefs, intentions and so forth."[31] Hence, the fact that physical systems can also be intentional systems does not entail that physical systems can be intentional agents. To be an agent, a system must be capable of actions, and actions are behavioral episodes that have intentional explanations, *realistically understood.* Now, it is in this gap between intentional systems and intentional agents that the skeptic finds the source of concern. It is no puzzle to the skeptic that many natural systems may be treated *as if* they were agents. Nor does it puzzle the skeptic that it is sometimes useful to predict and explain a natural system's behavior on the assumption of its rationality. What the skeptic professes to find puzzling is the notion of a natural system that really does act for reasons of its own.

Of course, if an independent case could be made for maintaining that intentional explanations may not properly be understood other than as predictive instruments, the problem of natural agency (as currently formulated) simply disappears. Without such an independent case, however, the Dennett–MacKay thesis begs the question against the skeptic who seeks to understand how responsible agency is possible in the natural order. For realism about actions (and hence, about intentional explanations) does seem to be a presupposition of our ethical perspective. The condition of control expresses a requirement on holding an agent morally responsible that we assume to hold or not to hold as a real matter of fact. It is because behavior counts as the agent's exercise of control that we are justified in regarding it, *ceteris paribus,* as open to moral assessment; it is not that a pragmatic decision to treat the agent's behavior from the intentional stance constitutes it as open to moral assessment. As Dennett remarks in clarifying MacKay's position[32] – and this is now the second limiting feature of the complementarity thesis – intentional systems do not *thereby* count as morally accountable.

One reason for this is clear: Intentional systems need not even be capable of exercising *their own* control. Dennett rightly observes that the intentional stance, though it is not "a moral stance . . . is a precondition of *any* moral stance, and hence if it is jeopardized by any triumph of mechanism, the notion of moral responsibility is jeopardized in turn."[33] It must also be said, however, that even though understanding a system's behavior from the intentional stance is (clearly) not jeopardized by "mechanism" (or "naturalism"), there may still be grounds for fearing that the moral stance remains in such jeopardy. There may be reasons for believing that part of what must occur if a system is *actually to exercise its own agent-control* has no smoothly intelligible place in the natural causal order.

An Emphatic Aside: Realism About Action

Before we consider what those reasons could be, it is imperative to underscore a point that has now emerged. *The problem of natural agency is a problem only for realists about action.* Realism about action seems to be a crucial presupposition of our ethical perspective. And if an action is understood as behavior that is correctly given an intentional explanation, realism about action entails realism about intentional explanation and the intentional states to which such explanation refers. Those who reject any of these "realisms" – or the claim that the ethical perspective requires them – simply do not have the problem we are discussing.

Some philosophers do have independent reasons for rejecting realism about action. I think, of course, of those "eliminative materialists" who reject ontological commitment to the folk psychological states used in intentional explanation, on the grounds that they are the theoretical posits of a bad theory.[34] (Their reasons for rejecting folk psychology are in fact largely independent of any concern with the problem of the natural possibility of action.) These philosophers, then, escape the problem of natural agency. They have a different problem, however: namely, to explain away the apparent commitment of our ethical perspective to realism about actions. And that is, I believe, a tall order. Any pragmatic or mind-dependent (or group-mind-dependent) view of what it is for an agent to satisfy necessary conditions for moral responsibility will, I believe, so reconstrue our ethical perspective that any claim to have achieved a reconciliatory naturalist position thereby will be quite empty. So although the flight into antirealism quickly solves (or rather, dissolves) the skeptical problem of natural agency, it is not to be recommended for serious reconciliatory naturalists.

But what exactly does our present problem come to, if it is, indeed, independent of determinism? The clash of explanation-types formulation may be on the right track; but we have not yet uncovered any plausible reason for supposing that premise 3' might be true – that there is something special about intentional explanations, realistically construed, that precludes their coapplication with naturalistic explanations.

IV. THE CORE OF THE PROBLEM OF NATURAL AGENCY – AND A PLAUSIBLE SOLUTION

The Agent-Causation Formulation of the Problem of Natural Agency

Gary Watson has written,

We would lack free will in a deterministic world, incompatibilists think, because there we would not determine our own behaviour – we would lack *self*-determination. But the denial of determinism does not ensure, by itself, that *we* determine anything. So an incompatibilist who affirms freedom – conventionally called a *libertarian* – must say what more is needed besides the absence of [100 percent] causal determination to get "self-determination." The . . . skeptic . . . suspects that the freedom demanded by the [libertarian] – a "self-determination" that could not obtain in a deterministic world – obtains in no possible world.[35]

This, I believe, hits the nail on the head. What makes action problematic from a naturalistic perspective is that actions – exercises of an agent's own control – are understood as essentially involving determination of events *by the agent*. Thus, what comes about through action needs to be explained, it seems, as *agent-caused:* as determined by an agent through an exercise of that agent's control. But from the perspective of natural science, if events are understood as "determined" at all, it is just in the sense that their occurrence is *event-caused* – which is to say that they occur in accordance with deterministic or probabilistic laws, given antecedent (and perhaps also, concurrent) events and states of affairs. Actions thus seem essentially to involve something that natural science does not recognize.

Exactly how, then, should the skeptic's problem of natural agency be formulated? The immediately foregoing remarks might suggest that we can now vindicate the clash of explanation-types formulation as the correct way to express the skeptic's doubts. For it might seem that the central flaw with that formulation has now been overcome. The flaw was, of course, that there seemed no good reason for rejecting the possibility that an intentional explanation might apply to an explanandum that *also* had a complete explanation of a natural scientific kind. But now, it seems, we can offer a reason for rejecting this possibility. Intentional explanations (realistically construed) make reference to the *agent's* determination of events. So if intentional explanations apply, some natural events will be agent-caused. But as natural events, they will be naturalistically explicable as event-caused. The coapplication of intentional and natural explanations, then, requires that the same events can be both agent-caused and event-caused – and this, the skeptic may claim, is impossible.

The trouble with this view of the matter, however, is that there may be as much difficulty about justifying the claim that the same event cannot be both agent- and event-caused as there was about justifying the alleged impossibility of coapplicable intentional and natural explanations in the first place. So it may be unhelpful to see the present account of the skeptical problem of natural agency simply as an extension of the problem on its clash of explanation-types formulation. It is better, I think, to abandon this formulation and to understand the skeptic as arguing just that the natural perspective denies the possibility of the existence of something that appears essential if the concept of action as used in our ethical perspective is to be instantiated.

Essentially, then, the problem of natural agency is an ontological problem – a problem about whether the existence of actions can be admitted within a natural scientific ontology. If both the ethical and the natural perspectives are to apply, actions must exist as part of the natural order. But it seems that they cannot because they appear to be essentially constituted (at least in part) by agent-causal relations – by the "bringing about" of events by agents. But such agent-causal relations do not belong to the ontology of the natural perspective. Naturalism does not essentially employ the concept of a causal relation whose first member is in the category of person or agent (or even, for that matter, in the broader category of continuant or "substance"). All natural causal relations have first members in the category of event or state of affairs. Of course, statements whose surface structure contains references to causal relations whose first member is a substance can be true of the natural world. Consider, for example, "the tree caused these pipes to crack." But the meaning of such statements will always be capable of analysis in terms that eliminate the reference to this kind of causal relation in favor of references to causal relations between events and/or states of affairs. "The growth of the tree's roots caused these pipes to crack." (I shall have more to say about this kind of analysis shortly.)

Thus, what creates the problem is not exactly that the events that (from the ethical perspective) seem to have to be regarded as agent-caused also have to be seen as event-caused from the natural perspective – through this will indeed be a consequence of coapplying the two perspectives. Rather, the problem is that the natural perspective *positively rejects the possibility that any natural event should be agent-caused*. From the natural perspective, all events have the status of *happenings,* and the problem is that the ethical perspective requires some events that are *doings* and for which, other things being equal, an agent may be held morally responsible. But how can any happening also constitute a doing? The skeptic doubts that it can. We can thus offer a very simple agent-causation formulation of the skeptical argument at the core of the problem of natural agency, using only two premises:

1*. If the ethical perspective applies to the world, then there exist agent-causal relations.

2*.   If the natural perspective applies to the world, then agent-causal relations cannot exist.

If both these premises are true, it follows straightforwardly that the ethical and the natural perspectives cannot both apply to the world.

Further Advantages to the Agent-Causation Formulation

There is a further minor respect in which the agent-causation formulation may improve on its clash of explanation-types predecessor. The clash of explanation-types formulation could at best express a problem for the possibility of *intentional* actions within the natural order. But perhaps the problem is more general? As previously acknowledged, it is at least arguable that only a subclass of the genus "action" is such that its members have intentional explanations for their occurrence. Intentional actions, it is true, always and noncontingently have their occurrences explicable through intentional explanations. But perhaps there are forms of behavior that count as action even though they are not intentional? Perhaps there are actions that are merely *voluntary*? (I have in mind idle exercises of control, such as ear scratching and finger tapping.) It would be unwise to be dogmatic here because a case may be made for denying the classification of "action" to any behavior that is not intentional under some description.[36] Nevertheless, it is a minor weakness of the clash of explanation-types formulation that it wouldn't explain why there was a skeptical problem about putatively nonintentional actions.

This minor weakness is overcome under the agent-causation formulation because if there are merely voluntary actions, they involve agent-causation just as much as intentional actions do. Furthermore, the perspective of the agent-causation formulation enables us to reinterpret the "dilemma" formulation as expressing, in different ways in the arguments of each of its horns, the claim that where states and events "do the determining," there is no room for the agent to act. Thus, the real concern expressed in the argument of the second horn is not that an element of chance is incompatible with agent-control but rather that where events and states of affairs determine an outcome (albeit only probabilistically), there is no room for the agent-causation that is constitutive of genuine action.

This diagnosis of the skeptical problem of action almost automatically suggests its resolution.[37] For our ethical perspective to apply, actions must exist in the natural world. These actions are understood as essentially involving agent-causation – episodes of self-determination in which an outcome is produced through the agent's exercise of control. There will be a real clash with the natural perspective only if this understanding of action is itself fully warranted. But perhaps it is not. Perhaps we can show that properly understood, the notion of action that we need for our ethical point of view does not involve ontological commitment to agent-causal relations of a kind foreign to our naturalist ontology. It is exactly this claim that the *Causal Theory of Action (CTA)* purports to establish; for CTA's crucial negative ontological claim is that, whatever our commonsense "ethical perspective" concept of an action may be, actions are not, in fact, essentially constituted even in part by relations of agent-causation.

The positive ontological claim of CTA is motivated by the thought that actions are done "for reasons." Actions typically occur *because* their agents had reasons for performing them, and these reasons, it seems, consist in sets of mental states – beliefs, desires, intentions, and the like. Thus, CTA proposes that an action consists in an event (or events) with a special kind of mental *event-causal* history: Actions are events caused by mental states that they "match". Behavior matches a set of mental states, in this sense, when it counts as reasonable in the light of the behaver's being in those states – or to put it another way, when those mental states constitute the agent's reasons for performing behavior of that kind. Thus, according to CTA, behavior that we suppose counts as action because it is agent-caused in fact counts as action because it "matches" and is *event*-caused by relevant mental states of the agent. The relevant mental states will be those that constitute the reasons the agent has for performing the action. It is therefore a commitment of CTA that intentional explanations do not involve reference to agent-causation but only to the event-causation of behavior by the agent's mental states. Just in that sense, if not in any other, CTA holds intentional explanations to be like most natural scientific explanations in explaining their explananda in terms of prior states or events that are their causes. If CTA is true, there can be no more mystery about how agency can belong to the natural order than there is about how the natural order can accommodate mental causes of suitably matching events.

Of course, there may still be a mystery about the place of "the mind" in the natural order and how it is that mental states and events can play a causal role. So the problem of natural agency might remain even if a satisfactory version of CTA can be found just because there is still a problem about how to give a naturalist account of mental states, events, and processes and their place in the causal order. As I have already warned in the Introduction, I shall not have anything to say on this more fundamental problem. I shall just assume that a naturalist account of both consciousness and intentionality is possible. My efforts are here directed solely at those who find reasons for doubting the natural possibility of morally responsible personhood that go beyond any reasons for skepticism about a naturalist resolution of the mind/body problem.

In this chapter I have examined one traditional source for skepticism of precisely this kind – namely, doubts about how the kind of freedom of action necessary for moral responsibility could be instantiated in a natural causal order. I have argued that this kind of skepticism amounts essentially to a doubt about how to accommodate *agency as such* within the natural causal order, whether it be deterministic or otherwise. There is, I have maintained, a skeptical problem of natural agency, which is to understand how an agent's exercise of control (whether relatively free or unfree) can be situated within the constraints of a naturalist ontology that has no room for real agent-causal relations. I believe that satisfactory naturalist solutions both to the mind/body problem and to the problem of natural agency will in fact suffice for a full naturalist account of moral agency. However, as admitted in the Introduction, reconciliatory naturalists may need to resolve a further skeptical problem of natural moral autonomy beyond the problem of natural agency since agency is only necessary and not also sufficient for moral responsibility. I shall have more to say about this topic in Chapter 6, where I shall be considering the limitations of CTA in the context of the full reconciliatory naturalist program. In the meantime, my business is to consider whether the skeptical problem of natural agency as such has a satisfactory solution.

It is clear that skepticism of this kind can be resolved if the Causal

Theory of Action is correct. I speak of "the" Causal Theory, but of course there can be a whole family of such theories because there are many specific ways in which it could turn out that actions are constituted by behavior with a special kind of mental causal history. To defend "the" CTA, then, it is necessary to find an acceptable way of filling out its basic ontological claim. This is what I shall try to do in what follows. In Chapter 3, I shall consider how such a theory might initially be formulated and developed in the face of various difficulties. And there is no doubt that there will be difficulties. If a CTA is indeed correct, it is certainly not obviously so. Causation of behavior by one's mental states (whether deterministic or indeterministic) seems, on first consideration, to have little chance of turning out, under certain conditions, to be equivalent to action. Even if it is my own mental states that cause me to behave, surely such behavior must fall short of a genuine action of mine in which *I* contribute to determining what happens?

Before trying to explain how a CTA might be developed in the face of this and other difficulties, I wish first to consider whether CTA does indeed hold the most promising key to solving the skeptical problem of natural agency. If correct, CTA would solve the problem – but might there not be more tractable alternatives? In Chapter 2, then, I shall first show the importance of CTA for traditional discussions of the debate over compatibilism and then consider whether there are alternative approaches to resolving the problem of natural agency that may merit consideration before CTA.

NOTES

1 Ludwig Wittgenstein, *Philosophical Investigations,* 3d ed., G. E. M. Anscombe, trans. (Oxford, England: Blackwell, 1972), §621 p. 161ᵉ.
2 This commitment of our ethical perspective to the existence of actions might be broken if a moral point of view that employs no notion of moral responsibility were a viable possibility. Only a retributivist morality, it might be suggested, need raise the question of responsibility, and a consequentialist one avoids it altogether. But this is a mistake: Good consequentialist justifications are available for practices that hold agents accountable for outcomes, and offer such differential responses as praise and blame, punishment and reward. (For example, consider a justification of punishment in terms of its deterrent effects.) But such practices can be beneficial only if the various responses are to be made strictly in accordance with desert. And an agent's behavior can be deserving of praise, censure, sanction, excuse, or whatever only if it satisfies general conditions of accountability or moral responsibility. Daniel Dennett argues per-

suasively that only the nihilist can do without a concept of moral responsibility – and nihilism, of course, is an abandonment of the ethical perspective altogether. See his *Elbow Room: The Varieties of Free Will Worth Wanting* (Oxford, England: Clarendon Press, 1984), chap. 7.

3 *Pace* Donald Davidson, who because he maintains that only language users can have beliefs – see "Thought and Talk," *Inquiries Into Truth and Interpretation* (Oxford, England: Clarendon Press, 1984), Essay 11 – is presumably committed to the view that only language users can perform genuine actions (for an agent could exercise its own control, surely, only if it had some beliefs about the context in which it did so). I have argued elsewhere that Davidson's arguments for this claim are unpersuasive: "More Thought on Thought and Talk," *Mind,* **89** (1980), 1–16.

4 For an example of this style of incompatibilist argument, see Richard Taylor's "refutation" of soft determinism: *Metaphysics* (Englewood Cliffs, N.J.: Prentice-Hall, 1963), p. 44.

5 There are several distinct versions of the thesis of determinism; for a useful discussion see Storrs McCall, "Freedom Defined as the Power to Decide," *American Philosophical Quarterly,* **21** (1984), 329–38, pp. 331–2. The formulation given here will be adequate for the present, but it will be important later to note that some current arguments for skepticism about action under determinism rest on the following stronger version of the thesis: For every event *e,* the statement that *e* occurs can be derived as a deductive consequence from the laws of nature plus a true statement of the total state of the universe at *any* time prior to that at which *e* occurs.

6 Most notably, Harry Frankfurt, "Alternate [sic] Possibilities and Moral Responsibility," *Journal of Philosophy,* **66** (1969), 829–39.

7 To show that an agent was not morally responsible is one way of excusing behavior, but it is not the only way. Many excuses acknowledge moral responsibility, while arguing for one reason or another that the usual standards for judgment do not apply.

8 Daniel Dennett, "I Could Not Have Done Otherwise – So What?" *Journal of Philosophy,* **81** (1984), 553–65.

9 For the details, see Frankfurt, "Alternate Possibilities," pp. 835–6. A useful description of the general form of Frankfurt-style counterexamples is offered by John Martin Fischer, "Responsibility and Control," *Journal of Philosophy,* **79** (1982), 24–40, who describes this type of example as "the case of the counterfactual intervener." Dennett is mistaken in describing Black as "the over-determiner" (*Elbow Room,* p. 132). Black's actual behavior can hardly *over-*determine Jones's *a*-ing since it isn't even a cause of his *a*-ing! (Donald Davidson is similarly mistaken. See his *Essays on Actions and Events* (Oxford, England: Clarendon Press, 1980), p. 75.) This mistake leads Dennett to downgrade the importance of Frankfurt's counterexample and to treat it as the exception that proves the rule (*Elbow Room,* pp. 132–3). Dennett's overall position on the CDO principle is confused. On the one hand, he suggests that in assigning responsibility, "it is seldom that we even *seem* to care whether or not a person could have done otherwise" (p. 133), yet he devotes a whole section of Chapter 6 to suggestions about the proper analysis of this condition about which we don't seem to care (sect. 3, pp. 144–52). He remarks that "even if we are right to abandon allegiance to the 'could have done otherwise' principle as a prerequisite of responsible action, there is the residual problem (according to the incompatibilists) that under determinism, we can never do anything but what we in fact do" (p. 144), and then proceeds to suggest ways of dealing with this "residual problem." But if it is correct to reject the CDO principle, how can it be

a "residual problem" for the defense of compatibilism that we can never do other than we in fact do? Peter van Inwagen's diagnosis seems correct: Although Dennett advertises himself as rejecting the CDO principle, he actually accepts it and then faces the usual compatibilist task of explaining how the CDO condition may be satisfied in a deterministic universe. See van Inwagen's reply to Dennett's "I Could Not Have Done Otherwise," *Journal of Philosophy*, **81** (1984), 565–7.

10 Peter van Inwagen argues along these lines in Chapter 5 of *An Essay on Free Will* (Oxford, England: Clarendon Press, 1983). He concedes that the CDO principle is false yet claims to "exhibit three principles which entail that free will is necessary for moral responsibility, which are not open to Frankfurt-style counterexamples" (p. 164). Since van Inwagen holds that "to be able to have acted otherwise is to have free will" (p. 162), it looks as if he is himself committed to the truth of some form of CDO principle. Yet he does not clearly distinguish between the version of the CDO principle that he concedes to be false and the version of it that is entailed by (each of?) his three "Frankfurt-immune" principles. In the absence of a clear distinction here, it can seem that van Inwagen fallaciously claims to establish the truth of three principles, each of which entails a principle he concedes to be false! Besides all this, I agree with Robert Heinaman, "Incompatibilism Without the Principle of Alternative Possibilities," *Australasian Journal of Philosophy*, **64** (1986), 266–76, that Frankfurt-style counterexamples can in fact be constructed for each of van Inwagen's three principles. Heinaman also correctly observes, in effect, that Frankfurt's counterexamples by themselves cannot be used to refute incompatibilism because the incompatibilist may maintain that CDO *under some contracausal construal* is necessary for moral responsibility (pp. 275–6).

11 Thomas Nagel, *Mortal Questions* (Cambridge, England: Cambridge University Press, 1979), p. 25.

12 There remains a further aspect to the problem of moral luck – namely, to account for our practice of not treating equally agents who make the same partial causal contribution to different outcomes. A similarly negligent driver who has no need to brake suddenly is not judged as blameworthy as his unlucky counterpart. The solution lies, I believe, in distinguishing between, on the one hand, a notion of the extent of an agent's liability to compensate or pay retribution for a wrong deed (or to receive praise or reward for a good one) and, on the other, some notion of the intrinsic value of the deed, perhaps as revealing the agent's character. The former is, whereas the latter is not, crucially affected by what actually happens. Our two negligent drivers, then, make the same input into their respective causal contexts. Each deed is intrinsically as bad as the other, but the driver whose negligence unluckily causes the greater harm pays the greater penalty.

13 When G. E. Moore, in Chapter 6 of his *Ethics* (Oxford, England: Oxford University Press, 1912), explicated "I could have done otherwise" as "I could have done otherwise, if I'd chosen," he was not offering an *analysis* but rather pointing out a *grammatical marker* for a special sense of "could have," which is used in the attribution of active powers. It is this very sense that I mean to indicate here by the device of hyphenation. However, Moore's suggestion that "to avoid a possible complication, perhaps we had better say, 'that I *should, if* I had chosen'" (p. 131) initiated a justly famous controversy about the analysis of the condition of control, on which I shall comment in Chapter 2, Section V.

14 Peter van Inwagen's "Consequence Argument" is of this general type. See his *Essay on Free Will*, chap. 3. An actual formulation of his argument is considered in Chapter 2.

46

15 Roderick Chisholm, "Freedom and Action," in Keith Lehrer, ed., *Freedom and Determinism* (New York: Random House, 1966), pp. 11–44.

16 Ibid., p. 16.

17 This view is argued by C. D. Broad, "Determinism, Indeterminism and Libertarianism," *Ethics and the History of Philosophy* (London: Routledge & Kegan Paul, 1952), who concludes, "it is . . . highly probable that the notion of categorical obligability [sc. action for which the agent is morally responsible] is a delusive notion, which neither has nor can have any application" (p. 217).

18 I mean a *genuine* further option – not the counterfeit third alternative that Chisholm himself offers. He professes to avoid the dilemma by rejecting its basic assumption that for every behavioral sequence, either its antecedent events do or do not (100 percent) causally determine it. Chisholm suggests as a third possibility that behavior might be caused *by the agent*. But since he requires that whatever is agent-caused is *not* also event-caused, his position is actually a classically libertarian one. We shall consider later whether an appeal to agent-causation can discharge the libertarian's obligation to deal with the argument of the second horn of Chisholm's dilemma.

19 Peter van Inwagen has recently claimed that no one has held such a view: "Compatibilistic Reflections," *Australasian Journal of Philosophy*, **63** (1985), 349–53. That he is mistaken is shown by the examples of Donald Davidson and Keith Lehrer. No commitment to the impossibility of action in an indeterministic world is entailed by Davidson's defense of compatibilism in Essays 1 and 4 of his *Essays on Actions and Events;* and Lehrer explicitly says that "whatever evidence I have that I could have done otherwise *in no way bears on the question* of whether or not there is some unbroken causal or deterministic chain [terminating in my behavior]"; see "Self-Profile," in R. J. Bogdan, ed., *Keith Lehrer* (Dordrecht, Holland: D. Reidel, 1981), 3–104, p. 9.

20 Compare Dennett's discussion of David Wiggins's similar remarks in Daniel Dennett, *Brainstorms: Philosophical Essays on Mind and Psychology* (Hassocks, England: Harvester Press, 1979), pp. 287–8.

21 Quoted by Dennett, *Elbow Room*, p. 144.

22 Ibid., pp. 169–70.

23 Dennett, *Brainstorms*, p. 233. I suggest that "mechanism" here is used with the same meaning as "naturalism" in the previous quotation (footnote 22).

24 Following the lead of G. E. M. Anscombe, *Intention* (Oxford, England: Blackwell, 1957), p. 9.

25 Dennett, *Brainstorms,* p. 235. This terminology has a dual connotation: Explanations "by reasons" refer to the agent's "intentional states" (or propositional attitudes), and when they apply, they yield a description under which the explanandum counts as an intentional action.

26 A useful review of these differences and their significance is offered by Davidson in "Actions, Reasons and Causes," Essay 1 in *Essays on Actions and Events.*

27 See Davidson, *Essays on Actions and Events,* p. 233; "we cannot turn this mode of explanation [sc. intentional explanation] into something more like science." Essays 11 and 12 provide arguments for this judgment.

28. D. M. MacKay, "Seeing the Wood and the Trees," in William Maxwell, ed., *Thinking: the Expanding Frontier* (Philadelphia: Franklin Institute Press, 1983), 5–12, p. 7. Compare also his "Selves and Brains," *Neuroscience, 3* (1978), 599–606.

29 See Dennett, *Brainstorms,* pp. 237–9; the quotation is from p. 238.

30 Ibid., p. 243.

31 Ibid., p. 238.

32 Ibid., pp. 239–43.

33 Ibid., pp. 242–3.
34 See, for example, Paul Churchland, "Eliminative Materialism and the Propositional Attitudes," *Journal of Philosophy*, **78** (1981), 67–90. For a recent reply to eliminativist arguments, see Terence Horgan and James Woodward, "Folk Psychology Is Here to Stay," *Philosophical Review*, **94** (1985), 197–226.
35 Gary Watson, ed., *Free Will* (Oxford, England: Oxford University Press, 1982), p. 9. See also Thomas Nagel's more recent, similar statement of the problem, *The View from Nowhere* (Oxford, England: Oxford University Press, 1986), p. 110.
36 See Davidson, *Essays on Actions and Events*, Essay 3, especially pp. 44–6.
37 Or so it seems to me. Nagel, however, manages to arrive (*View from Nowhere*, Chap. VII) at a pessimistic assessment of the prospects for solving the problem of natural agency without even mentioning the type of solution I am about to discuss.

2

The value of a causal theory of action

I. A TRADITIONAL APPROACH TO THE PROBLEM OF NATURAL AGENCY

In Chapter 1, I argued that the skeptical problem of natural agency is not to be identified with the traditional problem of freedom under determinism. Nevertheless, this traditional problem remains one instantiation of it: namely, that obtained by assuming that the natural order is deterministic and that "freedom" labels nothing more than an agent's power to exercise control over outcomes. Accordingly, although the traditional debate is not at the precise core of our problem, it is by no means irrelevant to it.

Indeed, a methodological justification may be given for beginning any inquiry into the problem of natural agency with an examination of the well-trodden paths of debate about compatibilism. Should it be possible to establish the compatibilist claim that behavior can count as action in a deterministic universe, it would follow immediately that it is mistaken to remain skeptical about how agency could be a natural possibility *under any natural causal order whatsoever.* So it seems sensible to start by considering whether we may defend a thesis whose truth would exclude such total skepticism about action in the natural order. Nevertheless, proving traditional compatibilism would not provide a fully general solution to the problem of natural agency because some compatibilists have argued that agency is not merely *consistent* with determinism but actually *positively requires* it. And for them, skepticism about action would follow were macroscopic behavior to turn out *not* to be 100 percent causally determined.

Would it not be best, then, to try resolving the problem of natural agency by sticking closely to the terms of the traditional debate? The following procedure seems suitable: First, consider whether compatibilism is defensible; if it is, skepticism about action in *any* natural order will have been defeated. A fully general solution will then require defending the possibility that behavior that lacks 100 percent causal determination should nevertheless count as the behavior's action. But this same thesis will also be required to defeat skepticism if traditional compatibilism turns out to be false: for, in that case, actions will be possible only if they are not 100 percent causally determined by prior states and events. Should we not, then, follow tradition by bifurcating the problem into two separate debates about the possibility of action under determinism and indeterminism, respectively?

In Chapter 1, I contended that this is not a perspicuous way to structure the issue. I claimed that there is a single fundamental problem of natural agency – namely, to understand how there can be room for real "doings" in a sequence of "happenings" – and this problem remains essentially the same, whether happenings belong to a deterministic system or not. This fundamental problem, I suggested, can best be solved by defending a Causal Theory of Action. My purpose in this chapter is to reinforce this approach, by showing just how valuable the Causal Theory of Action is even when we start by dealing with the problem in its traditional, bifurcated form. Thus, I shall argue that if we try to defeat skepticism about action under determinism and skepticism about action under indeterminism separately, we shall find ourselves drawn, in each case, into defending a Causal Theory of Action (CTA). Therefore, although my intentions are progressive, I shall in this chapter take a deliberate backward step to consider how the debate about natural agency, in its traditional, bifurcated form, is being handled by leading contemporary philosophers. I believe I shall be able to show that the question of the truth of a CTA should be located at the core of this debate and that much that is unsatisfactory about contemporary discussions stems from a failure to recognize this fact. My showing this will thus provide an appropriate prolegomenon to the formulation and defense of CTA, which occupies the remaining chapters.

Those impatient of further prolegomena, who are already convinced that a CTA offers the best hope for overcoming skepticism about natural agency, might perhaps proceed at once to Chapter 3. If they do so, however, they will miss not only some polemical engagements with influential protagonists in the current traditional debate but also some important clues for the correct formulation of CTA. It is useful, I believe, to explore the relevance of CTA to the traditional debate before proceeding to any more precise formulation of it than we have at present – namely, as a theory that says that what constitutes behavior as action is its having the right kind of mental causes. Accordingly, in Sections II and III, I consider the possibility of agency under determinism and under indeterminism in turn. The work of an influential contemporary libertarian, Peter van Inwagen, provides a useful critical focus for my discussion here. I shall argue that van Inwagen's "Consequence Argument" against the possibility of agency under determinism is unsuccessful – essentially because it begs the question against the truth of a CTA. But van Inwagen is dangerously close to being a closet skeptic about agency under any natural causal order since he also has doubts about understanding how agency is possible under indeterminism. However, I shall argue that these doubts are ill founded and that a suitably "probabilistic" version of CTA (if correct) would vindicate the natural possibility of action in an indeterministic universe.

My criticisms of contemporary treatments of the traditional debate are not, however, confined to those who profess a libertarian line. I also aim in this chapter to support my belief that defending the CTA is the best approach to defeating skepticism about natural agency. And to achieve this, I shall need to consider alternative contemporary suggestions for establishing the compatibility of agency with the presuppositions of the naturalist worldview. Thus in Section IV, I examine Daniel Dennett's approaches to the defense of natural agency and argue that he fails to provide intelligible "elbow room" for action precisely because (as a result of his instrumentalism about intentional states) he lacks the resources for defending a CTA. Finally, in Section V, I argue that the direct defense of a CTA is a superior strategy to the compatibilist's traditional appeal to a "conditional analysis" of free action. Chapter 2, then, seeks to drive home an appreciation of just how important the question of the truth of the Causal Theory of Action is for the problem of natural agency and, therefore, for the overall reconciliatory naturalist project of understanding how our ethical perspective can apply to the natural world.

II. IS ACTION POSSIBLE UNDER DETERMINISM?

I begin, then, with the first (and more common) form of skepticism about natural agency, which is relative to the assumption that from the natural perspective, behavior must be understood as 100 percent causally determined. Skepticism of this kind has as its core the thesis commonly known as *incompatibilism:* the claim that actions are impossible in a deterministic universe. (Of course, as I have already observed in Chapter 1, skepticism about action under determinism need not lead to skepticism about natural agency altogether because incompatibilists can be libertarians, who affirm the existence of action but draw the conclusion that the universe cannot, therefore, be a deterministic system.) In this section, I aim to show the relevance of CTA for the debate about incompatibilism and to make some observations about what a fully formulated CTA would have to include in order to deal with this particular species of skepticism about natural agency.

An argument for traditional incompatiblism was sketched at the start of Chapter 1: It turned on rejecting the possibility that behavior that could not but have happened relative to past events and the laws of nature might also be behavior that the agent could have avoided. A contradiction does indeed result if it is necessary for action that there could have been an alternative behavioral outcome even given the very same circumstances. But as we saw in our discussion of the Frankfurt counterexamples, this condition (the CDO condition on its "alternative outcome" construal) is *not* necessary for action, and so the case for incompatibilism cannot be as straightforward as this initial sketch makes it seem. Are there, then, reasons for thinking that conditions that *are* necessary for action are unrealizable under determinism?

To count as action, an agent's behavior must count as the use of a power the agent possesses – as an exercise of the agent's control. It is necessary for action, then, that the agent employ a power that the agent could have used otherwise – but as already argued, this requirement does not entail the CDO condition on its alternative outcome construal. It is tempting to argue that because behavior that is 100 percent causally determined is necessary relative to the laws of nature and facts about the past, it cannot also constitute the exercise of the *agent's* power. But of course, this begs the question whether such relative necessity is inconsistent with the exercise of an agent's control. It is evidently fallacious to infer from the fact that the truth of a statement about the agent's behavior is deductively necessitated by certain other truths that, therefore, the agent is necessitated to behave as he or she does and so does not exercise his or her own control. This is the well-known fallacy that deduces fatalism from determinism.

The Consequence Argument for Incompatibilism

What does clinch the incompatibilist's case, according to some philosophers, is the fact that 100 percent causally determined behavior is necessary relative to states of affairs that are *themselves also necessary* in a sense that excludes agent-control. Peter van Inwagen puts the argument (the "Consequence Argument") this way:

> If determinism is true, then our acts are the consequences of the laws of nature and events in the remote past. But it is not up to us what went on before we were born, and neither is it up to us what the laws of nature are. Therefore, the consequences of these things (including our present acts) are not up to us.[1]

We are to take it that *consequences* here means "deductive consequences" and that it is a necessary condition for behavior to count as action that its occurrence was "up to the agent," that is, an exercise of the agent's control.

If we define the modal operator, N, thus:

$Np =_{df} p$ & it is not under the agent's control that p,

then the logical form of the Consequence Argument may be represented as follows:

(1) Ns
(2) $N(s \supset p)$
(3) Np

where p is the statement that the agent performs behavior b, and s is the statement of facts about the (remote) past which, together with the laws of nature, entail that p. Thus (2) is a deductive consequence of the truth of the (relevant) laws of nature, and so is itself not under the agent's control (i.e., its truth is modified by the operator N).

The Consequence Argument thus assumes the truth of the following general principle:

$$(N\alpha \ \& \ N(\alpha \supset \beta)) \supset N\beta$$

which, following Michael Slote,[2] I shall call the *main modal principle* (henceforth, MMP). That is, the argument assumes that events whose occurrence is a deductive consequence of conditions that are not under an agent's control are therefore not themselves under that agent's control. Van Inwagen, in effect, takes the truth of MMP to be obvious.[3] But in fact, its use in attempts to prove incompatiblism is open to question, as Slote's recent discussion of the Consequence Argument and its relatives[4] nicely reveals.

Questioning the Main Modal Principle: Slote's Implicit Appeal to CTA

Michael Slote has argued that although the equivalent of MMP holds for *Np* interpreted as "it is logically necessary that *p*" under standard systems of alethic modal logic, it does not hold for certain other epistemic, deontic, and metaphysical modalities. Slote argues, in other words, for the falsity of the general principle, MMP*,

$$(N) \; [N\alpha \; \& \; N(\alpha \supset \beta)) \supset N\beta]$$

where *N* ranges over all forms of necessity representable as modal propositional operators. Slote terms "selective" those forms of necessity which falsify MMP*. Epistemic "necessity" offers perhaps the best example of a selective modality since, by omitting to make the relevant inferences, people can fail to know the deductive consequences of what they already know. The operator "It is obligatory (for *M*) that . . ." is also arguably selective because, for example, I may have an obligation to visit Jones and an obligation to call in on Smith (Jones's neighbor) if I should ever be in Jones's neighborhood without having any obligation *tout court* to visit Smith. And "nonaccidentality" is apparently also selective since, for example, it is no accident that I am writing this sentence; neither is it any accident that my being alive at this moment is a necessary condition of my doing so, yet the fact of my continued existence until now (as this sentence concludes) may plausibly be "something of an accident."[5]

Slote thus disposes of one possible basis for taking the truth of MMP to be obvious. Admittedly, proponents of the Consequence Argument (and its ilk) have never explicitly sought to support MMP by deriving it from the alleged truth of MMP* – although the fact that the equivalent of MMP holds for logical necessity may well have subconsciously fueled their sense of its obviousness. But Slote is – appropriately – not content simply to shake the complacency of incompatibilist faith in the obviousness of MMP by casting doubt on the general truth of MMP*. He goes further to offer positive argument for the claim that "unavoidability" (i.e., necessity as far as the agent's control is concerned) is a selective kind of necessity. That is, he claims that MMP itself is false and that, therefore, the Consequence Argument is invalid.

There is considerable interest (for present purposes) in the way Slote seeks to justify his claim that unavoidability is selective. Selectivity arises, he suggests, for forms of necessity that are in a certain sense relational – that is, when to say that some state of affairs or event obtains necessarily is to say that it is necessary *relative*, for example, to some body of knowledge (epistemic necessity), to some obligation-creating performance (deontic necessity), or to some specific agent's plan (nonaccidentality). How could selectivity arise, then, for the necessity that attaches to events in virtue of their occurring outside the agent's control? Slote says this:

The particular kind of factor in relation to which unavoidability exists at any given time, the factor "selected" by such necessity, is, simply, some factor, or set of factors, that brings about the unavoidable things *without making use of an explanatory chain that includes the desires, etc., the agent has around that time.*[6]

It is important to recognize that Slote is here implicitly advancing a theory about what it is for something to occur under an agent's control – that is, a theory of action. In suggesting that the "unavoidability" of an occurrence is its coming about through an "explanatory chain" that *does not* include "the desires, etc., the agent has" around the time of the occurrence, he is committing himself to the view that, for control, for *lack* of "unavoidability," behavior must complete an explanatory chain that *does* include "the desires, etc., the agent has" around that time.[7] Slote's view would therefore seem to be that behavior counts as action only when it terminates a causal chain (for that is surely what his talk of explanatory chains must come to) that passes through certain of the behaver's recent mental states ("desires, etc."). Now a view of this kind is right at the core of the Causal Theory of Action. Under CTA, to count as action it is essential that behavior have a causal history suitably involving the behaver's mental states. So the situation is that to show the selectivity of the kind of necessity involved in the Consequence Argument, Slote appeals to the core claim of CTA – a claim that can itself be made good only by defending a specific account of how an explanatory chain terminating in behavior has to involve the behaver's "desires, etc." if that behavior is to count as action. To drive home Slote's criticism of the Consequence Argument, then, we shall need to formulate and defend a Causal Theory of Action.[8]

Additional Note: Earlier Criticisms
of the Consequence Argument

I believe it is possible to show that earlier criticisms of van Inwagen's Consequence Argument, which were directed against his initial formulation of it, also need to make an implicit appeal to a CTA in order to rebut it. The essential point made independently by André Gallois, David Lewis, and John Martin Fischer[9] may be put like this: The version of MMP on which van Inwagen's initial version of the Consequence Argument relies comes to the claim that if p suffices for q, and p obtains, then an agent M could have rendered it false that q only if M could have rendered it false that p. But the locution "M could have rendered it false that p" is ambiguous, as between an attenuated and an unattenuated sense.

In the attenuated sense, it means that M had the capacity to perform some action, a, such that, if M had done a, it would have been false that p. In this sense MMP is (almost trivially) true, but the compatibilist may maintain that it can be true of agents that they could have *in this sense* rendered false facts about the past or even, according to Lewis,[10] the facts of natural law. Certainly, the compatibilist will have no difficulty in agreeing that in a deterministic universe, if an agent had acted other than he or she did, some truths about the past would have been false. Thus, on this construal, the compatibilist will hold false one of the premises of the Consequence Argument, namely, that M could not have rendered it false that s, where s states actual past causes of M's behavior. Accordingly, the Consequence Argument begs the question if this reading of "could have rendered false" is employed.

But there is an alternative, unattenuated construal of the locution on which it means that M had the capacity to perform the action of "making it false that p" – that M could have, directly or indirectly, *caused p* to be false. In this sense, no agent can render the past or the laws of nature false, so both crucial premises of the Consequence Argument will have to be accepted as true. But what of MMP, on this construal? It will read thus: If *p* suffices for *q*, and *p* obtains, then *M* could have rendered it false that *q* only if *it was within M's capacity to perform the action of making it false that p*. Now this claim might perhaps be true, but *compatibilists* certainly believe that it is false. According to compatibilism, a remote past state of the universe may be deductively sufficient, given the laws of nature, for an agent to perform behavior that counts as the agent's own action. But this claim can be made plausible in the face of the incompatibilist intuition of the truth of MMP as formulated on the unattenuated construal only if some account is given of how a deterministic causal chain can terminate in events that count as action. And this can be done, as Gallois suggests, by saying that in such a case, the causal chain will include "as an essential constituent, [the agent's] process of deliberation"[11]; however, this statement implies commitment to some version of CTA since, of course, the "process of deliberation" will be a sequence of mental states and events.

The Place of CTA in Compatibilist Responses to the Consequence Argument

We may thus understand Slote and other critics as arguing, in effect, that the main modal principle of the Consequence Argument is false because the core claim of the Causal Theory of Action is true. The remote past and the laws of nature will indeed be unavoidable – beyond the agent's control. But if the agent's behavior, which is the *deductive* consequence of these unavoidable states of affairs, is also the *causal* consequence of the right kind of states of the agent, the agent's behavior will fulfill conditions sufficient for it to count as action. If facts about the remote past cause present behavior via the right sort of causal chain, the causal consequence of what is unavoidable will actually constitute a case of something that comes about through agent-control.

It is not surprising, I believe, that these critics of the Consequence Argument appeal (though admittedly without much explicit fanfare) to the truth of a CTA. For, this appeal meets a requirement that I believe has to be met if we are to establish that the Consequence Argument is, indeed, unsound. As I have said, van Inwagen's strategy in the Consequence Argument is to treat

MMP as virtually self-evident. And there is little doubt that MMP does have considerable prima facie plausibility: How can my present behavior be under *my* control if its occurrence is literally fixed by (i.e., is a deductive consequence of) a conjunction of conditions none of which either is or was itself under my control? Prima facie plausibility, of course, is not the same as self-evidence, and one takes a significant though minor step in criticizing the Consequence Argument to observe as much. But to show that the argument is unsound, we need to show that MMP is false – or at least, that van Inwagen's compatibilist opponent will have good reason to believe that it is false (so that, strictly, the argument is unsound because it begs the question, rather than because it proceeds from a known false premise). Now, for MMP to be false it is going to have to be possible for happenings that are under my control to be fixed by events and states of affairs not under my control. But this – of course – is exactly what the compatibilist believes *is* possible! Indeed, compatibilism might fairly be *defined* as the thesis that MMP is false; so if the burden of proof in this argument rested with the incompatibilist, the Consequence Argument would conspicuously fail to discharge it.

However, the admitted prima facie plausibility of MMP effectively shifts the burden of proof. The compatibilist's claim that I can be in control of behavior whose occurrence is a deductive consequence of factors quite beyond my control will seem somewhat fanciful unless the compatibilist can provide a plausible account of how this could be possible. Without such an account, the most the compatibilist can claim is that van Inwagen's use of MMP begs the question against mere compatibilist intuitions – in which case, the debate degenerates into an exchange of contrary intuitions. And on those (unsatisfactory) terms van Inwagen is likely to win – or so my own modest personal survey of intuitive responses to the question of the truth of MMP would predict. Thus, although the Consequence Argument rather obviously fails as a disproof of compatibilism, it succeeds in making skepticism about agency under determinism sufficiently respectable for the compatibilist to be forced into explaining in positive terms how some – and only some – 100 percent causally determined behavioral episodes can have the status of action.

Therefore, to rebut the Consequence Argument, the compatibilist stands in need of *a positive argument for the falsity of MMP* –

that is, a putatively good reason for thinking that behavior fixed by conditions beyond the behaver's control can nevertheless count as that behaver's own action. Now if CTA is true, there are good prospects for supplying exactly the sort of argument the compatibilist needs here. In fact, it is my opinion that a positive case for the falsity of MMP can be achieved only by affirming a suitable version of CTA. In Sections IV and V of this chapter, I shall try to support this opinion, although (unsurprisingly) I have no a priori proof that the compatiblist must unavoidably be committed to some version of CTA. In the meantime, however, the importance of CTA for compatibilism will be quite adequately demonstrated if we can show that its truth is at least sufficient for the falsity of MMP.[12] And surely the truth of CTA does have this implication? If its having a causal history (appropriately running through the behaver's mental states) is essential for behavior to count as the behaver's own action, then, surely, actions can be fixed by conditions that are themselves quite beyond the agent's control?

A CTA Sufficient to Defeat the Consequence Argument Will Need to Be Deterministic

Obviously, one clear option for the incompatibilist at this point is to admit that were CTA true, MMP would be false (and conversely) but to argue that there is a good reason for thinking that CTA is false. To make this option work, of course, the incompatibilist will have to tell us what that good reason is, and in doing so, to go beyond merely asserting the truth of MMP (otherwise the question will simply be begged). Since CTA is well known to be controversial, this approach holds promise. Incompatibilists would do well to rally around the slogan that to act is one thing, to be caused to behave by one's own mental states, quite another.[13] All the doubts people continue to have about how action could possibly consist purely in behavior with suitable mental causes can be brought to bear on the incompatibilist side of the debate. Incompatibilists do, I think, face a little-noticed dilemma if they take this apparently very promising line – and I shall explain this presently. But first, I wish to consider a different option for the incompatibilist, which does not require outright rejection of CTA.

Incompatibilists might try to argue that although actions may indeed count as such because they have a suitable mental causal history, this does not entail that behavior can be completely fixed by conditions beyond the agent's control and still count as action. That is, they might argue that on any correct version of it, CTA will not, after all, entail the falsity of MMP – in which case, of course, the intuition that CTA is true would not tell against allowing ourselves to be persuaded by the plausibility of MMP. And incompatibilists have, indeed, taken this line. Typically, they have insisted that "internal" 100 percent causal determination of behavior is just as exclusive of agent-control as any "purely external" causal determination could be. They have claimed, that is, that causal determination of behavior by the agent's (relevant) mental states excludes it from counting as action, at least *where this causal determination occurs within a deterministic system.*

To establish the falsity of MMP, then, the compatibilist will need to defend not just any version of CTA but one that we may describe as *deterministic,* according to which behavior may count as action when it is 100 percent causally determined by the behaver's (appropriate) mental states or events and where these mental states or events are themselves 100 percent causally determined by antecedent conditions. Provided the case for CTA in general can successfully be made, the compatibilist may presume that deterministic versions of CTA are also acceptable. But this presumption is, of course, overturned if incompatibilists can provide arguments to show that behavior caused by suitable mental states would necessarily fall short of action *in a deterministic world,* although it might not in nondeterministic worlds. What might such arguments come to? I hope it is obvious that it will not be dialectically in order for incompatibilists merely to rehearse the Consequence Argument again in reply to this question. Such a procedure would, at this point, blatantly beg the question. In case this is not obvious, try considering the matter in this way: The force of the Consequence Argument lies in the initial plausibility of MMP; but the compatibilist has, in effect, sought to match this force by appealing to the initial plausibility of an unrestricted, deterministic, CTA; since MMP and a deterministic CTA are contraries, and initial plausibility is claimed for each, incompatibilists can make progress only by means of arguments that do not already simply presuppose that MMP is true. But appealing to the Consequence Argument itself to exclude the possibility of a deterministic CTA would, of course, simply presuppose MMP.

The Case Against a Specifically Deterministic
Causal Theory of Action

It turns out, I think, that there are no persuasive reasons for thinking that a specifically deterministic CTA would fail that go beyond the question-begging reiteration of the Consequence Argument. Arguments that seem to offer such reasons would, in fact, if they succeeded at all, be enough to cast doubt on CTA altogether – or so I hope to establish.

There are two distinct points at which incompatibilists might attack a specifically deterministic CTA while leaving open the possibility that a nondeterministic version of the Theory would turn out to be correct. First, they might focus on the causal link between mental states and matching behavior and argue that for the latter to count as action, this link cannot be deterministic. And second, they might focus on the causal antecedents of the mental states that (perhaps even deterministically) cause the matching behavior and argue that these cannot be deterministic if the behavior is to count as action. I shall consider these possibilities in order.

Some incompatibilists might well urge that the notion that, for example, my action of raising my arm is constituted by my arm going up as a causal consequence of my intention to raise it is flawed because, on this picture, once I form my intention to raise my arm, my arm's rising is then no longer up to me. My control ends once I perform that mental event (whatever it is; I here use intention only for the sake of example) that forms part of the proximate cause of my resulting bodily movements. Yet, they would claim, my behavior can count as my action only if I am exercising my control *throughout* its occurrence. Even as I form the final intention to raise my arm, it must still be "up to me" (they would say) actually to raise it. This is an important argument, but it is an argument against the CTA in general and not simply against a deterministic form of it. Even if the causal link between intention and behavior is probabilistic, there is still the same problem about how the behavior itself can count as being under my control, as it needs to do if it is to be my action. If my final intention to raise my arm can at best be an essential part of a causal condition that makes it probable to a degree less than 1 that my arm will go up, we still seem to be operating with a model of action that has the unsatisfactory feature that once I form my intention I just have (so to speak!) to sit back and wait for events to take their course. (As we shall see shortly, van Inwagen is bothered by this kind of argument in the context of the possibility of action in an indeterministic universe.)

So there is a problem here that will indeed have to be dealt with by any CTA defender: namely, to reconcile CTA with our intuition that it is under the control of the agent whether his or her intentions actually issue in action or not. This is a problem because it suggests that any causal account of what it is for behavior to count as action will have to involve reference to further exercises of control on the part of the agent, and so introduce circularity. But this problem is quite unaffected by whether or not the causal link from intentions to behavior is deterministic.

How about the second approach? How might the incompatibilist argue that although behavior might count as action if 100 percent causally determined by antecedents essentially including the agent's reasons for such action, it could not do so if *the agent's having these reasons* were itself 100 percent causally determined? There is a familiar incompatibilist argument by analogy that may be offered at this point – it requires us to perform the following thought experiment: Suppose that a clever neurophysiologist has deliberately produced the states that constitute having reason r in agent M, by appropriately stimulating electrodes planted in M's brain.[14] Now consider whether matching behavior caused by the states that realize r could, under these circumstances, count as an exercise of M's control – as an action of M's.

There is an inclination to say that it could not count because all the power to act here seems to be in the hands of the neurophysiologist. But this inclination may be resisted. Influencing agents to act by causing them to have good reasons for so doing may sometimes diminish their autonomy – although the imagined neurophysiologist's interference need have no more tendency to do so than other quite practicable techniques (e.g., by placing agents under nonstandard perceptual conditions that they do not recognize as such, or by lying effectively to them). But behavior that falls short of fully autonomous action does not necessarily fail to count as genuine action. Arguably, it is still *an action* of M's that results from the neurophysiologist's influence. Although it is an actual rather than a counterfactual intervener in this case, I suggest that the intuitions generated in a Frankfurt-type example (discussed in the previous chapter) are appropriate here: M acts under constraint, indeed, but not under such constraint that his or her behavior is no longer an exercise of M's control.

But suppose that the kind of interference involved in the imagined neurophysiologist case were *global*. Suppose that a superhuman "neurophysiologist" were responsible for deliberately inducing all of our most fundamental reasons for action. Or suppose, as van Inwagen does, that a device implanted by Martians in each of us shortly after birth "causes us to have desires and beliefs appropriate to the decisions [the Martians want to] cause us to make."[15] Would it not then follow that our behavior, although caused by mental states of ours that constituted good reasons for performing it, was nevertheless not action of our own at all? If so, will not any account of action as behavior with appropriate mental causes (any CTA) have to impose restrictions on the genesis of those mental causes themselves? And – to meet the intuitions generated by the present thought experiment – one of these restrictions will have to be that the mental causes that CTA holds to be definitive of action are not themselves caused by the systematic action or operation of a superhuman neurophysiologist or Martian-implanted device. But in that case, will it not also be necessary to require that the mental causes of actions not be themselves 100 percent causally determined by antecedent conditions? For, is not the uniform 100 percent causal determination of reasons by antecedent events just as apt to undermine genuine action as the systematic determination of reasons by highly powerful external agents? That, at least, is what the incompatibilist may claim. Thus, CTA may be correct, but only on versions of it that require that the mental states and events definitive of action are not themselves 100 percent causally determined. A deterministic version of CTA, which would vindicate the possibility of action under determinism, is therefore impossible.

This line of argument may be resisted at several points. First, even if our behavior could not count as action under the superhuman neurophysiologist or Martian hypothesis, that fact need not by itself show that 100 percent causal determination of reasons would prevent them from causing genuine actions. The basis of the intuition that we should not be agents under these hypotheses may have purely to do with the fact that they depict us as pervasively under the control of some other very powerful agent. But 100 percent causal determination by antecedent events and conditions need involve no other agent's action at all.

Second, I doubt whether we ought to concede in the first place that people fitted unwittingly with the Martian device or under the control of a superhuman neurophysiologist would therefore fail to qualify as genuine agents. What prompts such a view is presumably the belief that under such circumstances people's behavior would be systematically subject to manipulation. I am unsure whether such wholesale determination of our reasons by an external agent need necessarily count as manipulation (suppose, for example, that it is a Beneficent Spirit, which puts good desires and true beliefs into our hearts and then leaves it up to us to reassess them if we like and act on them as we will), but even if this is manipulation, it is not clear that it deprives us of agency altogether.

It is true that an agent who has been manipulated by another agent's control of his or her acquisition of beliefs and desires will usually have a good excuse for whatever he or she did subject to the manipulation. But the fact that M's behavior is excusable because N manipulated M into it does not entail that M ceases altogether to be responsible for it. For example, suppose I arrive late because someone deliberately reversed the signpost at the crossroad to delay me: My lateness is indeed excusable, but surely I retain responsibility in some measure for the actions I performed on the basis of the false information? Indeed, if I had not been exercising my own control in deciding to follow the misleading sign, the question of excusing me for the consequences of my so doing would just not arise. Were we all victims of a manipulative Superagent, we should thus be, not mere automata, but rather genuine agents with a constant supply of good excuses! There might, I agree, be significant defects in the manipulative Superagent universe – it would probably lack the most valuable forms of interpersonal relationship, for example. But the controlled beings of such a universe would still be agents nonetheless.

Were we forced to carry the second of these responses this far, the incompatibilist would have achieved a minor victory. The impossibility of a deterministic CTA would not have been shown, but its potential to dispel skepticism about the coapplicability of our ethical framework with any form of naturalism committed to determinism would have been diminished. If human action under determinism were relevantly equivalent to human action under the control of a manipulative Superagent, a deterministic universe would arguably necessarily lack fully autonomous action. No complete solution to (what I called in the Introduction) the 'skeptical problem of natural moral autonomy' would then be possible, even if the skeptical problem of natural agency were to be resolved through a successful defense of CTA.

However, we are not forced into this position. The first response is quite good enough: The analogy between determination by a Superagent and 100 percent causal determination just will not bear the weight the incompatibilist seeks to place on it. What do these two conditions have relevantly in common? What remains when we subtract from the Superagent hypothesis the feature that gives it its intuitive power – namely, the determination of reasons by an external, powerful agent – and then compare it with the formation of reasons under determinism? Just this: that, in each case, the reasons that then go on to yield the agent's matching behavior *themselves come into existence as a consequence of events beyond the agent's control.*[16] And this fact is enough to persuade the incompatibilist that the resulting behavior cannot itself count as action, as an exercise of the agent's control. But of course, the incompatibilist is simply relying on MMP once again – the principle that conditions beyond the agent's control cannot be sufficient for what comes about through the exercise of the agent's control. And in the present context, this argument begs the question: The incompatibilist is looking for an argument against a deterministic CTA that is independent of the mere assertion of MMP.

Although the manipulative Superagent thought experiment fails to sustain an effective incompatibilist argument against the possibility of a deterministic CTA, it may express a deeper concern about the defense of the CTA generally. The underlying intuition here may simply be that although behavior that counts as action can be caused (deterministically or probabilistically) by mental states constituting the agent's reasons, it can do so only if this causal link is itself under the agent's control. Either those mental states must themselves have arisen through the agent's control, or their causal efficacy in yielding matching behavior must itself be subject to the agent's control (or, of course, both). Thus, according to this intuition, actions can be causally determined – but only by a chain of events including an action of the same agent. If this claim is true, no CTA can succeed: There will be an inherent circularity in any account of action as behavior with a special kind of causal history. This incompatibilist argument, then (as indeed the first one we considered), is best seen simply as a challenge to the defender of CTA to produce a causal analysis of action that *does not itself involve further implicit references to the exercise of the agent's control.*

Should Incompatibilists Seek
to Reject CTA Altogether?

There seems, then, to be no adequate case for the view that a CTA could succeed only if it were not deterministic. Still, there may be potential joy for incompatibilists in any argument that *undermines the whole basis of a Causal Theory of Action altogether.* If it can be shown that actions are not completely constituted by behavioral episodes with a certain kind of special mental causal history, compatibilism will be in trouble. A Slote-style defense of the selectivity of the necessity operator used in the main modal principle of the Consequence Argument will no longer be possible. As things stand, the suggestion that actions are just events with special causal antecedents is a powerful counter to the admittedly intransigent incompatibilist intuition that what is determined by factors outside my control cannot be a controlled action of mine. However, should a CTA decisively fail, this incompatibilist intuition will surely have its head.

Why, then, have dedicated incompatibilists (such as van Inwagen) not spent time attacking the Causal Theory of Action as such? My suggestion in Chapter 1 that the core of the skeptical problem of natural agency is independent of determinism and best solved by a CTA offers an answer. When incompatibilists are also libertarians (that is, when they are not skeptical about the possibility of action in *every* kind of natural order – it is only its possibility under determinism that they reject), they need to defeat skepticism about action in an *indeterministic* universe. If I am correct in holding that CTA best provides what is needed to solve the general problem of natural agency, then CTA will offer the best solution to this particular version of it. And so incompatibilist libertarians will be burning their bridges if they seek to undermine the CTA itself in order to establish that action is impossible in a deterministic world. They will be undermining the very theory that offers the best prospects for defending the natural possibility of action at all!

To reinforce this diagnosis, let me now turn to the second part of the problem of natural agency, which (for present purposes) we are approaching in the traditionally bifurcated way. We have seen that defending a CTA offers real prospects for the defense of compatibilism about action under determinism. Can we now establish my claim that if it succeeds it will also explain how action is possible under indeterminism?

III. IS ACTION POSSIBLE UNDER INDETERMINISM?

In an indeterministic system, some events are not 100 percent causally determined. Presumably, doubts about how action is possible in indeterministic systems specifically must be based on a belief that 100 percent causal determination is somehow *required* for action. This belief is usually itself based on a view that takes it as intrinsic to actions that they are done for reasons and that regards it as necessary to construe this relation as causal. But as already observed, even if this view is correct, why should the causal relation here not be probabilistic? There must be more to doubts about action under indeterminism than sheer neglect (or deliberate rejection) of the possibility of probabilistic causation.

Perhaps it is possible to revamp the Consequence Argument so that it expresses grounds for doubting the possibility of action under indeterminism as well? Could it not be suggested that where behavior is caused by antecedent conditions beyond the agent's control, it fails to count as his or her action whether the causation is deterministic or probabilistic? Perhaps. But the claim is not so intuitively compelling under indeterminism as it was under determinism. Although it does seem clear that behavior that occurs completely at random can't count as action, there is, nevertheless, some attraction to the idea that antecedent conditions that simply "probabilify" the behavior somehow leave room for the agent's control – even though those antecedents are themselves beyond his or her control. Once deductive certainty relative to antecedent conditions is abandoned with the rejection of determinism, the threat to genuine agency seems to wane. Yet reflection suggests that the difference between 100 percent and, say, 99 percent probability of the effect, given the cause, should not really make the difference between mere behavior and genuine agency. If there are grounds for skepticism about agency under determinism, it seems likely that they will surface in some new guise as grounds for doubting that an indeterministic system can contain actions.

Nevertheless, I doubt whether there is any argument for the conclusion that action is impossible specifically under indeterminism that carries the same initial force as the Consequence Argument does for the conclusion that action is impossible under determinism. However, one can raise a skeptical challenge to the believer in action under indeterminism that is entirely parallel to the skeptical challenge issued against the compatibilist, which as we have just seen, is the useful residue of the Consequence Argument once its failure as a proof is recognized. The effect of the Consequence Argument was not to compel compatibilists to recant, but rather to challenge them to produce an account of how it can be that some (and only some) behavior that is 100 percent causally determined counts as action. Correspondingly, then, those who believe that actions can (or if they are libertarians, must) fail to be 100 percent causally determined may be challenged to explain what it is that makes the difference between action and mere indeterministically caused behavior.

Agent-Causation

Some philosophers have thought that this challenge is best met by an appeal to the notion of *agent-causation*.[17] Behavior counts as action when and only when it is caused *by the agent* rather than by antecedent states or events, whether deterministically or not. But this appeal is unsatisfactory – although not, as has sometimes been alleged,[18] because the notion of agent-causation leads us into an irresolvable dilemma. The alleged dilemma is presented as follows: Consider the agent's causing of the action, which according to the view that we may label *agent-causationism*, is essential for behavior to count as action – is this 'causing' *itself* an action or not? If it is, then to count as such it, too, must be agent-caused and so on, ad infinitum. But if it is not, then it is quite mysterious how something that merely "happens to" the agent can be such that when it does happen, his or her behavior becomes an exercise of the agent's own control. The difficulty dissolves, however, once we expose the misunderstanding of the agent-causationist's view that generates it. The theory is that actions consist in the causing by their agents *of certain events or states of affairs.* Thus, agents are not held to agent-cause their *actions* (as the constructor of the dilemma implicitly assumes) but rather the events or states of affairs that are, so to say, *intrinsic* to their actions.

Nevertheless, mere appeal to agent-causation is no help in explaining how actions differ from other behavioral episodes that are not 100 percent causally determined. All the notion of agent-causation can do is to perform the function for which we used it in Chapter 1, namely, to *label* what is problematic about fitting actions into the natural causal order by emphasizing our commonsense understanding of actions as controlled exercises of the agent's power. So merely to assert that actions involve a relation between the agent and certain events, and to call this relation (perhaps somewhat misleadingly?) agent-causation, can hardly be expected to offer any resolution of the problem. Of course action differs from other behavior in that the agent brings it about, but the problem is how to accommodate such bringing about within a naturalist ontology.

The tendency to expect too much of agent-causation, and to see it as part of the solution to the problem of natural agency rather than as an ingredient in its statement, is in fact confined to libertarians. But of course, soft determinists would be equally misguided if they supposed that a theory of agent-causation could assist them in distinguishing actions from other 100 percent causally determined events. Typically, what soft determinists actually do is to offer a Causal Theory of Action to serve this purpose. And it is my contention that libertarians ought to take a leaf from their rivals' book and advance a CTA to make the distinction they need between indeterministic action and mere indeterministic behavior. If it can be shown, as the CTA asserts, that actions consist in behavior with suitable mental event–causal antecedents, the problem of natural agency is solved for both the libertarian and the soft determinist, but with one important proviso: *The correct version of the CTA must permit the causal relations definitive of action to be either deterministic or probabilistic.* At the end of Section II, I argued that if a CTA can succeed at all, there is no special reason why it can't apply in a deterministic universe. Now I wish to argue that the same is true for an indeterministic universe – and in particular, one in which the sort of behavior that can count as action need not be 100 percent causally determined by antecedent events. This argument will enable me to conclude that the proviso just mentioned is satisfied: A successful CTA could be used to establish the possibility of action under both determinism and indeterminism.

First, let us ask whether there is any reason to believe that if a CTA works at all, it does so only given that the mental states definitive of action are its deterministic causes. In other words, is a probabilistic CTA a possibility? The idea that if it were to any extent a matter of chance whether matching behavior would follow an agent's reason-constituting mental states, that behavior would not count as the agent's exercise of control, gains its persuasiveness from the fact that if an outcome is to any extent a matter of chance, no agent can ensure its occurrence. And what no agent can ensure, surely, can hardly constitute an exercise of any agent's control? Hence, it is concluded, behavior that is merely probabilistically caused cannot count as action. Evidently, such an argument needs further articulation. This has recently been provided by van Inwagen, who is seriously bothered by the threat the argument poses to his libertarianism.[19] His way of putting the argument comes to this:

> Consider a mechanism that on the push of a button flashes either a red light (with 50 percent probability) or a green (with 50 percent probability). Then an agent who pushes the button has no control over which light flashes. Now if the mental states that constitute an agent's reasons caused matching behavior only probabilistically, by parity of reasoning, the agent would have no control over whether that matching behavior was produced or not. Hence, actions cannot be behavior with merely probabilistic mental causes.

This is a very bad argument, but it is instructive to see precisely what is wrong with it.[20] Certainly a false analogy is being drawn – but in what way, exactly? One might initially observe that an agent's deliberations or reasons (if they issue in something like a volition or an "all things considered" judgment to do *a*) make it much more likely that the agent will perform *a*-ing behavior than not. Hence, a proper analogy might rather be with a mechanism in which pushing the button has, say, a 90 percent probability of producing a red flash and only a 10 percent probability of a green. But this can hardly be the nub of the matter, for it still remains the case that once an agent pushes the button on such a mechanism, it is not *up to that agent* which light flashes, even if one result is much more probable than the other.

The misleading nature of the analogy can be seen once we tumble to the fact that even if the probability of a red light flashing once the button is pushed is 100 percent (that is, the causal link is deterministic), *once an agent pushes the button* the flashing of the light is not as such an exercise of that agent's control. Admittedly, with this deterministic mechanism, an agent who has complete control of the button also has complete control over whether the mechanism flashes a red light or no light at all. But that the mechanism works as it does need not itself be an exercise of the agent's control. (Of course, it may be because the machine may have been designed for the purpose by the agent who is now using it – although even in that case it is very unusual for the agent to be exercising control over how the machine operates at the very time it is being used for its designed purpose.) Thus, once we understand the link between reasons or deliberations and matching behavior according to the model of pushing the button on a mechanism that operates independently of the agent's control, then *whether that mechanism is deterministic or probabilistic,* the outcome (the behavior) will fail to count as the agent's action.

The moral is, of course, that this model is misconceived. On any of the light-flashing mechanisms described, an agent would have to press the button *in order to* get a light to flash. The agent would directly control the button, and only indirectly control the light: He or she would make a light flash *by* pushing the button. But the relationship between an agent, *M*'s, reasons for doing *a* and his, her, or its *a*-ing behavior is not that *M* directly controls *M*'s deliberations in order to exercise only indirect control over *M*'s behavior. Rather, *M*'s behaving as *M* does is itself an exercise of *direct* control. So it is patently true that it is not up to the agent whether an outcome that can only be indirectly controlled will actually eventuate, once the agent has done all that can be done by way of direct action in order to achieve it. But this fact has nothing whatsoever to teach us about any constraints that may apply to the relationship between agents' reasons and the behavior in which they exercise direct control for those reasons. In particular, no reason has been given for excluding the possibility that this relationship might be one of probabilistic causation.

We are bound to be seriously misled if we interpret a causal theory of an agent's *direct* exercise of control by using a model of *indirect* agent-control over an outcome – and this applies whether our CTA is probabilistic or deterministic. For, when an agent indirectly controls an outcome, there is always a stage in its production at which what happens (whether the mechanism is deterministic or probabilistic) is not up to the agent – namely, the stage at which the agent has exercised all the *direct* control open to him or her in the attempt to achieve the outcome. Thus, if we assimilate the kind of caused behavior that the CTA holds action to be to an indirectly controlled outcome, we shall be led to the conclusion that the behavior's occurrence was not up to the agent, and hence was not his or her own action. In any case, we could hardly expect a model of indirect control to be totally adequate as an account of action since such a model *already employs the notion of a direct exercise of control.* To pursue the analogy with the light-flashing mechanism, what the CTA offers is a theory of what it is for a *pushing of the button to be an action,* not of what it is for the flashing of the light to be so. Accordingly, any conclusions about the flashing of the light not being up to the agent, *given that the agent has pushed the button,* are just not transferable to the causal link between an agent's reason-constituting mental states and his or her matching behavior. Agents do not in general indirectly control their outer behavior by directly controlling their inner mental states, even if control of inner states is a genuine possibility.

This "argument from the model of indirect control" may thus be dismissed as powerless to rule out the possibility that an agent's direct control might consist in causal relations between mental states and behavior that are themselves probabilistic. As I have noted, had the argument worked, it would also have ruled out the possibility that such causal relations might be deterministic. So the argument's rejection is equally a defense of the possibility of a deterministic CTA. Nevertheless, as I have emphasized before, it is by no means obvious that an agent's direct control over his or her behavior is constituted by a causal relation (deterministic or probabilistic) between appropriate mental states and behavior. Intuitively, we think of agents as *carrying out* their intentions or *acting in accordance with* their practical reasons, and this seems different from (simply) being caused to behave by those intentions or reasons. Defenders of CTA must reverse (or somehow cope with) this intuition; my point now is just that this task presents itself quite independently of whether the natural causal order is assumed to be deterministic or not.

I conclude, then, that the traditional bifurcation of the skeptical problem of natural agency leads to a recognition that the very same philosophical theory – namely, the Causal Theory of Action – would, if correct, suffice to defeat both versions of skepticism. And this, surely, is good evidence that the truth or falsity of determinism is indeed irrelevant to the core of the problem, as I suggested in Chapter 1. Contemporary skeptics about natural agency (among whom, it seems, we have to number van Inwagen!) remain so, either because they don't recognize the power of CTA to answer their doubts or because their doubts extend to CTA itself. If they are to remain rationally entrenched in their skepticism, they must at least show that doubts about the truth of CTA are well founded.

But perhaps skeptics have good prospects of showing this? In Sections II and III I have tried to dispel arguments only against particular versions of CTA – deterministic and probabilistic, respectively. There still remains a real possibility of a persuasive argument against CTA as such; indeed, some such arguments have been sketched or hinted at in the present discussion, and so we now have a better idea of what might be needed for an adequate defense of CTA. Before advancing to a direct consideration of how to formulate and defend a CTA in the light of these doubts, however, there is one further unavoidable preliminary. All I have claimed is that CTA's truth would *suffice* to dispel skepticism about natural agency. It thus remains open that there might be alternative ways of refuting skepticism about natural agency that are independent of and superior to a defense of CTA. Perhaps we can deal with skepticism without having to maintain a theory of action which (as I have been loudly admitting) has some initially counterintuitive elements to it?

If this were so, CTA would hardly merit the extended discussion I offer in the three chapters following. So I want first to explain why I think that CTA is, in fact, the most promising approach to resolving the problem of natural agency. I cannot establish, as a matter of logical necessity, that natural agency is possible only if CTA is true. But I can compare the CTA approach with some representative contemporary alternatives; and this comparison, I believe, indicates very clearly that it is (so to speak) dialectically necessary to defend CTA in order to resolve skepticism about natural agency. Sections IV and V are devoted to this final preliminary.

IV. A COMPARISON WITH DENNETT'S *ELBOW ROOM*

In his recent book, *Elbow Room*,[21] Daniel Dennett has attempted to resolve the problem of natural agency without defending any Causal Theory of Action. Does he succeed? If he does, further pursuit of CTA may be abandoned to those who happen to have an interest in it for its own sake. In this section, however, I shall argue that Dennett does not succeed – and that furthermore, the gaps in his argument are tailor-made to be filled by a CTA. I also want to reveal a strange irony in the very existence of Dennett's *Elbow Room* – if, that is, he conceives of it as going beyond the solution to the problem of natural agency he effectively proposed in earlier writings. (Of that, more later.) But I hope that the overall moral will be clear: In the debate about natural agency, it is possible for reconciliatory naturalists as well as skeptics to underestimate the importance of the Causal Theory of Action, and Dennett is a classic case in point.

Dennett's Negative Case for Reconciliatory Naturalism

The negative side of Dennett's case for reconciliatory naturalism is to argue that skepticism about natural agency stems from the abuse of dangerous "intuition pumps." Of these, the two most insidious are, first, the tendency to assimilate causal determination to determination by some powerful agent (discussed previously) and, second, the fear that causal determination dooms us to "*Sphex*ishness" – to being at the mercy of tropistic responses to stimuli from whose grip we cannot escape, rather as the digger wasp, *Sphex ichneumoneus,* cannot break out of its set routines for nest building should it encounter an abnormal obstacle.[22] Dennett does a splendid job of shoring up our resistance to seduction by these overworked analogies, and he even manages to modify some of them to provoke contrary, compatibilist, intuitions.[23] His positive case for a reconciliatory neutralism about agency is less impressive, however.

Reconstructing the Natural Evolution of Agency: Its Independence of the Metaphysical Problem

On my account, reconciliatory naturalism requires a way of accommodating agent-control within a naturalistic ontology. It is not so much that we fear *Sphex*ishness; rather, we find difficulty in understanding *how it could be possible* for a physical system to count as an agent, given that we don't help ourselves to something like emergent agent-causation. By squarely locating his enterprise within the Kantian tradition of philosophical explanation,[24] Dennett makes it clear that it is this "how possible?" question he seeks to answer. After quoting Chisholm's agent-causationist belief that "each of us, when we act, is a prime mover unmoved," Dennett undertakes the task of discovering whether we can "find a naturalistic account of the self or agent that avoids this obscure and panicky metaphysics while distinguishing agents sufficiently within the causal fabric."[25] But his execution of this task[26] underestimates the strength of skepticism about the place of action in the kind of natural order envisaged by modern science. For, in order to establish that a genuine agent may be "sufficiently distinguished from a mere domino in a chain," Dennett tells a "just so" story about how complex, purposive, and adaptive behavior could have evolved from less complex kinds of adaptation. The kind of evolutionary story Dennett tells can, I think, be adequately gleaned from the following quotation:

What has been found to be special about naturalistically conceived selves? Only some of the portions of the physical universe have the property of being designed to resist their own dissolution, to wage a local campaign against the inexorable trend of the Second Law of Thermodynamics. And only some of these portions have the further property of being caused to have reliable expectations about what will happen next, and hence to have the capacity to control things, including themselves. And only some of these have the further capacity of significant self-improvement (through learning). And fewer still have the open-ended capacity (requiring a language of self-description) for "radical self-evaluation." These portions of the world are thus loci of self-control, of talent, of decision-making. They have projects, interests, and values they create in the course of their own self-evaluation and self-definition. How much less like a domino could a portion of the physical world be?[27]

Although Dennett's story about how agency evolved may be quite credible, it fails to address the *metaphysical* doubt that the "how possible?" question about agency expresses. If you already accept that agency is possible in the natural world (understood as a world without irreducible agent-causation, unmoved movers, and the like), Dennett's account will provide at least a plausible sketch of how *what you already believe to be metaphysically possible* could actually have come about. But what if it really is the metaphysical question that bothers you? What if you genuinely *cannot (yet) understand* how a network of physical states and events in however complex a set of causal relations could accommodate agency? If this is your predicament, sketched evolutionary histories will just beg the question you want answered. For, of course, skeptics about natural agency will maintain that no account could provide the natural history of agency because according to them, agency cannot have a natural history! There is nothing in Dennett's story *as he tells it* that precludes it from applying under determinism; but telling the story has no rational power to persuade those who accept van Inwagen's Consequence Argument out of their incompatibilism. For libertarians, for example, Dennett's account could be true only of a world in which agency is possible – namely, an indeterministic one. Or again, there is nothing to stop a convinced agent-causationist from maintaining that Dennett's story tells the tale *of the emergence of a quite new type of ontological item,* namely, episodes of agent-causation! So this line of argument fails: Natural histories of agency *presuppose* a resolution of the problem of natural agency, and cannot therefore resolve it.

Dennett's Epistemologizing of the Free Will Problem

Dennett does not proceed as if he takes his reconstructed natural history of agency by itself as enough to defeat skepticism about natural agency. Having told his evolutionary tale, he continues to address the skeptic's anxieties. In Chapters 5 and 6 of *Elbow Room,* he seeks to show that, under determinism, it remains possible for an agent to have a range of real opportunities for action and to exercise an active power that could have been exercised in other ways. Let us see, then, how his argument goes, noting at the start that his discussion restricts itself to a defense of traditional compatibilism – that is, the refutation of skepticism about agency under determinism.

Dennett observes that an agent who deliberates must regard himself as facing a range of options, such that it is "up to him" whether they eventuate or not. Thus, for all the deliberator knows, the future could branch in any of several directions. "It is this *epistemic* openness," Dennett says, "this possibility-for-all-one-knows, that provides the elbow room required for deliberation."[28] Conceding this point, however, does not suffice to defeat incompatibilism. Deliberators may indeed have to think of themselves as facing a restrictedly open future, but the question is whether they are correct in so doing. To defeat incompatibilism, we must show that belief in real opportunities for action is more than a necessary illusion of deliberators under determinism.

D. M. MacKay has argued that the existence of a real opportunity must be relativized to the agent, so that an outcome that under determinism is in principle "predictable-for-detached-nonparticipants need not be inevitable-for-the-agent."[29] Although questions can be raised about the cogency of the argument that leads MacKay to this conclusion,[30] a more serious doubt arises about his whole relativizing strategy. Does the relativized noninevitability for the agent of a causally determined outcome really give the compatibilists all they need? It is instructive that MacKay himself concedes that "of course, the mere fact that a future event is indeterminate for an agent would not of itself imply that that agent had any responsibility for determining it," and goes on to suggest what seems to be a Causal Theory of Action with his remark that events for which an agent is responsible are those "whose form depends . . . on the outcome of the cognitive information-processing activity we call making a decision."[31]

Dennett, too, realizes that a further step is needed to defeat incompatibilism[32] – but he does not follow MacKay's hint in the direction of a CTA. His strategy is first to maintain that there can be real chances in a deterministic world[33] and then to infer the existence of real opportunities for action from that. "If our world is determined," he says, "then we have pseudo-random number generators in us,"[34] which, he seems to suppose, are sufficient to ground real opportunities for action. However, not all events that have a real chance of happening are events that an agent has a real opportunity to bring about. This fact is well illustrated by the example Dennett gives of an "entirely non-metaphorical use" of the concept of chance by Richard Dawkins: "a germ-line cell division is one where the genes being duplicated *have a chance* of being the ancestors of an indefinitely long line of descendants" (Dennett's emphasis).[35] One might therefore concede that real chances can belong in a deterministic universe, and indeed, are necessary if a process of evolution is to be possible,[36] while still remaining puzzled about how such a universe can accommodate real opportunities for action.

But Dennett has another bite at the cherry. He suggests that we may resolve our doubts about the possibility of action under determinism by recognizing that there is something "fundamentally epistemic" about the sense of "can" in which we require that genuine agents "can" act other than they do. Just what Dennett means by this suggestion is somewhat obscure. If he is simply repeating the MacKay-derived point about the noninevitability of the future for the deliberating agent, no progress has been made. But there appears to be more to the suggestion than this. As a result of his reflection on Slote's reply to arguments like van Inwagen's Consequence Argument, Dennett claims that Slote "overlooks the possibility that the form of selective necessity he describes is in fact disguisedly epistemic."[37] That is, Dennett proposes that the modal operator, N, defined as $Np =_{df} p$ & it is not under the agent's control that p, is some form of *epistemic* necessity. But what kind of epistemic necessity Dennett does not say; and yet he needs to say, for if it is just relativized inevitability-for-the-agent, the case against the incompatibilist has been taken no further. Besides, although Slote does use epistemic modalities as examples of modalities that are selective (failing of agglomerativity and closure under entailment), he can hardly be said to have overlooked the possibility that N as just defined might itself be an epistemic modality. Slote explicitly observes that the selectivity of epistemic necessity seems to have no bearing on the status of the necessity expressed on this definition of N since it involves "forms of situational inevitability and unfreedom that seem to be nomic and metaphysical matters, and Kripke's *Naming and Necessity* has surely taught us to be wary of arguing from . . . epistemological considerations to [corresponding] metaphysical or nomic conclusions."[38]

There is a further clue to the nature of Dennett's "epistemic turn," again related to his remarks about Slote. Considering Slote's example of Jules and Jim's accidental meeting at the bank, despite the presence of each being nonaccidental (offered by Slote as an example of a metaphysical modality that is selective), Dennett says,

This is apparently accidentality or coincidentality from-a-limited-point-of-view. We imagine that if we knew much, much more than Jules and Jim together know, we would have been able to predict their convergence at the bank; *to us*, their meeting would have been "no accident." But this is nevertheless just the concept of accidentality we need to describe the "independence" of a thing's powers or abilities from the initial conditions or background conditions in which those powers are exercised.[39]

The first two sentences here miss Slote's point: The accidentality of Jules and Jim's coincidental meeting is not a matter of its in principle unpredictability. Rather, it is a matter of its not belonging to anyone's plan,[40] and coincidence of this kind may belong to a deterministic – and "in principle" fully predictable – world, as is indicated by Dennett's own remarks about real chances under determinism. What is important for interpreting Dennett, however, is the final sentence, which makes a proposal about how to understand what it is for something to have an active power. What Dennett seems to be suggesting is that an agent exercises a power that could have been exercised otherwise if his or her behavior counts as "accidental," in the sense that it could not have been predicted "from a limited point of view." But what limited point of view does Dennett have in mind? If it is the point of view of the agent, we are back to the unsatisfactory suggestion that agents have real opportunities because, as deliberators, they must think of themselves as doing so.

But I don't think it is. The "limited point of view" that Dennett has in mind, I think, is any *finite* point of view, for which some systems within a Newtonian, deterministic world have to be regarded as "chaotic," in the sense that their behavior is unpredictable without "infinite precision of initial observation."[41] In response to the obvious question why the existence of such finitely unpredictable systems should provide the "elbow room" for freedom of action, Dennett says this:

Such chaotic systems are the source of the "practical" (but one might say infinitely practical) independence of things that shuffles the world and makes it a place of continual opportunity. The opportunities provided are not just *our* opportunities, but also those of Mother Nature. . . .[42]

But this simply repeats Dennett's earlier point: A deterministic universe can include real chances. All that has been added is an explanation of how this can be so in terms of its being characterized by chaotic Newtonian systems. And the same objection may be renewed: How can any of these real chances count as opportunities such that it is up to an agent whether to take them or not? Without an answer to this question, the problem of natural agency remains unsolved.

Dennett's epistemic defense of compatibilism seems, then, to have
a lacuna – and furthermore, one that could be filled by a satisfactory
CTA. To show, as Dennett does, that agents must think of themselves as faced with real opportunities and that real opportunities
are possible in a deterministic universe may perhaps clear valuable
ground for the compatibilist. But the compatibilist's case is made
only if the range of opportunities possible under determinism includes those such that for them to be taken is for an agent to
exercise his or her own control. Now, if a CTA is correct, this
condition is satisfied. If, as CTA claims, an agent's exercise of
control *just amounts to* that agent's exhibiting behavior with a suitably mental event-causal history, then some real opportunities in a
deterministic world can be opportunities for agents to act. Indeed,
if a CTA may be defended, Dennett's ground clearing is unnecessary since CTA goes straight to the nub of the problem by
claiming that the troublesome notion of agency is open to an
ontologically humdrum analysis.

It may therefore seem something of a puzzle that Dennett is
virtually silent on the claims of a CTA to resolve the problem of
action. But there is an explanation, and it lies in Dennett's attitude
to so-called folk psychology. The CTA's core ontological claim is
that action consists in behavior suitably caused by the behavior's
mental states. The mental states concerned, of course, are those
cited in intentional explanations – those that constitute the reasons
for which agents act: beliefs, desires, intentions, and so on. Our
practice of explaining behavior in terms of such intentional states is
widely thought of as significantly analogous to theoretical explanation in general – and, thus, as belonging to a theory labeled (somewhat pejoratively) "our folk psychology." The important point
here is that Dennett maintains that the "beliefs and desires of folk
psychology . . . are *abstracta* – calculation-bound entities or logical
constructs," and he adopts an instrumentalist construal of the
attribution of intentional states to a system.[43] Or at least, Dennett's
view is that *all that it is worth taking scientifically seriously* in folk
psychology must be understood as belonging to what he calls
intentional system theory – "a rationalistic calculus of interpretation
and prediction – an idealizing, abstract, instrumentalistic inter-

pretation-method that has evolved because it works, and works because we have evolved."[44]

Thus, although Dennett insists that agents really do have folk psychological intentional states, "just the way they really have centers of gravity and the earth has an Equator,"[45] it is clear that, for him, these "real" states have an abstractness that excludes them from being causes of behavior. Intentional explanations can be classified as causal explanations only in the minimal sense that they refer to causes and are "as unspecific and unhelpful as a causal explanation can get."[46] "Specific and helpful" explanations of behavior will, according to Dennett, cite *physiological* causes, or the theoretical entities of "a sub-personal cognitive psychology," having in common with the posits of folk psychology only "the intentionality of their labels."[47]

In the light of these views, it is unsurprising that Dennett does not offer a Causal Theory of Action as a way of explaining how action is possible in the natural causal order. What may seem surprising, however, is that he does not claim to have explained natural agency simply by appeal to intentional system theory – or rather, to the possibility of showing "how a system described in physiological terms could warrant an interpretation as a realized intentional system."[48] Provided it is warranted to treat some natural systems "from the intentional stance," it may seem that on his own terms, Dennett should have nothing more to explain about how agency can belong to the natural order. Traditional compatibilism would follow simply from establishing that some deterministic systems can also be intentional systems.

Indeed, even if we reject Dennett's neo-Rylean holistic logical behaviorism about folk psychological states,[49] we may still ask a more general question about the need for a CTA. The warrantability of teleological and intentional descriptions of natural systems has been widely defended;[50] why, then, aren't such defenses – if successful – sufficient to lay to rest any doubt about how agents can belong to the natural order?

The answer is clear: There are, so to speak, grades of teleology. All agents are, of course, teleological and intentional systems. But the converse is false. A teleological system need not be an agent; its operation can *serve* a purpose without its *having* a purpose that it acts to carry out. Teleological systems that also fulfill the criteria for intentional systems may appropriately be described *as if* they

81

acted for a purpose, but not all of them actually count as agents, who might, *ceteris paribus,* be held morally responsible for their behavior. Not all intentional systems exercise their own power of control; for only some of them can it be true that the way things turn out is (at least partially) up to them. Dennett himself is willing to include chess-playing computers and even plants among the "mind-havers": "My view," he says, "embraces the broadest liberalism, gladly paying the price of a few recalcitrant intuitions for the generality gained."[51] Well, Dennett is entitled, perhaps, to this semantic choice. But if "mind-havers" have also to be agents, our reluctance to include computers and plants among them may not, in the present context, justifiably be dismissed as a recalcitrant intuition. There may be prima facie grounds (the Consequence Argument, for instance) for doubting whether agency can belong to the natural order that are evidently inapplicable to intentional systems – in which case, a defense of the natural possibility of intentional systems falls short of defending the natural possibility of agency.

Is it possible that Dennett's bothering to write *Elbow Room* indicates an obscure awareness of this shortcoming? Could the very existence of *Elbow Room* fairly be seen as testimony to the inadequacy of the Dennett–MacKay complementarity thesis – and, therefore, also to the unsatisfactoriness of antirealism about intentional states? Perhaps so. But there can certainly be no doubt that given antirealism about intentional states, Dennett's earlier position (the Dennett–MacKay complementarity thesis) is all that is needed to defend compatibilism and, indeed, reconciliatory naturalism about agency generally. If we share this antirealism, all the further arguments of *Elbow Room* are so much unnecessary rhetorical icing on a perfectly adequate metaphysical cake. Is it, then, just mischievous to suggest that, conversely, if the *Elbow Room* arguments are intended as more than rhetorical, antirealism has implicitly been abandoned? However, if skepticism about natural agency rests on realism about actions (and hence, about intentional states) – as I have argued in Chapter 1 – then more is needed to defeat it. But what Dennett offers in *Elbow Room* is inadequate. We need something better than Dennett's combination of a reconstructed natural history of agency and a regressive epistemic turn – and that something better seems to be an argument for CTA.

There is a well-known argument for traditional compatibilism that might appear as a viable alternative to CTA: the *conditional analysis argument* (CAA). First, it is claimed that M's doing a at t counts as M's action if and only if M could have done other than a at t.[52] Then, this condition is held to be equivalent to the claim that "*if M had chosen to do other than a at t, M would have done other than a at t.*" Alternative renderings of this conditional analysis are available, and it may be important whether the main verb in the antecedent assigns to M an action (such as choosing, deciding, willing, or trying) or a mental state or event that is not an action (such as, wanting, preferring, desiring, or even intending). The next step is to argue that the conditional analysis can be true under determinism. Given its equivalence to the "could have done otherwise" condition, it then follows that action is a possibility in a deterministic universe.

How is the CAA related to the CTA? Evidently, the CAA is usually intended to show only the possibility of action under determinism. But I see no reason why it shouldn't be generalized to cover the indeterministic case as well. A conditional of the form "if M had chosen to do other than a at t, M would have done other than a at t" can surely be true as well in an indeterministic as in a deterministic universe. So the CAA might on this score be equally as promising an approach to resolving the problem of natural agency as the CAA.

In fact, CAA and CTA seem closely allied. The Causal Theory of Action affirms that action is constituted by behavior with a suitable mental history, whereas CAA holds that to say that an agent could have exercised his or her power otherwise is equivalent to saying that if certain mental antecedents had occurred, the agent would have acted otherwise. If to act is to behave as a causal consequence of suitable mental antecedents (CTA), then *to be able to act* is to be such that different mental antecedents would cause correspondingly different behavioral outcomes (CAA). Thus, for a CTA to be true, it seems, the ability to perform actions must be a causal power of the agent, in the sense defined by Donald Davidson: namely, "a property of an object such that a change of a certain sort in the object causes an event of another sort."[53] Accordingly, CTA and CAA seem to be equipollent in the defense of compatibilism. As van Inwagen has himself acknowledged,[54] if the conditional analysis is correct, the main modal principle of his Consequence Argument for incompatibilism is false – a conclusion, of course, that is also entailed by the truth of CTA.

This suggestion that the fortunes of CTA might be inextricably linked to the success of CAA may provide some anxiety since the conditional analysis of the ability to act has had rather a bad press, even among philosophers of a compatibilist persuasion. (I particularly have Keith Lehrer in mind; his case for the wholesale rejection of conditional analyses of the capacity to act is discussed later.) Let us, therefore, briefly review the familiar reasons why CAA is thought to fail. I shall seek to show that although CTA is indeed committed to treating the ability to act as a causal power in the given sense, the problem of natural agency is better resolved by defending the view that a certain special kind of event-causal history is sufficient and necessary for action (as CTA claims) than it is by defending CAA. In fact, I shall maintain, a CAA could work only given an adequate CTA.

Problems for the Conditional Analysis Argument

For ease of exposition, we shall "standardize" our discussion with reference to an agent *M*, who at time *t* performs the action of *refraining from* doing *a*, so that the "could have done otherwise condition" amounts to the claim that *M* could have done *a* at *t*. For simplicity, I shall not keep repeating the time reference.

According to CAA,

(1)   *M* could have done *a*

is equivalent to

(2)   If *M* had chosen to do *a*, *M* would have done *a*.

This suggested analysis may immediately be dismissed since (2) is consistent with

(3)   *M* could not have chosen to do *a*

and (3) entails not-(1) (since *M* could not have performed any action that *M* could not have chosen to perform). An obvious improvement at once suggests itself, namely, that (1) is equivalent to

(4)   If *M* had chosen to do *a*, *M* would have done *a*, and *M* could have chosen to do *a*.

84

However, if the analysis given by (4) is sound, it will be to no avail in using a CAA to secure compatibilism since there will be as much reason to doubt whether the second conjunct of (4) can obtain under determinism as there is to doubt whether (1), the analysandum, can.

The obvious trouble with (2) as an analysans for (1) is the reference in its antecedent to an *action* of M's. In adding, as we must, to the analysans to obtain (4), we thus reintroduce a "could have done otherwise" condition of the very sort whose satisfiability under determinism is at issue. The cure is to follow Davidson[55] in seeking an alternative antecedent for (2) that avoids reference to actions like choosing, willing, or trying. For example, one might consider the following:

(5)   If M had wanted to do a, M would have done a.

Of course, we have the same reason to expand (5) as we did (2), as follows:

(6)   If M had wanted to do a, M would have done a, and M could have wanted to do a.

But because wanting is not an action but rather a mental *state*, the second conjunct of (6) can mean no more than "it could have been the case that M wanted to do a," which, of course, can be true under determinism. It may seem, then, that provided the antecedent of the condition proposed as the analysans refers to a suitable mental state or a combination of them, the conditional analysis may succeed.

Lehrer's Rejection of Conditional Analyses

Keith Lehrer has argued, however, that all proposed conditional analyses of the capacity to perform actions will fail because "it is logically consistent to suppose that any condition that is causally sufficient for a person performing an action should also be causally necessary for the person being able to perform the action, and that the condition should fail to occur."[56]

We may put the point as follows: Consider the hypothesis, *(H)*, that

(7) M could have done a

may be given the following conditional analysis:

(8)   If C, M would have done a

where C stands for whatever constitutes the right combination of mental states. *(H)* evidently entails

(9) M could have done a if and only if, if C, M would have done a.

Now Lehrer's claim, *(L)*, is this: that (8) is consistent with

(10)   If not-C, it is not the case that M could have done a

and also with

(11)   not-C.

Given *(L)*, since (10) and (11) entail not-(7), and (8) is consistent with (10) and (11), it follows that (8) is consistent with not-(7), which implies that (8) does not entail (7). Therefore, (9) is false (for it is the assertion that (7) and (8) mutually entail one another), and so *(H)* must itself be rejected. Hence, all conditional analyses will fail because this argument makes no assumptions about the actual content required for C.

All this shows, however, is that *(H)* and *(L)* are inconsistent with one another. It does not amount to a disproof of *(H)*. One might just as well argue that *given (H)*, the set of statements *(L)* holds to be consistent are actually not so. Given *(H)*, and substituting appropriately in (10), we get

(12)   If not C, it is not the case that, if C, M would have done a.

Given (11), we may infer that

(13)   It is not the case that, if C, M would have done a

which, of course, contradicts (8). So if *(H)* is correct, (8), (10), and (11) are not mutually consistent, as *(L)* claims.

Are there, then, any independent reasons either to support or to reject *(L)*? The question is whether a condition that is sufficient for M to perform action a could also be necessary for M to *have the capacity* to do a. Davidson has argued that it cannot, given that the capacity to act receives a conditional analysis. He observes that the issue applies not just to agency but to powers and dispositions generally, and he notes that were Lehrer's argument sound, it would exclude, for example, a conditional analysis of solubility.[57] Davidson puts the point thus:

The correct response to Lehrer is simply that if one analyses solubility by a causal conditional, one can't consistently allow that what causes dissolving is also a necessary condition of solubility, *since in that case the only soluble things would be dissolved.* Similarly for conditional analyses of freedom.[58]

In the emphasized clause Davidson seems to offer an independent reason for rejecting the possibility that what causes dissolving is also a necessary condition of solubility, and thus a way of showing that the inconsistency between this possibility and a conditional analysis of solubility offers no threat to the latter. Accordingly, given that the point is generalizable, he offers grounds for regarding a conditional analysis of agency as immune to Lehrer's objection. But it is hard to see how its entailing that the only soluble things are actually dissolved gives a reason for concluding that what causes dissolving *cannot* be a necessary condition for solubility. Perhaps having to accept that nothing is soluble unless actually dissolved would rather defeat the point of having a concept of solubility at all, but no self-contradiction is implied. Arguably, we have a genuine use for the idea that something has a power, disposition, or ability only if its possession is possible without its exercise. But there is no self-contradiction in the assertion that something possesses a "transient" ability only when conditions suffice for its exercise. Granted, there is a problem about how we could know whether a certain occurrence counts as the exercise of such an ability. We will not wish so to trivialize the notion of an ability that *any* property exhibited by an object involves the exercise of the object's transient ability to yield that property. (The existence of such abilities is not to be guaranteed just because whatever is actual is also – logically – possible.) So, some independent account of the *physical basis* for a disposition or ability will be needed. Given such an account, however, we cannot exclude the strange possibility that a system might have the feature that it exhibits the physical basis for the ability to exhibit property *F* only transiently, and only when conditions guarantee that it will exhibit *F*.

Thus, it is not part of *what it means* to say that a thing has a certain ability that this ability can be possessed independently of its exercise. We understand well enough what it means to say that things are soluble only under conditions that suffice for them to dissolve; and we understand just as well what it means to say that an agent can perform the action *a* only if there obtain conditions that are sufficient for the agent actually to do a. So Davidson does not seem to be successful in giving us a way to show independently that (L) is false and that Lehrer thus has no grounds on which to object to (H). In fact, our remarks show that the set of statements that (L) claims to be consistent may indeed be so for some actions, a, and this is enough to show that (H) cannot purport to offer a general analysis of the *meaning* of "M could have done a."

Revising the CAA Strategy

But why should it be necessary for the success of CAA that it provide a successful conditional analysis of the meaning of possessing the capacity to act? Will CAA not go through provided that for some actions at least, (H) does express a conditional *equivalence* – provided, that is, that (7) and (8) mutually entail one another? Although it may not be part of the meaning of an ability to act that the agent may have that ability without exercising it, *in fact* most abilities are stable and do persist when not exercised. (We should hardly have come by the notion of an ability in the first place if this had not been so.) For an ability of this kind, then, it may be possible to find a conditional of the form "if C, then M does a," which both entails that M has the ability to do a and is satisfiable under determinism. Given that this is an ability that can be possessed without being exercised, it follows that C will not turn out to be necessary for M to have the ability to do a. And if such a conditional may be found, traditional compatibilism is proved. Notice that *mutual* entailment between the conditional statement and the ability claim is not needed. As Lehrer himself makes clear, this proof of compatibilism requires only that the conditional statement entails the ability statement.[59] In the terms we have used, all we need to show is that (8) can be true under determinism and that (8) entails (7).

The Impotence of CAA without CTA

If CTA is correct, then, the ability to act must indeed be a causal power of the agent, and there must be a conditional claim of the form "if C, M would do a" that is equivalent to "M could do a" – but this equivalence need not be an equivalence of *meaning*. Mutual entailment will be quite enough. Given this qualification, the possibility of conditional analyses of the capacity to act remains

88

open. Of course, a search must be made for a suitable filling for *C*. In general, what sort of condition is it that suffices for *M* to do *a* such that this sufficiency itself entails that *M* can do *a*? It is clear that the answer to this question will be provided by specifying what sort of causal history is required for behavior to count as action – in other words, by pursuing a Causal Theory of Action.

But there is another reason why the strategy underlying CAA requires defense of CTA. The conditional analysis argument works only if there is a conditional claim that suffices for freedom of action that is *itself* unproblematically satisfiable under determinism (or since our concern is the more general one, under the constraints imposed by our naturalist ontology). How is this requirement to be met? Suppose we have arrived at a conditional statement sufficient for *M* to be able to do *a*, namely,

(C)   If *C*, then *M* does *a*.

If we interpret the consequent of *(C)* as referring to an action, we shall have got nowhere, for the whole problem is to explain how action is possible in the natural order. If there is a difficulty in understanding how actions are naturally possible at all, then there will be equal difficulty in understanding how they are possible under certain natural conditions. Thus, we must "unpack" the consequent of *(C)*, to show that it refers only to the occurrence of events that belong unproblematically within a naturalistic ontology – bodily movements and the like. Presumably, to do so, we will need to take "*M* does *a*" to mean "*M* exhibits *a*-type behavior."

But this still leaves a problem: It could be argued that *(C)* can be a sufficient condition for *M* to be able to do *a* only if *(C)* is interpreted to mean something like

(C*)   If *C*, then *M*'s exhibiting *a*-type behavior is *made to happen* by *M*.

That is, it might be held that any conditional statement that suffices for an agent to have the ability to act must be understood as making implicit reference in its consequent to agent-causation – and if so, the possibility of such a statement holding true in the natural order is problematic. Indeed, it is the very problem with which we are seeking to deal. So CAA can work only if the conditional it offers as sufficient for *M*'s being able to do *a* does not irreducibly have a form like *(C*)*. But this can be guaranteed only by defending a CTA. The conditional analysis argument requires an *event-causal* conditional statement of the form given by *(C)* to be sufficient for an agent to have the capacity to act. Such a conditional statement can be produced, however, only by derivation from a successful causal analysis of what it is for behavior to count as action. And this is just what we shall need to specify in order to defend CTA. Thus, the preliminaries are over, and we may now consider how a causal analysis of action may be constructed.

NOTES

1 Peter van Inwagen, *An Essay on Free Will* (Oxford, England: Clarendon Press, 1983), p. 56. Two matters need attention. First, as noted in Chapter 1, this kind of argument does not rest on assuming the CDO principle under its alternative outcome construal, although this fact is somewhat obscured by van Inwagen's first elaboration of his Consequence Argument, namely, the "First Formal Argument," p. 70, which was the version originally offered in his "The Incompatibility of Free Will and Determinism," *Philosophical Studies,* **27** (1975), 185–99. On this version, *M*'s behavior, *b*, is taken to count as an action only if *M* "could have rendered false the statement that *M* does *b*." This may seem like an expression of the alternative outcome CDO condition; but if the argument is to be of any interest, it must rather be construed (as is certainly possible) as an expression of the condition of control. Second, the definition of *determinism* that van Inwagen uses is stronger than the one with which I have been working. In effect, van Inwagen takes the thesis of determinism to be the claim that for every event *e*, the statement that *e* occurs can be derived as a deductive consequence from the laws of nature plus a true statement of the total state of the universe at *any* other time (see his *Essay on Freewill,* pp. 58–65). The differences between this definition and the one I have so far assumed are mostly unimportant for assessment of the Consequence Argument. I shall note an exception to this in footnote 16.

2 Michael Slote, "Selective Necessity and the Free Will Problem," *Journal of Philosophy,* **79** (1982), 5–24.

3 Van Inwagen's discussion (*Essay on Free Will,* pp. 96–102) simply elaborates his intuitive sense that the inference rule corresponding to MMP is valid.

4 In "Selective Necessity," p. 5, Slote identifies arguments similar to van Inwagen's in the work of Carl Ginet, "Might We Have No Choice?" in Keith Lehrer, ed., *Freedom and Determinism* (New York: Random House, 1966), 87–104; James Lamb, "On a Proof of Incompatibilism," *Philosophical Review,* **86** (1977), 20–35; and David Wiggins, "Towards a Reasonable Libertarianism," in Ted Honderich, ed., *Essays on Freedom of Action* (London: Routledge & Kegan Paul, 1973), 31–61; and for this reason, refers to the Consequence Argument as the "GLVW Argument."

5 Slote, "Selective Necessity," p. 16. Slote remarks that "anyone who assumes the validity [of the rule of inference corresponding to MMP] would seem to be tacitly assuming that the necessity expressed in operator, 'N' is both agglomerative [i.e., satisfies the principle $N\alpha \ \& \ N\beta \supset N(\alpha \ \& \ \beta)$], and closed under logical implication [i.e., satisfies the principle $N(\alpha \ \& \ (\alpha \supset \beta)) \supset N\beta]$" (p. 10). With each of his examples of selective necessity, Slote is at pains to show that they fail either agglomerativity or closure under logical implication or both, and this may create the impression that Slote believes that failing either or both of these principles *entails* that the form of necessity concerned fails the equivalent of MMP. But

90

Thomas P. Flint has recently claimed that it is "of course, conceivable" that MMP could hold even if agglomerativity or closure under logical implication failed ("Compatibilism and the Argument from Unavoidability," *Journal of Philosophy,* **84** (1987), 423–40, footnote 6, p. 427). Though Flint offers no argument for it, his claim is, I believe, correct. For example, the relational necessity operator, "It is an obligation of mine *to Jones* that . . .," arguably does yield a true instance of MMP*, although it clearly fails the principle of closure under logical implication. (To illustrate: I do not acquire an obligation to Jones to be alive tomorrow just because I have an obligation to visit him tomorrow; however, if I am not only obliged to visit him but also have an obligation *to him* not to let it be the case that I visit him without bringing my niece to visit him as well, then I do have an obligation to Jones to bring my niece with me on the visit.) It is thus important to note that Slote's case against the general applicability of MMP does not depend on assuming (it would appear mistakenly) that failure of agglomerativity or closure under logical implication *entails* failure of MMP. Slote offers convincing direct counterexamples to MMP for epistemic necessity and for the operators "It is obligatory (for *M*) that . . ." and "It is nonaccidental that. . . ."

6 Slote, "Selective Necessity," p. 19; his emphasis.
7 Note that to say, in Slote's terms, that an event is not "unavoidable" for an agent is simply to say that it occurs through the agent's exercise of control, and this – as Frankfurt's counterfactual intervener examples show – is *not* equivalent to saying that given the circumstances, the event could have failed to occur. Thus, an agent who acts in the presence of a counterfactual intervener – so that in the circumstances there could have been no alternative outcome – does not thereby behave in a way that is, in the present sense, "unavoidable". Kadri Vihvelin's recent claim that "Slote's [causal] account of ["avoidable" behavior] doesn't work because it delivers the wrong verdict in cases of causal pre-emption" is mistaken at this very point: "The Modal Argument for Incompatibilism", *Philosophical Studies,* **53** (1988), 227–44, p. 235.
8 Flint objects to Slote's case against the Consequence Argument on the grounds that "the failure of *one* purported analysis of unavoidability . . . by no means implies that *no* analysis can succeed" ("Compatibilism and the Argument from Unavoidability," p. 430). This objection misunderstands the dialectical position. To rebut the Consequence Argument successfully, the compatibilist has only to show that there is an interpretation of the "unavoidability" operator that is such that (a) MMP fails for it and (b) an event counts as intrinsic to a genuine action if and only if its occurrence is not "unavoidable" on that interpretation. Flint's misunderstanding is perhaps attributable to Slote's lack of emphasis on (b), which I here seek to rectify by stressing Slote's implicit commitment to CTA.
9 André Gallois, "Van Inwagen on Free Will and Determinism," *Philosophical Studies,* **32** (1977), 99–105; David Lewis, "Are We Free to Break the Laws?" *Theoria,* **47** (1981), 113–21; John Martin Fischer, "Incompatibilism," *Philosophical Studies,* **43** (1983), 127–37.
10 For a critical examination of Lewis's argument, which concludes that "there is no single definition of 'can render false' that will serve van Inwagen's purposes," see Terence Horgan, "Compatibilism and the Consequence Argument," *Philosophical Studies,* **47** (1985), 339–56. p. 351.
11 Gallois, "Van Inwagen on Free Will and Determinism," p. 104.
12 For an ingenious attempt to establish the falsity of MMP without an appeal to CTA, see Vihvelin, "Modal Argument for Incompatibilism," pp. 235–40. In the Consequence Argument, the state of affairs expressed in the first premise is

distinct from, and temporally prior to, the behavior whose occurrence is stated in the conclusion. Neither of Vihvelin's counterexamples to MMP have this feature, and thus invite dismissal through the appropriate restriction on MMP. Furthermore, each counterexample rests on a contestable assumption. The first assumes that agents have no control over the causal consequences of their basic acts unless these are foreseen (an assumption, which, I believe, wrongly conflates control with *intentional* control). And the second requires agreement that winning a lottery can *as such* count as an action (i.e., over and above the action of buying a ticket that has a chance of being the winner).

13 As argued by Roderick Chisholm, "Freedom and Action," in Keith Lehrer, ed., *Freedom and Determinism* (New York: Random House, 1966), p. 13, "If what we say [the agent] did was really something that was brought about by his own beliefs and desires . . . then, since *they* caused it, *he* was unable to do anything other than just what he did do."

14 This supposition may require a certain suspension of disbelief from those who interpret M's reason r as consisting in "broad" intentional states, whose content is determined by contextual features that may well include their having a certain causal history. For a recent discussion of the extent to which reference to broad intentional states is indispensable in psychological explanation, see Philip Pettit, "Broad-Minded Explanation and Psychology," in P. Pettit and J. McDowell, eds., *Subject, Thought and Context* (Oxford, England: Clarendon Press, 1986), 17–58.

15 Van Inwagen, *Essay on Free Will*, p. 109. Compare van Inwagen's discussion, pp. 109–14.

16 Arguably, this account of what the thesis of determinism and the Superagent thesis have in common applies only given the stronger version of the thesis of determinism, mentioned in Chapter 1, footnote 5, and Chapter 2, footnote 1. If determinism requires only that every event should be 100 percent causally determined (as on the weaker version of the thesis I have been using since the definition given in Chapter 1), then it is at least logically possible that under determinism, actions should be causally determined only by antecedent conditions falling under the agent's control. For, M's coming to be in intentional state s at time t_1 (one second after the origin, t_0) could be caused by M's having been in intentional state s' at $t_{1/2}$ (half a second after the origin); and M's coming to be in s' could itself have been caused by M's being in s'' at $t_{1/4}$ (one-quarter of a second after the origin); and so on. In this way, every event in the system could be 100 percent caused, yet because the causes of M's being is s come to a limit at t_0, the state of the universe before t_0 need not, together with the laws of nature, have it as a deductive consequence that M comes to be in s at t_1. Although it seems quite implausible, it could conceivably be maintained that an agent's control over his or her reasons would be secured by such a setup – in which case, the present incompatibilist argument would (at best) establish the impossibility of action only under a deterministic system of the stronger kind.

17 As C. D. Broad puts it in "Determinism, Indeterminism and Libertarianism," *Ethics and the History of Philosophy* (London: Routledge & Kegan Paul, 1952), pp. 214–15, what libertarians "would like to say" about a responsible action is that

it is literally determined *by the agent or self*, considered as a substance or continuant, and not by a total cause which contains as factors *events in* and *dispositions of* the agent. If this could be maintained, our puttings-forth of effort would be completely determined, but their causes would neither be events nor contain events as cause-factors.

Compare Chisholm's use of the notion of "immanent" causation ("Freedom and Action," pp. 20ff.) and John Thorp's appeal to agent-causality in *Free Will: A*

Defense Against Neurophysiological Determinism (London: Routledge & Kegan Paul, 1980), pp. 96ff.

18 For example, by Donald Davidson, *Essays on Actions and Events*, (Oxford, England: Clarendon Press, 1980), p. 52.

19 Van Inwagen, *Essay on Free Will*, pp. 142ff.

20 Van Inwagen himself fails to recognize what is wrong with it, although he realizes as a libertarian he is committed to its rejection. He says (ibid., p. 149):

> I must reject the following proposition:
> If an agent's act was caused but not [100 percent] determined by his prior inner state, and if nothing besides that inner state was causally relevant to the agent's act, then that agent had no choice about whether that inner state was followed by that act.

But he goes on to say, "I must admit that I find it puzzling that this proposition should be false," and so ends up on his own admission having to choose between "the puzzling and the inconceivable" in order to believe that there are free actions. (His conviction that action is inconceivable in a deterministic universe rests, of course, on his confidence in the Consequence Argument.) This is an extremely unsatisfactory conclusion to have to come to. I here seek to show that the reasons why van Inwagen thinks it puzzling that action should be possible in an indeterministic universe are even less persuasive than those that convince him that its possibility in a deterministic universe is inconceivable.

21 Daniel Dennett, *Elbow Room, The Varieties of Free Will Worth Wanting* (Oxford, England: Clarendon Press, 1984). Patricia Smith Churchland has recently described this as "the best recent discussion of the free will issue," in *Neurophilosophy: Toward a Unified Science of the Mind-Brain* (Cambridge, Mass.: M.I.T. Press, 1986), p. 322.

22 See Dennett, *Elbow Room*, pp. 10–17.

23 For a sample of this, see Dennett's "delightful case of the well-informed, truthful oracle who indirectly manipulates a person's brain by bombarding his ears with lucid and accurate warnings, made all the more irresistible by the citation of all the evidence in their favour and a frank account of the entire evidence-gathering operation" (ibid., p. 65). Note also Dennett's warnings against reliance on "clear cases of everyday causation" in generating intuitions about the possibility of deterministically caused action (pp. 31–4).

24 Ibid., p. 49, footnote 30.

25 Ibid., p. 76.

26 Ibid., chap. 4.

27 Ibid., p. 100.

28 Ibid., p. 113.

29 D. M. MacKay, "Seeing the Wood and the Trees," in W. Maxwell, ed., *Thinking: The Expanding Frontier* (Philadelphia: Franklin Institute Press, 1983), p. 10. MacKay here usefully summarizes the core of an argument he has developed in many previous papers.

30 See, for example, my own discussion, "Thought, Action and the Natural Order," in D. Perkins, J. Lochhead, and J. Bishop, eds., *Thinking: The Second International Conference* (Philadelphia: Lawrence Erlbaum, 1987), 3–18, especially pp. 13–16.

31 MacKay, "Seeing the Wood and the Trees," p. 10.

32 See Dennett, *Elbow Room,* p. 115.

33 Ibid., pp. 120–2.

34 Ibid., p. 121.

35 Ibid. Quoted from Richard Dawkins, *The Extended Phenotype* (New York: W. H. Freeman, 1982).

36 Dennett remarks, "what evolution requires is an unpatterned generator of raw material, not an uncaused generator of raw material" (ibid., p. 150).

37 Ibid., p. 149, footnote 13.
38 Slote, "Selective Necessity," p. 11.
39 Dennett, *Elbow Room*, p. 149.
40 See Slote, "Selective Necessity," p. 17.
41 Dennett, *Elbow Room*, p. 151.
42 Ibid., p. 152.
43 Daniel Dennett, "Three Kinds of Intentional Psychology," in Richard Healey, ed., *Reduction, Time and Reality* (Cambridge, England: Cambridge University Press, 1981), 37–61, p. 46.
44 Ibid., p. 42.
45 Ibid., p. 46.
46 Ibid., p. 50.
47 See ibid., pp. 53–7.
48 Ibid., p. 60.
49 See Dennett, "Three Kinds of Intentional Psychology," pp. 50–3, for a fuller development of this position.
50 See, for example, Ernest Nagel, "Teleology Revisited," *Journal of Philosophy*, 74 (1977), 261–301; and Jonathan Bennett, *Linguistic Behaviour* (Cambridge, England: Cambridge University Press, 1976), chap. 2.
51 Dennett, "Three Kinds of Intentional Psychology," p. 60, footnote 35.
52 Following our discussion of the Frankfurt examples in Chapter 1, this condition must be read as the condition of control and not under the alternative outcome construal.
53 Davidson, *Essays on Actions and Events*, p. 64.
54 Van Inwagen, *Essay on Free Will*, pp. 123–5.
55 Davidson, *Essays on Actions and Events*, p. 69.
56 Keith Lehrer, "Self-Profile," in Radu J. Bogdan, ed., *Keith Lehrer* (Dordrecht, Holland: D. Reidel, 1981), 3–104, p. 24. See also Davidson's reference to this view of Lehrer's, *Essays on Actions and Events*, p. 69.
57 Davidson, *Essays on Actions and Events*, p. 69.
58 Ibid., p. 70, footnote 7; my emphasis.
59 Keith Lehrer, "Preferences, Conditionals and Freedom," in Peter van Inwagen, ed., *Time and Cause* (Dordrecht, Holland: D. Reidel, 1980), 187–201, p. 187. In this paper, Lehrer suggests that the following condition is sufficient for M's refraining from doing a to be a free act: Had M preferred to do a, M would have done a, and had M preferred to prefer to do a, M would have preferred to do a, and so on, ad infinitum. Lehrer thinks that this condition has the merit that it eliminates all reference to further capacities on the part of the agent. But it is far from clear whether this elimination can really be achieved. As Krister Segerberg argues, "[Lehrer] has believed that kicking the modal residue upstairs, one step at a time, would be enough to kick it out of existence; but in fact it was only kicked out of sight" ("Could Have but Did Not," *Pacific Philosophical Quarterly*, 64 (1983), 230–41, p. 239). It is surprising that Lehrer does not find it necessary to defend his argument against his own general objection to hypotheses that hold a conditional statement of the form "if C, then M would do a" to be sufficient for "M can do a." Yet were that objection sound, it would apply here as elsewhere. Is it not possible that a person could have a perfectly integrated set of counterfactual preferences with respect to a-ing, yet not be able to do a because actually having any one of the preferences in the hierarchy is a necessary condition for possessing the capacity to do a? The fact that Lehrer reaffirms his general objection to conditional analyses of the ability to act in his "Self-Profile," which was published after "Preferences, Conditionals and Freedom," suggests that the explanation cannot be that Lehrer has changed his mind on the power of this general objection.

94

3

Developing a causal theory of action

I. CAUSAL ANALYSES OF ACTION

If the Causal Theory of Action is correct, the skeptical problem of natural agency is solved. As argued in Chapter 1, the problem is to accommodate apparent agent-causation within a natural ontology that recognizes only event-causation, and CTA solves the problem by maintaining that agent-causation is *merely* apparent. For, the core of CTA is the ontological claim that action consists in behavior with an *event*-causal history running through relevant mental states of the behaver.

How may we show that CTA does succeed? We shall not defeat skepticism about natural agency merely by asserting CTA's ontological thesis; we need an *argument,* with this thesis as its conclusion. To establish that CTA's ontological claim is true, it will be necessary to show that its truth is consistent with our notion of action as essentially involving the exercise of the agent's own control over an outcome. From our investigation of the traditional, bifurcated version of the problem of natural agency in Chapter 2, it has clearly emerged that the onus of proof here is on the proponent of CTA. Initial intuitions quite strongly suggest that there must be something more to action than causation of behavior by the agent's appropriate mental states. To defeat skepticism about natural agency, these intuitions must be overturned.

One way to discharge this onus of proof would be to try to analyze what we mean by action in terms of event-causation by suitable mental states. The aim would be to provide a definition of action as behavior with specified mental event-causes. Such a definition would show that all we really mean by attributing an action is that the agent exhibits behavior with the specified type of event-causes. It would establish that our notion of agent-causation is the very same as the notion of event-causation of behavior by suitable mental states. Granted such a definition, there would not be even at the level of meaning anything more to action than appropriate mental causation of behavior. The production of such a definition, then, would be a decisive argument for the truth of CTA: If the notion of agent-causation is not after all really essential to our concept of action, and if all that is essential to it is event-causation by suitable mental antecedents, then the existence of action can pose no problem at all for a natural ontology that recognizes only event-causal relations. Successfully defining action in event-causal terms would undercut skepticism about natural agency altogether.

This is not the only way to defend CTA, however. Its core ontological claim may be supported without providing anything approaching a Platonic real definition of action as behavior with suitable mental event-causes. Consider it this way. The source of the skepticism we wish to defeat is the assumption that because our concept of action appears essentially to involve agent-causation, actions can exist in the natural order only if some events are agent-caused in the natural order – a possibility that our prevailing naturalism excludes. To defeat this skepticism, it will be enough to show that, even if to act does not *mean* to be caused to behave by one's reasons, nevertheless, actions can exist without the need for special agent-causal relations in nature *because actions are realized within complex sequences of events related only in event-causal ways to one another*. And CTA, of course, suggests just what sort of complex, causally related event-sequences do realize actions, namely, certain kinds of sequences in which the agent's mental states cause his or her behavior. Thus, agent-causation might be conceptually essential but not ontologically essential for action – and the latter is all we need to defend if we are to establish CTA.

But how could it be shown that belief in the existence of actions involves no commitment to the ontology of agent-causation? How may we refute the agent-causationist, who insists that agent-causal relations are essential for action ontologically as well as conceptually? To refute this claim we shall need to specify purely event-causal conditions for the performance of an action. And this specification, it is important to recognize, will need to state conditions that are both necessary *and sufficient* for action. If only necessary event-causal conditions are stated, it will be open to the agent-causationist to insist that there are further necessary conditions for action that include the existence of agent-causal relations.

But if we can show that an action occurs *when, and only when,* conditions of type C obtain, and conditions of type C make no reference to agent-causation, then will we not have enough to refute agent-causationism? I believe so. If, through empirical investigation, we simply turned up a correlation between C-type event-causal conditions and what we intuitively recognize as actions, then – perhaps – some room for reasonable skeptical doubt about natural agency might remain. It might be reasonable for the skeptic to insist that all we would have shown was that actions are regularly but contingently accompanied by C-type conditions, thus leaving open the possibility of continued puzzlement about how *the actions themselves* can be naturally realized.

But if the existence of such a correlation emerges from a conceptual investigation of agency, then it will be reasonable to argue that the correlated C-type event-causal conditions *constitute* actions – at least across all possible worlds with the same natural ontology and causal order as the metaphysics of naturalism holds the actual world to have. For, such a conceptual investigation will be driven by the question whether we can conceive of the hypothesized natural conditions obtaining independently of an action's being performed. So if we do find C-type conditions for which this is *not* conceivable, we will have a correlation that is sufficiently noncontingent to support the claim that in our sort of world, anyway, C-type conditions naturally realize actions. Thus, if a conceptual analysis of action yields, not a definition of it, but at least event-causal conditions of type C such that their obtaining is both sufficient and necessary for the occurrence of an action, it is reasonable to argue that C-type conditions *ontologically constitute* actions and, therefore, that actions can belong to the natural order. Resistance at this point would turn skepticism about natural agency into an uninterestingly dogmatic rejection of it.

The Causal Theory of Action provides a theory of what those "C-type" conditions are which, on conceptual investigation, turn out to be sufficient and necessary for the existence of an action. So far I have talked about CTA in general terms: "The CTA" has meant any theory of action according to which actions consist in behavior caused by suitable mental states (which I have described as the core ontological claim of a CTA). Thus "the CTA" is actually a family of theories, each of which, in some way or other, asserts the core ontological claim. But now that the time has come to defend CTA, and to defend it as resolving the skeptical problem of natural agency, I need to develop a version of CTA that has a chance of succeeding, at least in specifying event-causal conditions sufficient and necessary for action.[1]

Of course, if a full definitional analysis of action in event-causal terms could be provided, the problem of natural agency would be very clearly resolved. Since I don't want to rule out that possibility from the start, I shall risk saying that what I am looking for is an event-causal *analysis* of action (a *CTA analysis,* as I shall call it), provided it is understood that this need not be a definitional analysis. Thus, my aim is to argue for CTA's core ontological claim by supplying a successful CTA analysis. I grant, of course, that the core ontological thesis might in fact be true even though no one succeeded in providing a satisfactory CTA analysis. Merely promising that such an analysis is possible will not be enough, however. For, without actually providing such an analysis, no non-question-begging reason can be given for believing that CTA's core ontological claim is true in the face of skeptical doubts to the contrary. And those skeptical doubts, as I have been at some pains to show, do place the onus of proof squarely on the shoulders of the proponent of CTA. It will not do to argue that CTA has to be true because that is the only way we can think of to refute obviously misguided skepticism about natural agency!

A First Approach to a CTA Analysis

According to CTA, actions consist in events with a causal history *suitably* involving mental states of the agent. The qualification is needed since behavior can have mental causes without counting as action. For example, my sudden suspicion that I've inadvertently insulted my host might cause me to blush with embarrassment – but my blushing wouldn't count as an action despite its mental cause.[2] Thus, the first step in providing a CTA analysis will be to say what *suitably* means here by specifying the type of mental causal history that constitutes behavior as action.

A CTA analysis can be satisfactory only if it avoids any reference to actions, agent-causation, exercises of control, and the like. Thus, although there may be considerable plausibility in the suggestion that for *M*'s "outer" behavior to count as the action of *a*-ing is for it to be caused by M's *choosing, deciding, willing,* or *trying* to do a, it cannot serve as the basis for an adequate CTA analysis – unless there is a way of understanding choosings, tryings, willings (etc.) that does not construe them as actions.[3] To avoid circularity, the safest policy is to begin by finding appropriate mental causes for action that belong to a category clearly distinct from mental action. This can be done by taking mental *states* of some kind to be the constitutive causes of action. Being in a mental state seems necessarily distinct from performing any action, even a mental one.

But what sort of mental states could serve the purpose here? The answer is well known: Typically (even essentially?) actions are "done for reasons" – which is not (just) to say that they have causes, but rather that their agents have reasons of their own for performing them. Now for an agent to have a reason for a certain action is for the agent to be in a particular complex mental *state*. The composition of this complex state is a matter of some dispute – but it is broadly agreed that it must include both beliefs (or some other cognitive state) and desires (or some other conative state). To have a reason for doing a, M must desire (want, intend to achieve) some end and believe that a-ing is conducive to that end. Beliefs and desires can, of course, be formed through the agent's action – typically, as a result of an intentional attempt to answer a theoretical or practical question. But in general agents do not have to perform actions in order to form beliefs or desires. Beliefs about the immediate environment are formed involuntarily in perception, and our most basic desires arise directly from our natural needs and constitution. So no circularity will be introduced by a CTA that takes the constitutive causes of action to be mental states such as these.

Is a CTA Analysis in Terms
of Reasons Even Possible?

Therefore, the idea is to try a CTA analysis of actions as caused by the reasons their agents have for doing them. Some philosophers regard this idea as doomed a priori because they believe that reasons necessarily cannot be causes. Those who take an antirealist line about intentional states (such as Daniel Dennett) are in this camp; but then, as I have argued earlier, their very antirealism gives them an almost immediate solution to – or better, dissolution of – the problem of natural agency. However, there are philosophers who appear to be realists about intentional states but who deny that such states can be causes of the actions for which they are reasons. Typically, such philosophers express their view as a claim about the nature of intentional explanation (explanation "by reasons"). If reasons are causes for actions, the explanatory citing of reasons for action is a kind of causal explanation. But, they have claimed, it is not: Intentional explanations are quite distinct – logically and structurally – from the causal explanations of the natural sciences.

It would be tedious to review the arguments that have persuaded philosophers that reasons cannot be causes since an excellent job of debunking them was done by Donald Davidson more than a quarter of a century ago in "Actions, Reasons and Causes."[4] For example, he diagnosed the flaw in the famous "logical connection" argument, showing that there can be logical connections between descriptions of events genuinely related as cause and effect.[5] He pointed out that the agent's ability to know of his or her own reasons for action without observation or inductive inference does not entail that such privileged knowledge cannot be knowledge of causes.[6] And he argued that although an agent's reasons are dispositional states (rather than events), they can be causes nonetheless because they may be appropriately associated with genuine event-causes.[7]

Perhaps Davidson's most important observation was that "no particular law is entailed by any singular causal claim, and a singular causal claim can be defended, if it needs defense, without defending any law."[8] This enabled Davidson to argue that it is possible for reasons to be singular causes of action, even if (as he in fact maintains) there are no laws that subsume such causal relations under their psychobehavioral descriptions.[9] Davidson thus freed debate about CTA from its earlier focus on the question whether intentional explanations have, at least implicitly, the same "covering law" form as was taken to characterize scientific explanation generally.[10] He showed that this assumption adopts too narrow an understanding of causal explanations, according to which their explanatory force necessarily requires the citing of relevant covering laws. The explanatory force of an intentional explanation lies in exhibiting the reasonableness of the agent's behavior in the light of his or her reasons, but this fact does not entail that these reasons are not causes. Even if we stick with the covering law model of causal explanation, it is enough, for a reason to cause an action, just that *there should exist* a covering law under which this relation is subsumed; the *content* of that covering law plays no part whatsoever in the associated intentional explanation. Indeed, that content need not even be known for the explanation to succeed.

How to Make a Positive Case
for a Reason-Based CTA Analysis

In "Actions, Reasons and Causes," Davidson was, I believe, highly successful in rebutting what had been fashionable arguments against taking agents' reasons to be causes of their intentional actions. He thus protected the a priori possibility of a successful CTA analysis from the threat posed by those particular arguments. But this by itself, of course, falls short of the positive case for the CTA that is needed to defeat skepticism about natural agency. What, then, did Davidson contribute on the positive side?

Well, he did offer one simple but highly persuasive argument for the view that when agents act for reasons, their reasons must be causes of their behavior. Behavior that counts as an intentional action must have occurred not just *in the presence* of the agent's reasons for doing it but also *because* the agent had those reasons for doing it. This "because" condition is required to avoid collapsing the distinction between intentional action on the one hand, and, on the other, behavior that is rationally justified in the light of reasons for it that the agent happens to have at the time. For example, I might stay silent during an important meeting simply because my laryngitis renders me effectively dumb and yet, at the same time, have – and even be aware that I have – very good reason for keeping quiet. But what can this "because" condition mean except that the mental states that constitute the agent's reasons were causes of the agent's behavior?[11]

It is very important to realize, however, that this argument alone does not establish the truth of CTA. It shows only that it is a *necessary* condition for intentional action that the agent's reasons caused his or her behavior. But for CTA to be proved, we need to establish a CTA analysis that specifies purely event-causal conditions that are *sufficient* as well as necessary for the occurrence of action. For all that the preceding argument establishes, it could be that the reasons that are (indeed) causes of an agent's intentional action can be so only if the agent acts to *give those reasons effect* – in which case, reasons could be causes only in the presence of the agent-causation of the behavioral outcome. Thus, skepticism about natural agency might reasonably persist, even granted acceptance of Davidson's negative and positive grounds for holding that reasons are causes.

Nevertheless, Davidson's arguments are invaluable in showing the way to make progress in removing skepticism about natural agency – for they clear away obstacles to affirming a Causal Theory of Action and provide guidelines for formulating at least an initial CTA analysis. It is also notable that Davidson's insight about intentional explanations needing to make reference only to singular causal relations has a positive role to play in constructing an account of how intentional and physical explanations of the same behavior may be complementary rather than in competition with one another. In later work,[12] Davidson develops his view that the causal laws whose existence is referred to in intentional explanations are physical laws, linking mental causes *under their physical descriptions* to their behavioral effects. There is, therefore (at least in principle), a purely physical explanation of the behavior that constitutes an action – but it does not compete with the intentional explanation. In fact, the two explanations coapply *because they each cite the same causes,* although *under different descriptions:* the intentional explanation under their psychological descriptions as beliefs and pro-attitudes, and the physical explanation under their physiological descriptions as neural states.

Thus, Davidson explains the complementarity not (as Dennett does) by appealing to the pragmatic utility of treating some natural systems from the intentional stance, but by employing the principle that the same real state may be open to different levels of description. According to Davidson, the reasons that cause intentional action are real causes – as real as the physical states of the brain with which they are, in fact, token-identical. Davidson's complementarity thesis, then, adopts the realism about actions and mental states that is (as I have argued) a presupposition of our ethical perspective, and without which there is no significant skeptical problem of natural agency. It offers an attractive reconciliatory naturalist picture: The explanations that our ethical perspective requires to apply to certain natural events (namely, intentional explanations), though not by any means translatable into physical terms, refer to physical states that feature in coapplicable natural explanations of the same events.[13]

This attractive picture, however, depends on the tenability of CTA. The sketch we have just given is not an argument for CTA: It is an explication of the implications of accepting a CTA and, of course, a physicalist answer to the mind/body problem. If more is needed to constitute action than the suitable causation of behavior by mental states, then Davidson's complementarity thesis is a castle built on air. In particular, if the intuition remains that agent-causation is essential to action, the physicalist way with mental event-causation won't be enough to "naturalize" action. So the crucial thing is to prevent skeptical exploitation of agent-causationist intuitions by providing a CTA analysis.

It may therefore be appreciated just how significant it was that in "Actions, Reasons and Causes," *Davidson did not purport to provide a CTA analysis*. He clearly committed himself to CTA, speaking in his final sentence of "the states and changes of states in persons which, because they are reasons as well as causes, *constitute* certain events [as] . . . intentional actions."[14] But the most he offered toward a CTA *analysis* was an account of certain necessary event-causal conditions for intentional action[15] – and as I have argued, a CTA analysis cannot do its job unless it provides event-causal conditions that are sufficient as well as necessary for action. Davidson's account in that paper, therefore, fell short of the positive defense of CTA that is needed to defeat skepticism about natural agency.

Davidson had hoped to remedy this deficiency, but in later work he appeared pessimistic about so doing. In his essay "Intending," he describes the account of intentional action with which he "ends up" as "incomplete and unsatisfactory."[16] The source of his dissatisfaction is easy to discover: Davidson found that he had to abandon his earlier belief that it would be possible to provide a statement of sufficient event-causal conditions for intentional action.[17] He reached this opinion through reflection on the problem of causal deviance – the problem of specifying *the right sort of way* in which reasons have to cause matching behavior for a genuine intentional action to take place. In Chapters 4 and 5, I shall be considering this problem in some detail. My concern now is only to highlight the predicament in which Davidson places himself by abandoning even the possibility of producing an adequate CTA analysis.

If it is impossible to state event-causal conditions that are sufficient for action then it is impossible to provide a CTA analysis to back up CTA's core ontological thesis. Davidson tries to salvage the situation by claiming that "the reduction" CTA provides "is not definitional but ontological."[18] And as we have seen, it is indeed true that a successful CTA analysis could well fall short of a full definition of action. But it is not enough just to make this clarificatory point. If Davidson is right in thinking that we cannot get event-causal conditions that are sufficient for action, then there is no hope even of a nondefinitional CTA analysis. So Davidson is left in the predicament of maintaining CTA as the answer to our puzzle about "the possibility of autonomous action in a world of causality"[19], but lacking an adequate CTA analysis to back this answer up. In fact, his position looks worse (even self-contradictory) if we interpret him as affirming CTA while seriously believing that a CTA analysis is actually impossible.

So for the sake of reconciliatory naturalism, Davidson's pessimism had better not be right. By the end of Chapter 5, I hope to have shown that it is not: A CTA analysis can actually be supplied, and reconciliatory naturalists can breathe a sigh of relief. But this is to anticipate. First, we shall need to understand why Davidson was inclined to pessimism about upgrading his earlier causal account of intentional action to provide a full CTA analysis. And to do that, we need to start at the beginning by examining the kind of causal account of action with which Davidson began.

A First Hypothesis for a CTA Analysis

I therefore want to propose a first hypothesis for a CTA analysis based on Davidson's account in "Actions, Reasons and Causes." It will, of course, prove inadequate (I have, after all, just been noting that Davidson himself emphasizes that his initial account provides only necessary conditions for action), but it is important to see how and why this first hypothesis proves inadequate and to develop objections to it in an ordered fashion. For the sake of a label, I call this hypothesis *CTA-H*:

M performs the intentional action of *a*-ing if, and only if,

(1) M is in a complex mental state, r;
(2) M's being in r makes it reasonable for M to do a;
(3) M's being in r causes an outcome, b; and
(4) b instantiates the type of state or event intrinsic to the action of *a*-ing.

Some brief points of explication. First, the complex mental state, r, need not be such that M is consciously aware of each of its components – or even of any of its components – at the time of (or immediately preceding) the action of a-ing. Intentional actions need not be preceded by conscious deliberation of any kind.

Second, the condition – (3) – that M's being in r should cause outcome b does not, of course, require that r be the *sole* cause of b. M's being in r need not, by itself, be sufficient for b's occurrence; it need only be an explanatorily salient causal factor in this outcome.

Third, a remark on the notion – used in (4) – of an outcome's belonging to a state- or event-type that is *intrinsic* to an action: Each type of action is a bringing about by the agent of a specific type of event or state, and this is what counts as the event- or state-type intrinsic to that action. For example, the rising of an arm is the type of event intrinsic to the action of raising one's arm. An event of the type intrinsic to a-ing can, of course, occur without action a being performed – and indeed, the intrinsic event-types of many actions could be instantiated in a universe in which, in fact, no actions were ever performed. Thus, events and states intrinsic to actions are always open to descriptions under which they have an unproblematic place in a naturalist ontology, and CTA-H accordingly avoids any vicious circularity at this point. A reference to an event-type *intrinsic* to an action is not a reference to any kind of action.[20]

Fourth, through clause (2), CTA-H specifies the kind of mental cause constitutive of action as a *rational* cause, consisting in *intentional* states with "propositional" content, such as desires, intentions, and beliefs. To apply CTA-H's *rationality condition,* we will require a theory of practical reasoning – of the standards governing the rationality of action relative to given sets of intentional states. Again, in case there should be any further anxiety about circularity, the reference in (2) to a mental state that makes it reasonable to do a certain action is, of course, not a reference to action as such.

Given the rationality condition, behavior cannot count as intentional action unless it is rational in the minimal sense that it is reasonable *with respect to the intentional states that cause it.* So quite mad behavior can count as intentional action; but to do so, it will have to be reasonable relative to the mad beliefs and/or desires of the agent concerned. But totally irrational intentional action is a conceptual impossibility under CTA-H, which poses a problem by apparently ruling out the possibility of weak-willed or incontinent actions. In Section II, we shall consider how serious this difficulty is and what further development of CTA-H might be required to deal with it. More will then be said about what kind of complex mental state it is that both causes and makes relatively rational the behavior that thereby counts as action.[21]

Intentional Action and Action in General

Because CTA-H proposes an account of *intentional* action only, it might fairly be asked how CTA-H could pass muster even as an initial hypothesis for a CTA analysis capable of defeating skepticism about the natural possibility of action in general.

Obviously, agents sometimes act unintentionally. But according to Davidson, in all such cases there is a description of the agent's behavior under which it counts as an intentional action.[22] In other words, people do things unintentionally only in the context of some intentional project or other. For example, suppose I unintentionally offend the gardener by walking over a newly seeded lawn. My behavior will still be intentional under some other true description of it: taking the short cut to the parking lot, for instance. If this claim is correct, the notion of an intentional action is conceptually more fundamental than the notion of action in general. The general concept of action is the concept of action that is *intentional under some description*. Hence, ontologically, all action is intentional action, and a causal theory of *intentional* action will explain all that needs to be explained about how action is possible in the natural causal order.

This claim is controversial. Intuition may not exclude the possibility of *purely voluntary* actions, which are not intentional under any description of them. It seems possible for agents to exercise control for no reason whatsoever, not even the trivial reason that they "just wanted to." Are there not purely idle exercises of agent-control, such as finger tappings and ear scratchings, which are done with no intention whatsoever?[23]

The intuition that such purely voluntary actions are possible is not, I think, so robust that it would resist appropriate tutoring. It is far from ridiculous to hold that the idle finger-tapper has at least an unconscious intention to make those bodily movements. And it might be worthwhile running this line if that was all we needed to

106

do to upgrade a CTA analysis of intentional action so that it applied to actions generally.

Of course, even if there are purely voluntary actions, a CTA analysis of intentional action would be enough to establish that wholesale skepticism about natural agency must be mistaken. If we show how *intentional* action may be accommodated in the natural causal order, a fortiori we have shown that action as such is a natural possibility. Still, if we have to admit that our CTA analysis applies only to one kind of action (i.e., that the analysis is sufficient *but not necessary* for the existence of action), a degree of puzzlement about how other forms of action can be naturally realized might remain.[24] So it would be preferable to be able to give a naturalist analysis applicable to actions generally, even though a CTA analysis just of intentional action will suffice to dismiss skepticism about natural agency.

The possibility of purely voluntary action would, however, prove a serious problem for a CTA defender if we were to find that a reference to voluntary action is ineliminable from the CTA analysis of intentional action. In that case the conceptual priority would be the reverse of what Davidson suggests, and the defense of a reconciliatory naturalist view of agency would have to focus on explaining how purely voluntary action can be realized in an event-causal order. Thus everything depends here on whether a CTA analysis of intentional action can succeed. If it does, intuitions about purely voluntary actions need not trouble us, and should probably simply be revised. If such intuitions do come to trouble us, however, that will probably be because they seem to threaten a CTA analysis of intentional action. And so indeed they do, but only in the context of other difficulties faced by such an analysis, or so I shall maintain.

II. THE CHALLENGE OF AKRASIA

The question now is to consider where CTA-H (my hypothesis for a CTA analysis) is inadequate and to find out whether its inadequacies can be remedied. The most serious problem for CTA-H is that it counterintuitively counts as actions a whole host of causally deviant cases – and this is the problem with which I shall deal in Chapters 4 and 5. Before that, however, it will be useful to consider the challenge posed to CTA-H by the possibility of weak-willed (or *akratic*) intentional actions.

Akrasia is another of those contemporary philosophical topics that is often treated on its own – and I suppose it is interesting to ask how it can be that people can act quite intentionally against their better judgment. But the topic has a wider significance for the problem of natural agency, which I hope to bring out in this section. As Davidson recognized, to allow weak-willed action seems to be inconsistent with offering a CTA analysis, which takes it as essential for behavior to count as intentional action that it have a rational cause, at least relative to the agent's own relevant beliefs and desires. Weak-willed actions seem to be both intentional and *irrational* with respect to the agent's salient mental states. I shall argue that Davidson offers at least the structure of a correct solution to this problem. This solution, however, does require us to recognize that the rational causes constitutive of intentional action (the complex mental state, r, of CTA-H) cannot in general consist only in desires and beliefs and are best understood as necessarily involving an *intention*. Furthermore, there is an additional problem (the problem of final stage akrasia), which Davidson does not recognize and which actually poses a potentially deeper problem for CTA-H because it indicates that the hypothesized analysans may not be sufficient for intentional action.

Characterizing Weak-willed Action

In "How Is Weakness of the Will Possible?" Davidson offers the following characterization, which I shall refer to as *D*, of what is variously called weak-willed, akratic, or incontinent action:

In doing x an agent acts incontinently if and only if: (a) the agent does x intentionally; (b) the agent believes there is an alternative action, y, open to him; and (c) the agent judges that, all things considered, it would be better to do y than to do x.[25]

Some brief comments on this characterization: Condition (a) is intended to capture the difference between incontinent *action* and compulsive *behavior* – only what occurs under an agent's own control can count as weak-willed action. Incontinent action is also to be distinguished from erratic or whimsical action. It is possible, of course, to decide that it is better to do y rather than x and yet, when it comes to the point, to *change one's mind* and do x after all.

But this is not a case of doing x incontinently; for incontinence, one must act contrary to one's *current unamended* judgment about what it is best to do, all things considered. Thus, the judgment referred to in condition (c) must be the judgment made or sustained at (or just immediately before) the time of action. It should be noted, however, that making this all-things-considered judgment need not amount to an introspectively accessible mental episode.

It is important properly to understand the all-things-considered character of the judgment referred to in (c). It is not a judgment made in the light of all the *objectively* relevant evidence; rather, it is a judgment in which the agent weighs together all the considerations *that he or she recognizes as needing to be taken into account*. The all-things-considered clause is therefore *part of the content* of the judgment the agent makes, namely, that doing y is better than doing x, given evidence e, and e *is all the evidence to be taken into account*.

Finally, all-things-considered judgments are not to be confused with judgments of what morality requires, and correspondingly, incontinent action must not be equated with action contrary to known moral duty, even though it is true that continence is a moral virtue. In the first place, moral issues are just irrelevant to some all-things-considered judgments. But second, action in accordance with perceived moral duty may be incontinent if the agent has made an all-things-considered judgment *not* to do what morality requires. Conversely, intentional failures to carry out perceived moral duty are not all akratic. Some such failures are wilfully immoral, in which, out of egotism, cowardice, or whatever, the agents judge that it is best, all things considered, to act contrary to what they know to be their duty.[26]

Are Weak-willed Actions a Real Possibility?

Davidson offers no argument to support the claim that incontinent actions, as characterised by *D*, really can occur. He simply says this:

Does it never happen that I have an unclouded, unwavering judgment that my action is not for the best, all things considered, and yet where the action I do perform has no hint of compulsion or of the compulsive? There is no proving such actions exist; but it seems to me absolutely certain that they do.[27]

I have nothing to add here: It is, in my view, a fact of experience that incontinent actions (as characterized) are a real possibility. And so I allow that it would be a serious objection to a CTA analysis if it entailed that incontinent action was impossible. But it will be wise not to exclude in advance the possibility that should the CTA analysis not be modifiable to admit intentional but weak-willed actions, it would be preferable to argue that the phenomena we think of as akratic acts have been misdescribed, rather than to abandon the analysis. (There is, in fact, a further alternative: We could admit that there are weak-willed intentional actions, agree that a CTA analysis cannot accommodate them because its rationality condition is essential to it, but attempt to offer a CTA analysis of that large proper subset of intentional actions that are not akratic. This approach would indeed be enough to show how *some* actions are possible in the natural order, but it would not offer the satisfaction of a fully general account of the natural possibility of *all* that we recognize as action, and without such a general account, our solution to the problem of natural agency is incomplete. Here compare my previous remarks on whether merely voluntary action, if there is such a thing, poses a problem for CTA.) I wish to argue, however, that we can find a CTA analysis that accommodates akrasia, but first I shall explain more fully exactly why akratic acts pose a difficulty for CTA analyses. My explanation aims to improve on the somewhat confusing picture that Davidson provides.

How Akrasia Poses a Problem for a CTA Analysis

Davidson explains the difficulty by suggesting, in effect, that there is a principle, *P*, to which CTA is committed, whose truth excludes the possibility of intentional akratic actions. This principle may be put as follows:

P   If agents judge that it would be better to do *x* than to do *y*, and believe themselves free to do either *x* or *y*, then they will do *x* intentionally if they do either *x* or *y* intentionally.[28]

Although *P* apparently does entail that agents never act intentionally contrary to their best judgments, and hence that there is no incontinence as characterized by *D*, there seems little reason to suppose that CTA is committed to the truth of *P*. *P* does, as

Davidson observes, express the natural supposition that if reasons are causes, "the strongest reasons are the strongest causes."[29] But so what? Could not the proponent of CTA simply affirm that this natural supposition is a natural mistake, shown to be so by the possibility of akrasia? Good and sufficient reasons, after all, are only one of many kinds of causes of behavior and may sometimes be causally overridden, as Davidson himself points out: "a reason which is causally strongest need not be a reason deemed by the actor to provide the strongest (best) grounds for acting."[30]

Davidson's emphasis on the apparent inconsistency between *P* and the possibility of akrasia does not quite bring the difficulty into proper focus. The CTA can dispense with *P*, but it cannot dispense with some form of rationality condition because it is the rationality condition that marks off action from other kinds of behavior with mental causes. Of course, to count as action, behavior does not have to be rational in all its dimensions; one may act intentionally from beliefs irrationally held or from intentions misguidedly derived from fundamental desires. But if a CTA analysis is correct, part of the concept of intentional action is the idea of behaving in a way made reasonable, relative to *the relevant* intentional states of the behaver, however irrationally held these themselves may be. To make a CTA analysis work we have to say what "the relevant" sorts of mental states are. We have to find the type of complex mental state of the agent that both causes and makes relatively rational behavioral episodes that count as intentional actions. With respect to just what kind of complex mental state does behavior have to be rational in order to count as intentional action?

Principle *P* suggests an initially plausible answer to this question, namely, that the complex mental state relative to which behavior must be rational in order to count as intentional action is the agent's final, "summing up," judgment (however flawed) about what it is best to do, all things considered. Yet once we accept the real possibility of akratic intentional actions, we are committed to rejecting *P* and its associated hypothesis for specifying the rationality condition required by our CTA analysis. Akrasia, then, poses a problem for a CTA analysis because it excludes what might otherwise seem to be the most natural specification of the rationality condition for intentional action. To defend a CTA analysis, an alternative specification of the rationality condition is required, according to which even akratic acts can count as relatively rational

111

with respect to the defining mental causes of intentional action. And this may seem a tall order. What is puzzling is not that the mental states that give the agent the strongest reason for *a*-ing may be outweighed by some other causal factor to yield an alternative outcome. What is puzzling is how such outweighing can occur in akratic action and the CTA's rationality condition still apply so that the outcome still counts as rational relative to the agent's relevant mental states. What sorts of mental states could those possibly be?

How to Specify the Rationality Condition for a CTA Analysis: Davidson's Notion of an Unconditional Practical Judgment

In "How Is Weakness of the Will Possible?" Davidson effectively offers a specification of the CTA's rationality condition that accommodates incontinent actions. His proposal amounts to this: that we take the defining mental cause of intentional action to be, not the agent's all-things-considered judgment about what it is best to do, but rather the agent's all-out, or *unconditional,* judgment about what to do. Davidson's distinction between all-things-considered and unconditional judgments may be understood as follows.

In the earlier stages of practical reasoning, agents make *conditional* or relative judgments of the form "*x* is better than *y*, given evidence *e*," which constitute prima facie judgments about what is to be done. For practical reasoning to reach any conclusion, however, the agent must "add up" the various prima facie judgments and form a judgment about what it is best to do *all things considered.* Davidson stresses, however, that all-things-considered judgments still have the conditional form "*x* is better than *y*, given evidence *e*"; they differ from prima facie judgments only in possessing an additional clause to the effect that "*e* is all the evidence to be considered."[31] If practical reasoning is actually to issue in action, Davidson argues that a further step beyond an all-things-considered judgment of conditional form is required. The agent must make an *unconditional,* or "all-out," judgment about what to do. Normally, the agent arrives at this unconditional judgment simply by detaching the condition of his or her all-things-considered judgment – by making the following (emphatically nondeductive!) inference:

Doing x is better than doing y, given evidence e; e is all the evidence to be considered;

therefore,

doing x is better than doing y.

This schema may be taken to express a standard of practical rationality, which together with the requirement that to be rational, one should carry out those actions that one judges unconditionally to be best, forms what Davidson calls "the principle of continence."[32]

With these resources, Davidson is able to maintain that in akratic action, agents form and act on unconditional practical judgments that are at odds with their all-things-considered judgments about what it is best to do. Thus, their behavior can count as rational relative to their unconditional practical judgments, even though it is not rational relative to their conditional all-things-considered judgments. In effect, then, Davidson proposes a specification of CTA's rationality condition on which the mental state relative to which behavior must be rational in order to count as intentional action is the agent's unconditional practical judgment. Thus, P may be accepted, provided it is reconstrued thus:

P' If agents *judge unconditionally* that it is better to do x than to do y, and believe themselves free to do either x or y, then they will do x intentionally if they do either x or y intentionally.

Unconditional Practical Judgments Construed as Intentions

Davidson thus provides the CTA analysis with exactly what it needs to meet the challenge of akrasia – a kind of antecedent mental state with respect to which even akratic action counts as rational. The suspicion may be, however, that this solution is purely formal and ad hoc. The claim that there is a kind of practical judgment that is more "all out" and unconditional than a final evaluation of what it is best to do, all things considered, is psychologically implausible. It is not easy to get an independent grip on what unconditional practical judgments really come to, and this unclarity fuels the impression that the only reason for giving them a place in practical reasoning is that they need to be posited in order to accommodate the CTA's rationality condition so that it applies to akratic acts.

113

The odor of ad hocness may be somewhat dispelled, however, once we recognise that Davidson's unconditional judgments are not strictly evaluative judgments at all but are really to be identified as *intentions to act*. (Davidson himself would allow this identification since in his later essay, "Intending," he admits a distinct category of "pure intendings" among mental events and concludes that a pure intending is "simply an all-out judgment," a judgment, that is, to the effect that some action *is to be done*.[33]) Intentions constitute a sui generis category of mental states, whose content needs to be expressed in the imperative rather than the indicative mood.[34] Thus, given this identification, Davidson's suggestion amounts to the much more intelligible claim that for practical reasoning to issue in action, the agent must *form the intention* to execute the action that is judged best, all things considered. This "pure intending" is not any kind of judgment about *what is the case* but is something more like a self-directed command that something *be the case*. An akratic break occurs when the agent forms and carries out an intention to act contrary to his or her all-things-considered judgment about what it is best to do.

An Independent Argument for Admitting Intentions

However, a nuance of ad hocness may perhaps remain. There is little phenomenological evidence that prior to acting, akratics always consciously form an intention contrary to their best practical judgment, let alone that forming the intention consistent with this judgment is a standard step in normal practical reasoning. So the appeal to intentions may still seem a theory-driven contrivance. Hence, it is worth asking whether there is any reason, other than the need to deal with akrasia, that supports the positing of intentions as intermediaries between final practical judgments and action itself.

The answer, I suggest, is that there is. Consider what may be called "Buridan's ass choices," in which the agent judges, all things considered, that at least two of the mutually exclusive options for action are equally preferable. Agents so situated can and often do intentionally perform one of the equally desirable options for action. Once they have evaluated two options equally, agents in this situation just have to decide what to do. Independently of rational considerations, which *ex hypothesi* have been exhausted, they must plump for one of the alternatives. But what can this decision come to? What can settling on one alternative amount to, given that it cannot be a further evaluative judgment? It is natural to see it as the formation of an intention to perform one of the equally satisfactory options rather than the other. *Something* has to happen beyond the evaluative judgment if one of the actions is to be performed; what else can it be but the forming and execution of an intention?

Though persuasive, this argument is not conclusive. It might alternatively be claimed that in Buridan's ass choices, settling on one of the equally preferred options *just is the performance of the action itself*. Yet this can hardly be generally true: Deliberators who evaluate options equally do sometimes, without any further evaluation, consciously settle on one of them *before* they act. So reference to intentions is required in such cases. Nevertheless, the argument does not quite show that there is *always* an, albeit often unconscious, formation of an intention intermediate between practical judgment and action itself. It does not even show that this is an invariable feature of akratic action.

Still, we have said enough to dispel the suggestion that positing intentions as the final stage of practical reasoning has no other basis than a desire to save a CTA analysis from the embarrassment of having to deny the existence of akratic acts as characterised by *D*. The notion of an intention is not an ad hoc invention of proponents of the CTA (whereas this impression did rather attach to Davidson's description of the very same thing as an unconditional practical judgment more final than an all-things-considered evaluation). Thus, there is already something in our repertoire of concepts about action and practical reasoning to play the role required if a CTA analysis is to accommodate akrasia.

The argument for positing intentions might be further strengthened if there turn out to be other kinds of intentional action, apart from the akratic, that could meet CTA's rationality condition only if intentions rather than evaluative judgments are posited as the defining causes of intentional action. One might suppose that Buridan's ass choices belong to this category because where the agent evaluates at least two options equally, there just is no all-things-considered judgment that one action is best that could be the defining cause of an intentional choice under these circumstances. However, there is the evaluative judgment that assesses the two options equally, and there seems no reason why this should not be the defining cause of the action taken – although, of course, this judgment would have had as much claim to be the defining cause of the rejected alternative action. There is a problem for a CTA analysis here, but it is a problem for its causal rather than its rationality condition, and I shall return to it later. Buridan's ass choices, then, do not pose the difficulty that they fail to be made reasonable by the agent's final evaluative practical judgment (which would challenge the rationality condition); rather, they pose the difficulty that they are not made *uniquely* reasonable by that judgment.

However, there are cases somewhat similar to Buridan's ass choices that do seem to pose more of a problem for the assumption that the rationality condition is to be specified in terms of practical evaluative judgments. Michael Bratman has drawn attention to cases in which the agent is aware that one of only two options is superior to the other but recognizes that he or she is unable to tell which.[35] Bratman's example is of a canoeist who has to decide which fork to take in a river, knowing that only one stream leads to dangerous rapids, but unable to discover which. The canoeist may intentionally direct the craft down one stream rather than the other, and yet the defining cause of his action cannot be any kind of final evaluation of what it is best to do since he makes no such judgment, not even the judgment that either course would be equally preferable. Positing intentions is evidently useful here; without making any evaluative judgment about which is the better course, the canoeist simply *forms the intention* to direct the canoe down one fork in the river, and it is *with respect to this intention* that his behavior counts as reasonable. However, one could still maintain that in such a case, the agent judges that *for all he or she can tell at the point of decision,* each course is equally to be preferred, and so assimilate Bratman's case to a Buridan's ass choice in order to insist that the defining cause here is still an evaluative practical judgment.

I conclude, then, that it is only the challenge of akrasia that forces a CTA analysis to admit that intentions, rather than final evaluative practical judgments, may be the constitutive causes of intentional actions. Their admission is by no means purely ad hoc, although it would certainly have been nice to find a further conclusive reason, quite independent of considerations about akrasia, for requiring the

116

positing of intentions in the final stage of reasoning toward intentional action. Gratifyingly enough, we shall be able to find such a reason once we tackle a different kind of challenge to the causal component of the CTA analysis, following and in the next chapter. A certain consilience of grounds for positing final stage intentions does thus eventually emerge.

What amendments or elaborations does CTA-H require, then, to accommodate akratic actions? In Section I of this chapter, CTA-H was formulated as follows:

M performs the intentional action of a-ing, if, and only if,

(1) M is in a complex mental state, r;
(2) M's being in r makes it reasonable for M to do a;
(3) M's being in r causes an outcome, b; and
(4) b instantiates the type of state or event intrinsic to the action of a-ing.

Akratic intentional action is consistent with this analysis, provided it is understood that the complex mental state, r, need not be anything more than a final stage intention to do a. If r is construed as necessarily consisting in an evaluative judgment in favor of doing a, or some set of mental states (beliefs and desires, for example) that themselves justify such a judgment, then CTA-H is falsified by the possibility of akratic actions. From now on, then, we shall understand CTA-H so that r can consist merely in a final stage intention. It is worth noting that where r does consist only in a final stage intention, condition (2) becomes redundant. All the match we need between the outcome and the intentional content of r is, in fact, secured by the truth of (4).

The Possibility of Final Stage Akrasia

We have not, however, put the problem of akrasia entirely behind us by glossing CTA-H in this way. It might be suggested that there is a further form of *final stage* akrasia, in which an agent acts contrary to his or her final stage intention to act. What we have dealt with is the possibility of an akratic gap between all-things-considered best judgments and final stage intentions. It is now suggested that we have also to deal with the possibility of an akratic gap between final stage intentions and behavior.

Is final stage akrasia really a possibility? Take an example: Suppose a person judges that all things considered, it is better to go out for some exercise rather than stay inside in an armchair, and accordingly and continently, forms the final stage intention to get up. Is it possible that despite forming this intention, the person still doesn't stir? Well, if it is, then, given CTA-H as glossed, the agent's staying put could not be the agent's own intentional action (or more to the point, inaction). The agent must either be subject to some form of sudden incapacity to carry out the final stage intentions concerned, or else the truth must be that these intentions have not really been formed; the intention to get up has been displaced at the last minute by the final stage intention to stay put (that is, the agent has had a change of mind).

There can be no doubt that it is impossible for a person *intentionally* to remain in an armchair even though the person has formed a final stage intention to get up and retains the capacity to make the relevant bodily movements. But perhaps it can happen that the agent retains the relevant capacities yet fails to get up even though the final stage intention to do so is not displaced? Thus, there might be cases of *purely voluntary weak-willed action* contrary to the agent's final stage intention, even if intentional failures to carry out undisplaced final stage intentions are conceptually impossible. If we are prepared to enlarge Davidson's characterization D of incontinent action so that condition (a) now reads

(a*)   the agent does x voluntarily

then we may have to admit that there can be final stage akrasia.

However, it is clear that the possibility of final stage akrasia could offer no threat to the rationality condition of a CTA analysis of *intentional* action, such as CTA-H, since such final stage akratic acts would have to be merely voluntary actions. Indeed, provided we may rely on our earlier justification for defending CTA via a causal analysis of intentional action only, the suggestion that there might be final stage akrasia need not trouble us. Yet the (admittedly tentative) intuition that final stage akrasia is a possibility may lead us to grounds for reviewing the assumption, on which that justification was based, that intentional action is conceptually more fundamental than action generally. For, there is a further, and potentially more profound, respect in which akrasia may challenge a CTA analysis.

So far, we have treated akrasia as posing a problem for the specification of the rationality condition of a CTA analysis. However, it also raises difficulty for CTA's *causal condition,* and it is here that the possibility of final stage akrasia proves potentially most embarrassing. A CTA analysis will succeed in supporting CTA's core ontological claim – that actions are constituted by behavior with suitable mental causes – only if its causal clause refers purely to relations of ordinary event-causation whose place in a natural ontology is unproblematic. The analysis will fail if this causal clause needs to be interpreted as making essential reference to agent-causation. The possibility of akrasia raises a problem here because it shows that making a final evaluative judgment in favor of doing *a* (in a context where one has the capacity to do *a*) could at the very most be a merely necessary causal condition of intentionally *a*-ing. Thus, there must be further necessary conditions for intentional action. While these remain unstated, the suspicion may arise that they essentially include agent-causal conditions, such as that the agent, having made the judgment in favour of *a*-ing, must then bring about bodily events of a type intrinsic to *a*-ing. A CTA analysis needs decisively to exclude the agent-causationist's suggestion that an agent's reasons can be causes of his or her behavior only if *he or she* gives effect to them so that, strictly, *they* don't cause the behavior – rather, *the agent* causes it in the light of those reasons.

We should note that akratic action is not the only kind of intentional action that raises this problem. Actions that resolve a Buridan's ass choice do so also. For, here the final evaluative practical judgment and the required capacity for action patently cannot be sufficient for a particular intentional choice of either of the equally preferred options. Here too, the agent-causationist will maintain that an intentional action can occur only through *the agent's* causing the events intrinsic to the action chosen.

This difficulty may appear adequately resolved, however, by appealing to what we have already discovered in considering the problem akrasia poses for CTA's rationality condition, namely, that the mental states required as the rational causes of the intentional action need only be final stage intentions. Given this, we may suggest that although the possibility of akrasia and of resolving a Buridan's ass choice do indeed establish that a final practical *judgment* cannot be sufficient for action, there is an ontologically unproblematic causally sufficient condition for intentional action, namely, that the agent, having the relevant behavioral capacity, forms a final stage intention to act. Once a final practical evaluation is made, then, something extra does need to happen. But it is not anything ontologically suspect like *the agent's* causing matching behavioral events. It is a quite ordinary piece of event-causation, in which a final stage intention, caused as may be by prior mental states, itself causes a matching behavioral outcome. Thus, as foreshadowed, further grounds emerge for a CTA analysis to posit final stage intentions as essential components of chains of practical reasoning, which confer the status of intentional action on the behavior they cause.

This picture is spoiled, however, if we admit the possibility of final stage akrasia. For, if this is a possibility, even the formation of a final stage intention to do *a*, in the presence of the unimpaired behavioral capacity, cannot be a sufficient causal condition of performing the action of *a*-ing. And so the specter of an additional necessary condition for action that introduces agent-causal notions is raised once again. If indeed an agent can form the final stage intention to do an action that is actually within his or her capacity and still not perform that action, then agents do have to carry out their final stage intentions and the puzzle remains whether this can amount simply to some kind of ordinary event-causal relationship.

The belief that final stage akrasia is possible has nothing like the status of a central intuition, which could not be abandoned. Thus, if the only obstacle to a successful CTA analysis were the possibility of merely voluntary final stage akrasia, we would do well to take it as a corollary of the Causal Theory of Action that akrasia of this type is impossible. No doubt a case could be made for redescribing what we thought of as final stage akrasia in other terms (as sudden paralysis, last-ditch changes of mind, etc.). But such proposals for bringing intuitions into line with CTA raise the very question that is the subject of our next chapter: Are there other difficulties in establishing that the causal connections referred to in a CTA analysis are ontologically unproblematic and involve no hidden circular reference to the primitive notion of an action?

1 It might be suggested that all we need to resolve the problem of natural agency is to find a set of event-causal conditions that are *sufficient* for the occurrence of action – it does not matter whether they are necessary or not. (Here compare Keith Lehrer's recent account of how to establish traditional compatibilism; see Chapter 2, footnote 5.) Strictly speaking this suggestion is correct. However, unless our analysis gives event-causal conditions that are both sufficient and necessary for action, we will not be able to justify the claim that actions are *constituted* by suitable event-causal relations between complexes of states and events – and unless we can make this claim about what constitutes actions, we shall not have found a completely general way to understand how actions can belong to the natural order. If we give merely sufficient conditions, it will remain puzzling how the actions that fail to meet those conditions fit into the natural order, even though skepticism about the existence of *any* actions in the natural order will have been defeated. I shall, therefore, pursue the goal of a CTA analysis that offers both sufficient and necessary event-causal conditions for action. In practice, a search for merely sufficient conditions would, anyway, take us very much along the same track since the best way to progress toward such conditions is to keep conjoining individually necessary natural conditions for action.

2 See G. E. M. Anscombe's discussion of mental causation, *Intention* (Oxford, England: Blackwell, 1957), pp. 15–17. Anscombe believes, of course, that *all* mental causes exclude their behavioral effects from counting as actions. I take her view to be refuted by the arguments of Donald Davidson, discussed later.

3 Wilfrid Sellars has argued that there is an important distinction between mental "acts" and mental "actions": *Science and Metaphysics* (London: Routledge & Kegan Paul, 1968), p. 74, §33. In his view, "an action is the sort of thing one can decide to do." Thus, provided those mental events that are proposed as constitutive causes of actions are not themselves the kind of things "one can decide to do," there will be no threat of circularity.

4 Donald Davidson, *Essays on Actions and Events* (Oxford, England: Clarendon Press, 1980), Essay 1. My view of Davidson's arguments is by no means universally shared. Anscombe, for example, remains splendidly adamant in rejecting reasons as causes of actions. See her "The Causation of Action," in Carl Ginet and Sydney Shoemaker, eds., *Knowledge and Mind: Philosophical Essays* (Oxford, England: Oxford University Press, 1983), 174–90.

5 Davidson, *Essays on Actions and Events* pp. 13–15.

6 Ibid., pp. 17–18.

7 Ibid., pp. 12–13. Davidson accepts the principle that "mention of a causal condition for an event gives a cause only on the assumption that there was also a preceding event" (p. 12), and he argues that this principle is met for intentional explanations, on the grounds that although mental "states and dispositions are not events . . . the onslaught of a state or disposition is" (ibid.). If "onslaught" here means "formation," more will need to be said since agents often act for reasons that consist in beliefs and pro-attitudes of long standing. Arguably, in such cases (and perhaps generally?), the event-cause associated with the agent's mental states will be *the agent's using their contents in his or her practical reasoning*. Perhaps it is events of this kind that count for Sellars as mental acts but not as actions (see footnote 3). Further clarity will be gained on this question, once we recognise the need to offer a fuller characterization of the constitu-

tive mental causes of action than Davidson's initial account supplied (see Section II).

8 Ibid., p. 17.

9 Ibid. In Essay 1, Davidson remarks that "the laws whose existence is required if reasons are causes of actions do not, we may be sure, deal in the concepts in which rationalizations [sc. intentional explanations] must deal" (p. 17). Davidson's arguments for this claim are developed in Essays 11, 12, and 13. Davidson subscribes to the thesis of "psychophysical anomaly," that *in general* there are no strict laws linking psychological with physical properties (see especially Essay 11, sect. II, pp. 215–23).

10 See, for example, Carl Hempel's attempt to assimilate intentional explanations to the covering law model of scientific explanation in section 10 of his "Aspects of Scientific Explanation," *Aspects of Scientific Explanation and Other Essays in the Philosophy of Science* (New York: Macmillan, 1965), 331–496. The debate about the status of intentional explanations vis-à-vis scientific causal explanations still continues, and there is room for discussion about the significance of Davidson's work for this debate. Some philosophers, for example, have argued that given his thesis of psychophysical anomaly Davidson weakens the notion of causal explanation to such an extent that it means little to class intentional explanation as causal. See Dagfinn Føllesdal, "Explanation of Action," in R. Hilpinen, ed., *Rationality and Science* (Dordrecht, Holland: D. Reidel, 1980), 231–47; and Frederick Stoutland, "Oblique Causation and Reasons for Action," *Synthèse,* **43** (1980), 351–67. As far as resolving the problem of natural agency is concerned, however, this debate is somewhat at a tangent. Provided that the mental states referred to in intentional explanations are causes of the behavior explained, it does not matter whether such explanations meet further criteria arguably required for "scientific" causal explanation.

11 See Davidson, *Essays on Actions and Events,* pp. 11–12. Further arguments that reinforce the conclusion that reasons are causes of actions are usefully collected by Raimo Tuomela, "Explanation of Action," in G. Fløistad, ed., *Contemporary Philosophy: A New Survey, Volume 3* (The Hague: Martinus Nijhoff, 1986), 15–43, pp. 26–9.

12 Especially in *Essays on Actions and Events,* Essay 11.

13 In this connection, note that Davidson claims that "there is a sense in which the physical characteristics of [a state] *determine* the psychological characteristics . . . psychological concepts are *supervenient* on physical concepts . . . [in the sense that] it is impossible for two [states] to agree in all their physical characteristics . . . and to differ in their psychological characteristics" (ibid., Essay 13, p. 253).

14 Ibid., p. 19, my emphasis.

15 Ibid., p. 12, footnote 5.

16 Ibid., p. 87. Earlier, in "Freedom to Act," Davidson had concluded that 'we must count our search for a causal analysis of 'A is free to do x' a failure' (p. 80).

17 Ibid., Introduction, p. xiii., and p. 87, footnote 3.

18 Ibid., p. 88.

19 Ibid.

20 This notion of an action's intrinsic event is the same as G. H. von Wright's notion of the *result* of an action. See *Explanation and Understanding* (London: Routledge & Kegan Paul, 1971), pp. 66–9, 87–91. Although von Wright emphasizes that an action's result is not a causal consequence of it, I believe that the causal connotations of "result" in many of its uses can be confusing here, and so I avoid his terminology.

21 In "Actions, Reasons and Causes," Davidson takes this complex mental state to be a *primary reason*, consisting of a pro-attitude toward actions with a certain property and a belief that the behavior performed is an action with that property (*Essays on Actions and Events*, pp. 4–8).

22 "A person is the agent of an event if and only if there is a description of what he did that makes true a sentence that says he did it intentionally" (ibid., Essay 3, p. 46).

23 Kent Bach has argued, in "A Representational Theory of Action," *Philosophical Studies*, **34** (1978), 361–79, that the CTA is in trouble because the existence of merely voluntary actions such as these does have to be acknowledged. Accordingly, he develops a version of CTA ("Representational Causalism") for which behavior counts as action if and only if it is appropriately caused by "executive representations" (p. 366). Bach's position effectively collapses into the one he opposes if we are prepared to identify his executive representations as a species of intention – and to achieve this, all we need is to deny his contentious claim that intentions must involve explicit self-ascriptive thoughts of the form "I will do *A*." See pp. 363 and 371.

24 See my earlier remarks in footnote 1 on the limitations of an account that offers only sufficient natural conditions for action.

25 Davidson, *Essays on Actions and Events*, p. 22.

26 Such a judgment may exhibit weakness of will if the agent has the standing belief that he or she should let considerations of moral duty override all else in making all-things-considered judgments. But akrasia of judgment does not entail that the action carrying out the judgment is itself akratic. The case for allowing that beliefs may be held akratically is well argued by Amélie Rorty, "Akratic Believers," *American Philosophical Quarterly*, **20** (1983), 175–84.

27 Davidson, *Essays on Actions and Events* p. 29.

28 See *Essays on Actions and Events*, p. 23. Davidson does not state *P* as such but implicitly deduces it from two separate premises:

> P1. If an agent wants to do *x* more than he wants to do *y* and he believes himself free to do either *x* or *y*, then he will intentionally do *x* if he does either *x* or *y* intentionally; and
>
> P2. If an agent judges that it would be better to do *x* than to do *y*, then he wants to do *x* more than he wants to do *y*.

29 Ibid., p. xii.

30 Ibid.

31 Davidson's exposition is confusing at this point. He usefully suggests that a conditional practical judgment should have its form understood by analogy with probability judgments of the form "evidence *e probabilifies* that *p*" as follows: "evidence *e prima facie makes it the case that* doing *x* is better than doing *y*," which is represented under Davidson's symbolism as "*pf*(doing *x* is better than doing *y*, *e*)." But his use of "prima facie" in naming the relation employed in conditional practical judgments gives the false impression that because all-things-considered judgments have conditional form, they are also "prima facie" in the usual sense of being judgments subject to further consideration – which, of course, they can hardly be, given their all-things-considered character.

32 Davidson, *Essays on Actions and Events*, p. 41.

33 Ibid., Essay 5. Davidson here retracts his earlier view that all references to intentions as mental states can be reduced to attributions of intentional action – of acting *with* a certain intention – and admits that an agent can have an intention to act without ever acting with that intention.

34 For a recent survey of arguments in support of this view and against attempts to reduce intentions to complexes of beliefs and desires, see Myles Brand, *Intending and Acting: Toward a Naturalized Action Theory* (Cambridge, Mass.: M.I.T. Press, 1984), chaps. 5 and 6. See also Hector-Neri Castañeda's theory of practitions, *Thinking and Doing* (Dordrecht, Holland: D. Reidel, 1975), chaps. 10–11.
35 Michael Bratman, "Practical Reasoning and Weakness of Will," *Nous,* **13** (1979), 153–71.

4

The challenge of causal deviance

It is well known that behavior can conform to the conditions of CTA-H without counting as intentional action because there is something "deviant" about the way in which it is caused by the mental states that make it reasonable. That is, M's being in complex mental state r may make M's a-ing reasonable and cause an outcome, b, that instantiates the event type intrinsic to a-ing, and yet M nevertheless does not perform the intentional action of a-ing because the causal relation between being in r and b is not of the right kind. Thus, the causal condition of CTA-H needs to be supplemented so that it specifies what it is for the causal link between mental state and rational behavior to be of the right, nondeviant, kind for genuine intentional action to take place. Let us briefly review how the causally deviant counterexamples to CTA-H may be constructed.

With some of them, the causal chain from 'rationalizing' intentional state to matching behavior runs through conditions, such as nervousness or excitement, that deprive the agent of control over the outcome. Here the caused behavior is not only not an intentional action of the kind CTA-H says it should be – it is not even an action at all. This is the case with Davidson's climber,[1] whose reasons for letting go of the rope make him so nervous that he loses his grip, and also with Morton's avenger,[2] whose intention to shoot his insulter causes such excitement that his trigger finger jerks uncontrollably and he fires (more about these cases later). Another favorite way to construct counterexamples of this kind is to run the causal chain from intention to matching behavior through the intentional actions of a *second* agent. For ease of reference, we shall say that such causal chains from mental state to behavior are *heteromesial*. Thus it is with the victim of Peacocke's

125

knowledgeable neurophysiologist,[3] whose intention causes matching behavior only because the neurophysiologist recognizes it and stimulates the victim's otherwise inactive efferent nervous system to produce just those bodily movements that are required.

In other sorts of deviant counterexamples, the behavior does count as action, yet it fails to instantiate the intentional action that CTA-H predicts it should be. One sample formula for such cases is to let the agents' exercise of control fulfill their intentions, but in such a way that they do not realize it. This formula is exemplified by Peacocke's bank clerk, whose desire for more money and whose belief "that he could without detection write some accounts financially favourably to himself" distract him sufficiently to cause him "absent-mindedly [to] write his own rather than another's name on a line, which action . . . result[s] in a large payment of money to himself."[4] Another formula is illustrated by Daniel Bennett's case[5] of the man who tries to shoot an enemy, misses, yet with the noise of the shot stampedes a herd of wild pigs, which trample the victim to death. Here, although the agent recognizes that he has caused the fulfillment of his intention, we do not credit him with the performance of the corresponding intentional action because the means by which his end is achieved is so different from the means he intended.

How Deviant Cases Challenge CTA

The possibility of such causally deviant links between mental states and matching behavior might at first appear to pose only a trivial problem for CTA. All we need to do, it may seem, is to add the requirement that M's being in r causes b *in a causally nondeviant way*. But as long as we seek a CTA analysis to support the ontological claim that actions consist in behavior with a suitable event-causal history, the problem is by no means trivial. The deviant counterexamples show that a further condition is necessary for M to perform the intentional action of a-ing beyond those stated in the analysans of CTA-H. An event-causal CTA analysis will succeed only if this further condition can be expressed in terms requiring no essential reference to the notion of action or agent-causation.

Unfortunately, commonsense explanations of what makes for deviance in these counterexamples do appeal to the notion of an action or its equivalent. With Davidson's climber, for instance, it is natural to say that he did not let go intentionally because he "lost control of his grip," thus employing the concept of an exercise of control – not, of course, that there is anything mistaken about this response. The point is, if we can do no better than this, our attempted event-causal CTA analysis is back to square one, for we have had to make a circular appeal to the idea of an *agent's* doing something in order to exclude the deviant cases. Thus the challenge for the CTA analysis is to go beyond such commonsense responses and explain deviance without covert appeal to the notion of action.

If this point is not appreciated, debates about causal deviance will understandably seem purely academic. Irving Thalberg takes just such an attitude when he suggests that all the fuss about an example like Davidson's climber can be set aside by the simple observation that "the enfeeblement of one's grip is not something one can do, and hence is ineligible to be considered something one does either intentionally or unintentionally."[6] But in appealing to the notion of "something one can do," Thalberg is presupposing the concept of an action. In terms of CTA-H, he is requiring that mental state r should cause behavior b in such a way as to count as something the agent does.[7] If our analysis of intentional action thus helps itself to the notion of agency, it may escape deviant counterexamples – but it will forfeit any prospect of supplying an independent argument for CTA's ontological thesis that actions consist purely in behavior with a certain kind of event-causal history. Indeed, the whole rationale for seeking an analysis of specifically *intentional* action (as expressed in Chapter 3), rests on the expectation that it will *not* require appeal to the concept of action *tout court*.

Hence, the possibility of causally deviant counterexamples can serve as the main premise in an argument for the claim that intentional actions cannot be analyzed in purely event-causal terms – that is, that a CTA analysis is impossible. Put positively, this is the *thesis of agent-causationism,* namely, that actions must be understood essentially as events *brought about by the agent*. Roderick Chisholm[8] introduces his famous example of the murderous nephew (outlined later) in support of just such an argument, although the main justification Chisholm offers for agent-causationism is the claim that its truth alone provides a solution to the dilemma formulation of the problem of action (discussed in Chapter 1). However, as already argued there, appealing to agent-causation merely reformulates rather then resolves the essential problem of action, whereas it is the CTA that promises a genuine solution. Thus, in fact,

Chisholm's secondary argument for agent-causationism should become his main one: The possibility of deviant counterexamples really does threaten to block an event-causal analysis of intentional action, and so leave the core ontological claim of CTA unsupported and skepticism about natural agency unresolved. Much is to be gained, then, by showing that an event-causal analysis of intentional action can be elaborated so that the deviant counterexamples are clearly excluded.[9]

Match with the Action-Plan as Necessary for
Nondeviant Action

According to CTA-H, for M to perform the intentional action of a-ing, M must be in a mental state, r, that makes the outcome, b, *reasonable* under the description "a-ing." For brevity, let us say that an outcome, b, which stands in this relation to a mental state, r, "matches" r's content, and we shall refer to this requirement of a CTA analysis as its "condition of match." One suggested method for excluding deviant counterexamples relies on developing this condition.

I have already argued (when discussing akrasia in Chapter 3) that r need be no more than a final stage intention. Typically, however, the mental antecedents of action will be richer than this. In general, the mental state that initiates action will be the agent's *intending* a certain goal or end, e. Now, either e will be something agent M can bring about directly, or M will be able to achieve e only by bringing about other events or states of affairs as a means to it. Suppose that e is achievable only indirectly. Then we shall say that M's intention to achieve e is a *nonbasic* intention, and that its fulfillment is a *nonbasic intentional action*. To fulfill a nonbasic intention, M must form an *action-plan*: Given M's beliefs about the situation (both particular and general), M must reason toward a suitable means for achieving e – means that M can bring about directly without further practical reasoning. Successful practical reasoning thus culminates in a belief that performing a certain set of basic actions (in such and such an order) is, all things considered, an optimal (or perhaps just an adequate) means for achieving e. (Basic actions are those the agent can perform directly, without having to find other means for their achievement.[10]) Given M's intention to achieve e, and the belief that a certain basic action-sequence is the appropriate means for achieving e, M then forms the intention to perform the basic action-sequence specified in his or her action-plan. If all goes well, M performs the nonbasic intentional action of bringing e about by executing this action-plan. Evidently, if M originally intends an end that he or she can directly achieve, M already possesses a trivial action-plan for fulfilling such a "basic" intention.

With all nonbasic intentional actions, then, the mental antecedents include not just the original nonbasic intention but also *an intention to achieve it by carrying out the basic actions specified in the action-plan.* It is therefore natural to suggest that CTA's condition of match requires here that the outcome match the means the agent intended as well as the end. As Alvin Goldman[11] and David Armstrong,[12] for example, have suggested, we should add to CTA-H the requirement that r should cause *b in a way that matches the agent's action-plan* for achieving his or her goal.

This suggestion is promising. It does seem a typical (and, one might hope, universal) feature of the deviant counterexamples that although the outcome is what the agent intended, it does not come about *in the way* intended. Consider, for example, Chisholm's case of the murderous nephew.[13] A nephew's desire to murder his uncle in order to inherit his fortune causes him to drive so recklessly on the way to do the deed that he runs down a pedestrian, who, unknown to him, is his unfortunate relative, and so he inherits. Here the deviance is well accounted for as a failure of match with the action-plan: The nephew's intention causes its fulfillment by a causal route quite different from the kind intended. Indeed, the actual causal route could not have been intended – it would be incoherent to form a plan to kill Uncle Joe by accidentally running over an anonymous pedestrian who then turns out to be Uncle Joe. Perhaps, then, all the counterexamples will be excluded once we understand CTA-H to require that the agent's intention should cause its fulfillment in a way that matches the agent's plan of action.

Making Precise the Condition of Match with the Action-Plan

What exactly does match with the agent's plan require? In particular, how specific a statement of the agent's plan do events have to match to fulfill this condition? In the limiting case, an agent might have no plan at all, yet his or her intention might happen to cause its own fulfillment (agitated by the intention to inherit the fortune somehow, the nephew drives recklessly, runs down his uncle, and so inherits). Or the agent's plan might be so vague, that match with the outcome is too readily achieved (the nephew intends to kill his frail uncle by giving him a shock, and this intention causes the nephew to become so nervous that he has a horrifying accident, which, it so happens, the uncle witnesses, . . .). Neither of these are intentional killings, yet in a loose sense, match with the agent's plan is achieved. Evidently, we must require that what happens should match a *sufficiently specific* statement of the agent's plan. The question is to say what would count as such.

Agents develop action-plans, as we saw, to discover what basic actions (directly under their control) they should take in order to achieve ends not directly under their control. An action-plan is worthless unless it specifies a basic action (or sequence of them) that the agent may perform with the intention of achieving his or her end. Thus, an action-plan must at least fulfill this requirement if it is to be adequately specific for the purposes of the suggested condition. Null action-plans, or plans as vague as "killing him by giving him a shock," fail this test.

For an outcome to match a given action-plan that passes this test, at least the following three conditions are necessary. First, the agent must perform the basic acts specified in the plan. Second, the agent's doing so must be intentional under the description given in the plan. And, third, the agent must perform these acts *with the intention of* attaining the end the plan was formed to serve. Only if these three conditions are satisfied will the agent have what John Searle has called the right "intention in acting" for his behavior to count as an intentional action fulfilling the "prior intention" that causes it.[14]

To appreciate the power of the condition of match, so understood, let us see how its application disposes of some of the deviant counterexamples. Chisholm's murderous nephew fails the first component of the condition of match with the action-plan: Whatever his action-plan was, he does not carry out the basic acts it specified, and his evil intent causes its own fulfillment by a fluke. With Peacocke's bank clerk, the first component is present, for he performs just the right basic acts specified in his plan to transfer funds to his own account. But the second component of the condition of match fails since he performs these acts absent-mindedly (or perhaps, by way of a Freudian slip), and they are not intentional under the true description, "making a transfer into his own account." Conceivably, an agent's nonbasic intention could cause that agent *intentionally* to perform the basic acts specified in his or her action-plan, and yet the case would still be deviant because the third component is missing – because these basic actions are not performed by the agent with the intention of carrying out the plan.[15]

There is reason to think that we should recognize a further, fourth, component of the condition of match. Bennett's counterexample satisfies each of the three already mentioned components of the condition of match with the action-plan. Bennett's agent planned to kill his enemy by shooting him, and he intentionally performs the basic acts required by this plan with the intention of killing the enemy. However, because the enemy's death is caused by a quite unforseen causal route – the noise of the shot stampedes a herd of pigs, which trample the enemy to death – we classify the case as deviant, and we are inclined to explain the deviance as a failure of match with the agent's plan. This example suggests that a fourth component of the condition of match with the action-plan should be that the actual outcome must conform to the agent's beliefs (formed in his or her practical reasoning) about *how it would be* that the basic actions planned would yield the desired goal.

Admitting this fourth component, however, runs the risk of ruling as deviant some quite genuine cases of intentional action. Will a fastidious assassin, whose plan is to kill the tyrant with a shot through the heart, fail to kill intentionally if the bullet lodges in the victim's brain instead? Hardly! Of course, if we describe the intended action more specifically, as a killing-by-shooting-through-the-heart, there will be no intentional action of that type. But this expedient dodges the interesting issue: Why does our assassin count as killing intentionally, whereas Bennett's inadvertent pig-stampeder does not?

The correct hint here, I think, is that what matters is whether the actual causal sequence is of a type that the agent could have considered in reasoning toward his or her action-plan. Thus, if what happens fails to match the agent's plan but matches a way of achieving the goal that the agent should have been able to envisage as an option, we allow that the intentional action of achieving that goal has been performed. Given plausible background assumptions, the pig-stampeder could not have considered what actually occurred as a possible means of despatching his enemy, whereas our assassin could certainly have considered aiming at the tyrant's head and could also have recognized that shooting at the tyrant's heart might have resulted instead in his getting a bullet through the head.

I conclude, then, that there are good prospects for formulating the condition of match with the agent's plan precisely enough for it to be added to an event-causal CTA analysis. Perhaps some would argue that a reference to the agent's plan introduces something suspiciously like the agent-causal relation. But this doubt may be set aside. In referring to the agent's plan, as suggested earlier, we are simply elaborating, for the case of nonbasic intentional action, the general condition of match between a behavioral outcome and the content of the relevant intentional states of the agent that is an intrinsic feature of any CTA analysis – and that condition poses no difficulty provided we may presuppose (as I have been doing) a naturalist account of intentionality.

The Problem of Basic Deviance

Adding a requirement of match with the agent's plan to CTA-H does not, however, dispose of all the deviant counterexamples. For, counterexamples may be constructed in which the mental states that constitute an agent's reasons for performing a *basic* action cause the appropriate matching behavior, and yet the corresponding basic intentional action is not performed. Clearly, there can be no hope of excluding these cases (which I shall refer to as cases of basic deviance) by requiring match with the agent's plan since once an agent has a reason to perform a directly achievable action within his or her repertoire, there is neither need nor opportunity for further planning about how to carry out the action.

To illustrate, I shall consider a much-discussed deviant case of Davidson's: the case of the nervous climber (already mentioned previously). This is how Davidson states the example:

A climber might want to rid himself of the weight and danger of holding another man on a rope, and he might know that by loosening his hold on the rope he could rid himself of the weight and danger. This belief and want might so unnerve him as to cause him to loosen his hold, and yet it might be the case that he never *chose* to loosen his hold, nor did he do it intentionally.[16]

It will be useful to begin by considering the normal case from which this one deviates. What intentional action would the climber have performed had his letting go been caused without causal deviance? Well, it would have been a (morally repugnant!) nonbasic intentional action of ridding himself of the weight and danger of holding his partner on the rope; and the means by which he would have performed this nonbasic action would have been by performing the basic intentional action of letting go of the rope. We may represent the causal chain of events in this "normal" case as falling into two stages:

Reason-constituting states	—1→ Basic action	—2→	Final end
Desire to be rid of the weight and danger; belief that letting go is the means to this end	Letting go of rope		No longer bearing weight or risking danger

This kind of pattern, of course, is common to all nonbasic intentional actions. The link at stage 2, from basic action to final end, is frequently a causal link, but it need not be so, as this example shows. The bodily movements that constitute a basic action may generate the performance of a nonbasic intentional action because, given the circumstances, as a matter of fact or convention, making those bodily movements *just is* achieving the final end. Here, given that the weight and danger are due solely to holding his colleague on the rope, the climber's letting go of the rope *is* his becoming free of the weight and danger.[17]

In Davidson's actual example – the deviant case – the climber's desire and belief make him so nervous that he loses his grip and lets go, thus making the very bodily movements it is reasonable for him to make given his desire and belief. Here, the deviance *affects the causal link between mental states and basic action* – stage 1 in the diagram. In cases like Chisholm's murderous nephew or Bennett's pig-stampeding assassin, the deviance affects the link between the bodily movements intrinsic to the basic action – which is performed quite nondeviantly – and the final end (stage 2 in the diagram).[18] Only in cases like these, where the deviance enters at stage 2, can there be any point in considering match with the

133

agent's plan. At stage 1, since agents do not have to form action-plans for carrying out basic actions, there can be no issue about match with the agent's plan. Thus, Davidson's climber provides a counterexample even to a CTA analysis that includes a condition of match with the agent's plan.

It is true that it would be entirely apt for the climber to report his experience by saying that things did not go in accordance with his plan – that he never planned to let go. But the aptness of such a report does not show that the case involves a violation of the condition of match. What the report conveys is the climber's "nonobservational" awareness that the causal sequence, running as it did through nervousness, was not of the right type to realize an intentional letting go. Thus, "I didn't let go in the way I planned" has no more content than "My letting go was not intentional." Since the climber had no plan about *how* to let go (letting go was in his repertoire of basic actions), the condition of match is satisfied by the outcome being exactly that which he had reason to bring about, given his beliefs and desires.

Excluding Basic Deviance: The Causal Chain Must Constitute Practical Reasoning

How, then, may a CTA analysis be developed to exclude a counterexample such as the case of the nervous climber, in which it is the agent's reasons for performing a *basic* action that deviantly cause the appropriate outcome? What goes wrong in this case, of course, is that the causal chain passes through nervousness, and nervousness robs the climber of control. So what would we need for the climber to retain control? A natural first suggestion is that the agent's reasons should cause the matching behavioral outcome via a causal chain, part of which *counts as the agent's own practical reasoning*. If it is through the agent's own – however brief – deliberations about how to act that the matching outcome is produced, then surely the causal chain will be nondeviant? Perhaps so. But as it stands, this suggestion is problematic for an event-causal CTA analysis since it makes at least a surface reference to something the agent *does,* namely, to *reason* from certain mental states toward suitable behavior.

But perhaps this reference to an agent's reasoning is purely superficial? If we may take an agent's practical reasoning to amount to *the operation of a particular kind of causal mechanism* (as opposed to other causal mechanisms that might yield the same result), then indeed there will be nothing ontologically embarrassing about requiring that the causal chain should include the agent's reasoning.[19] But for this to work, we shall have to give a purely event-causal account of what distinguishes causal mechanisms that count as the agent's reasoning from those that do not. We shall need to specify *the sorts of causal paths that can count as the "right" way in which beliefs and desires must yield behavior for genuine intentional action to occur.* How might this be done?

One obvious solution is to regard the difference between deviant and nondeviant causal mechanisms here as depending on the kinds of intermediate steps through which the causal chain passes on its way from the agent's reasons to his or her matching behavior. Thus, on this view, a causal chain would count as someone's practical reasoning, not because it involves anything ontologically suspect like agent-causation, but because it passes through mental events of the kind that constitute practical reasoning. This suggestion will work, of course, only if it is possible to specify what sorts of intermediate mental events are sufficient and necessary for the chain to count as the agent's practical reasoning and, hence, as nondeviant.

I have already described the typical sequence of practical reasoning involved in nonbasic intentional action, and that account may be put to use here. Typically, a chain of practical reasoning begins with a nonbasic intention, proceeds to an all-things-considered judgment in favor of a certain sequence of basic actions, and culminates in a basic intention to carry out these actions. But this pattern is not exhibited in the nervous climber case. For a start, the initial cause is a combination of belief and desire, and this does not seem to be equivalent to an intention. (Agents often do *not* intend to achieve what they nevertheless desire). But of course, the example can easily be modified so that the initiating cause is a genuine intention to be rid of the weight and danger, and this intention then causes the nervousness that makes the climber let go.[20] This climber will not be quite so blameless as Davidson's, whose nervousness may well have been induced by the shock of realizing the moral repugnance of his desires. In the case as we now have it, the climber forms the morally blameworthy intention to be rid of the weight and danger of holding his partner on the rope. But in the event, he escapes responsibility for sacrificing his colleague by a deviant stroke of "moral luck."

However, in such a (slightly reformulated) case, there would still be something missing in comparison with the normal course of practical reasoning. For, the climber's intention to be rid of the weight and danger does not cause its fulfillment through evaluative practical judgments or intentions to perform basic actions. So, it may be hoped, if we are more precise about what sort of a causal route from initial intention to matching behavior can count as the agent's reasoning, we are in a position to develop CTA-H in order to exclude cases of basic deviance. In effect, we have to be much more explicit about r, the "complex" mental state that is the rational cause of intentional action: We have to see it as a *process* rather than as a state, as beginning with a nonbasic intention, and then moving through evaluative judgments to a basic intention and finally to action.

Unfortunately, matters are not so straightforward. It is obviously possible to construct a further variant on the climber case in which it is *making an all-things-considered judgment to let go* that induces the climber's nervousness and causes him to let go. But then, it will be replied, the causal route will still fail to count overall as reasoning since it doesn't pass through a basic intention to let go. As our discussion of akrasia in Chapter 3 has convinced us, it is possible for an agent to judge, all things considered, that it is best to do a yet fail to form the final stage intention to do a. Agreeably, then, it seems that a CTA will need to require basic intentions as intermediate between final practical evaluations and behavior in order to exclude a deviant case like this – which provides further confirmation in favor of positing final stage intentions.

But of course, there is causal space between even a basic intention and matching behavior, and therefore room to construct a further counterexample in which it is the agent's *basic intention to let go* that causes the nervousness that causes the loss of grip. One might reply that the distinction between deviance and nondeviance at this stage may still be characterized as a difference in causal intermediaries. After all, a basic intention is typically an intention to implement a whole sequence of basic actions at the correct times; so presumably, when the right time comes for each action in the sequence, an intention to perform the relevant basic act *there and then* (which we may call a *proximate* intention) is formed, which then causes the required behavior. This general point has less application to the climber case, although it might still be argued that there is a very swift transition between the basic intention to let go of the rope and the proximate intention to do so "right now." However, it won't do any good to specify our CTA analysis so that the causal chain must pass through a proximate intention, for the obvious reason that the strategy for manufacturing basic deviance may be applied yet again: Could not there be a case in which the agent's *proximate* intention to do *a* induces nervousness that yields an instance of *a*'s intrinsic event type?

Excluding Basic Deviance: Causation by Virtually Concurrent Intentions

Perhaps there is something wrong with the formula I have just been using to generate a succession of causally deviant cases. Is it really true that wherever there is causal space between mental events and behavior there can be deviance? Perhaps there is a relatively late stage in the normal process of practical reasoning beyond which deviance is just impossible – a stage at which, no matter how the mental state causes its matching outcome, genuine intentional action will occur?

Dorothy Mitchell has claimed as much.[21] She believes that intentional actions consist in behavior that matches and is caused by a *concurrent* intention. A concurrent intention is not strictly simultaneous with the caused behavior – it possesses only "the concurrence of everyday experience and not of scientific measurement": It virtually accompanies the behavior. (Mitchell's notion of a concurrent intention thus comes to much the same as my notion of a proximate intention, previously suggested). So Mitchell does not deny "the existence of causal processes between the [concurrent] intention and the action."[22] Her claim is just that such processes will not be deviant: Somehow, the concurrent intention is too causally close to action for deviance to intrude. Should nervousness intervene at this late stage, it will be a vehicle of the agent's control rather than an obstacle to it.

But why should this claim be accepted? Why cannot a concurrent intention, at the very last minute, cause the agent to lose the relevant capacity and yet (as it happens) to behave involuntarily just as intended? Mitchell offers no argument for excluding this possibility. Perhaps it might be argued that, since concurrent intentions are experienced as simultaneous with the behavior they cause, the difference between an allegedly deviant and a nondeviant causal link here would be experientially undetectable and that, therefore, there can be no such difference. But this argument does not pass muster. In the first place, the alleged undetectability of any putatively deviant case does not entail that such cases are impossible. And in the second place, there may be ways of detecting when a link between a concurrent intention and matching behavior is deviant that do not require experiencing a temporal gap between them. Indeed, agents themselves might tell the difference by the absence of the normal sense of exercising control over their bodily movements.

Although detecting the difference between deviant and nondeviant cases in the causal space between concurrent intention and matching behavior may be problematic, there can be no doubt that we may differentiate conceptually between them. Given that concurrent intentions are strictly temporally antecedent to the behavior they cause, it makes perfectly good sense to claim that an agent's concurrent (proximate) intention to do *a* induces a state that both deprives the agent of his or her normal power to do *a* and fortuitously causes the agent's body to move in the way required for *a*-ing. Furthermore, we can envisage this possibility without any knowledge whatsoever of the physical details of any actual such deviant case. Thus, although it is true that "intentional behavior is a prescientific concept and the nature of the causal processes from concurrent intention to action was unknown at the time the concept was forged,"[23] this fact does not establish that it is a conceptual truth that concurrent intentions cannot deviantly cause matching behavior. For, using only the resources of our "prescientific" concept we can coherently envisage the possibility of a concurrent intention causing matching behavior via a causal route that deprives the agent of control. Thus, we cannot accept a CTA analysis of basic action as behavior that matches and is caused by the agent's concurrent (proximate) intention to act. These conditions may be necessary, but they are not sufficient.

Excluding Basic Deviance: The Causal Immediacy Strategy

Mitchell's suggestion therefore fails. But it may be worth exploring a strengthened version of it, for which concurrent intentions are held to be strictly concurrent with the behavior they cause.[24] On this account, concurrent intentions are the *immediate* causes of matching behavior. Though explicitly rejected by Mitchell, this approach has been taken by Myles Brand.[25] In discussing cases of "antecedential waywardness" ("basic deviance" in our terms), Brand observes that they involve the *intervention* between mental antecedents and behavior of some condition depriving the agent of control. Were there no room for such intervention, Brand reasons, counterexamples of this type would be impossible. So he introduces the notion of *proximate* causation, in which a cause proximately yields its effect when there is no mediating cause linking them. He then suggests that genuine basic intentional action requires the mental antecedent to be the proximate cause of the matching behavior. Let us call this the *causal immediacy* strategy for developing a CTA analysis to exclude basic deviance.

There may well be something suspect about the very idea of proximate causation: Have we, for instance, any reason to suppose that it makes any more sense than a corresponding notion of "proximate" points on a line? Yet even if the coherence of the notion is granted, Brand faces the difficulty that intentions as realized in central neural states will never be causally proximate to the bodily movements that match them. To avoid this difficulty, he stipulates that the sequence of events constituting a basic action begins at the very point in the physiological chain at which mental antecedents end, and thus commits himself to the view that "the action of [e.g.] Richard's clapping his hands begins in the brain."[26] This notion of a physiologically extended action might, of course, be a fair price to pay for a solution to the problem of excluding basic deviance. But in fact, this manoeuvre does not genuinely solve the problem.

Suppose that a mental state is the proximate cause of the first element in a physiological chain that issues in matching bodily movements: Will the case thereby be guaranteed to be nondeviant? No, for as the nervousness cases show, the physiological chain may proceed via a condition that deprives the agent of control. Thus, if we try to exclude deviance between intention and action by insisting on proximate causation, the problem of excluding it breaks out anew with the need to specify what types of physiological chain, proximately caused by an intention and yielding behavior to match it, may count as realizing genuine action. The causal immediacy strategy will succeed in furnishing the event-causal CTA analysis we are seeking only if such a specification can be given.

Brand's suggestion for such a specification may be gathered from the following remark: "An action has occurred provided only that the causal chain has been initiated *in the right way* and the bodily movement has taken place . . . the route from the initial neurological events to the bodily movement is irrelevant."[27] The idea seems to be that the kinds of causal chain that realize genuine actions (of Brand's physiologically extended kind) are those that have been proximately caused by a suitable mental event "in the right way." But what can this constraint mean? As there is no causal space here for mediation, the difference between right and wrong ways cannot be a difference in types of mediating causal routes. But what other possibility is there? Brand does not say.

It follows that Brand's causal immediacy strategy makes no progress. The event-causal analysis we seek cannot rely on an appeal to an indefinitely specified difference between "rightly initiated" (nondeviant) and "wrongly initiated" (deviant) causal chains. What is needed for nondeviance, of course, is that the proximately caused physiological chain be of a kind that realizes rather than blocks the agent's control. But adding such a clause to our CTA analysis will frustrate its purpose, unless some event-causal analysis can be given of the notion of a causal chain realizing the agent's own exercise of control – yet this is what we have been trying to achieve all along. The causal immediacy strategy thus brings us full circle. Since it rests anyway on a notion of doubtful coherence (that of proximate causation), I conclude that there is no point in amending CTA-H to require that the defining mental causes of action should include a mental state (such as a concurrent intention) that proximately causes the matching behavior.

Excluding Basic Deviance: Volitions

We seem to have found a way of excluding some of the examples of basic deviance by specifying what sort of causal route could count as an agent's practical reasoning. The trouble is that this method deals with only some of these examples. There seems to be nothing incoherent about a case in which a basic intention (or a proximate intention, if we admit them) deviantly causes its own fulfillment. That is, it seems quite feasible that whatever mental state we take to

140

be the last stage in practical reasoning before action itself should be a deviant cause of matching behavior.

Advocates of volitions might suggest that they will do the trick for us.[28] Perhaps we can say that to be nondeviant, the causal chain from final stage intention must pass through a volition to perform the intended act. Evidently, for volitions to play this role they must be distinct from final stage intentions – a point that needs making since some philosophers[29] use the term *volition* to refer to what we have called a proximate intention. Some phenomenological evidence might be adduced in support of this proposal, to the effect that even after a final stage intention has been formed, it is still up to the agent to implement it. Indeed, the possibility of final stage akrasia (discussed in the previous chapter) might be taken to show that volitions need to be introduced to explain what is missing when an agent forms a final stage intention yet (despite no lack of capacity) fails to go through with it. Interestingly enough, this suggestion would provide us with a CTA analysis covering action in general, and not just intentional action specifically. The analysis will be simple: Behavior counts as action if and only if it is caused by a volition that (in our now familiar sense) it also matches.

Such simplicity suggests a mirage, and indeed, there is one. Appealing to volitions gets us nowhere, for what exactly are volitions? Either they are themselves in the category of action (as the alternative term *act of will* suggests), or they are not. If volitions are actions, their use in the CTA analysis will introduce circularity: The puzzle about how action is possible will simply be shifted into the "inner" realm. It may indeed be true that behavior "caused by" a volition to perform an action whose intrinsic event type it instantiates must be genuine action and cannot be a mere deviant counterpart. But this will be a trivial truth of no use to the project of providing a CTA analysis that resolves the problem of natural agency.

On the other hand, if volitions are not actions but mental events of some kind realized in central neural states, then causal chains from volitions to matching behavior will be in principle as much subject to causal deviance as are causal chains from final stage intentions. Indeed, on this supposition, we are in fact making volitions the final stage in practical reasoning, and so the problem about how that final causal link from practical reasoning to action can count as nondeviant will understandably still remain.

141

It seems, then, that talk of volitions is either talk of something like proximate intentions or talk about actions – in which case there is no need to introduce volitions at all.[30] Certainly, they offer no solution to our current problem, which is to find an event-causal analysis of intentional action that excludes *all* the cases of basic deviance.

May the Exclusion of Basic Deviance Be Left to Future Empirical Inquiry?

At this stage, in some desperation, seekers after an event-causal CTA analysis may be tempted to follow the suggestion, made for example, by Goldman,[31] that the task of excluding basic deviance be left for future empirical inquiry. Genuine basic intentional action is behavior caused by a basic (or proximate) intention in the right sort of way. If an event-causal CTA analysis is to be possible, the right sort of way must amount to a certain kind of mediating causal route from intention to matching behavior. We have failed so far to specify what kind of causal route this must be. But perhaps it doesn't matter. Perhaps – and this is what Goldman suggests – all we need do is point out that there must be such a specification and leave it to neurophysiology, as the relevant branch of empirical enquiry, to discover what that specification is.

This suggestion appears both liberating and tough-minded. But it is actually quite useless in the context of the search for a CTA analysis that will secure the possibility of agency in an event-causal natural order. Goldman's "solution" amounts in fact to a decision to abandon the problem. As McCann puts it,[32] a CTA analysis "cannot [justifiably] be made hostage to physiology" in this way. I think it is important to understand why this is so.

Although I agree with McCann, I don't think he offers the right reasons for rejecting Goldman's approach, because he takes Goldman's suggestion to be a proposal about the analysis of the *meaning* of the concept of a nondeviant intentional action. However, in fact there is no need to take it that way at all. McCann's objection is that Goldman

fails to do justice to the fact that whereas at present no one, physiologist or not, has the scientific information [he] calls for, we all usually *know* when changes that occur in our bodies count as the results of intentional actions on our part, and when they occur as mere involuntary responses.[33]

So McCann is arguing that since our practical mastery of the concept of intentional action indicates that we already know very well what we mean by it, the analysis of its meaning cannot essentially involve any unknown empirical information about the types of causal pathway that count as nondeviant. The general assumption (to which this argument is committed) that empirical discovery cannot enlarge our understanding of what we mean by a concept is, I think, a questionable one.[34] If we want to argue that reference to some not yet fully known empirical conditions cannot be part of what we mean by "action," it will be preferable, I think, to rest the case on a functionalist account of mental states and events. According to such an account, for a system to be in a given mental state is for it to be in any physical state that plays a specific role in the functional interrelation of the system's inputs, outputs, and central states; mental terms are, strictly speaking, names of functional roles, and these roles are multiply realizable.[35] The same type of mental state can be instantiated in – perhaps indefinitely many – different types of physical state. Now, if we do suppose that action is to be defined as behavior with the right sort of mental history, given functionalism, it will follow that actions too can be multiply realized. So empirical information about, say, the neurophysiological features of nondeviant causal chains in a particular individual or species will give no more than the facts about how genuine agency is *contingently* realized in that individual or species. In other individuals or species (or machines), nondeviant causal chains with the same functional characteristics may be realized rather differently in physical terms. Discoveries about the physiological basis of human basic action will not, then, yield a heightened understanding of what we meant all along by the notion of an action. They will simply tell us what happens neurophysiologically when *we* act.[36]

The point is, though, that defining the meaning of "action" need not be at issue. As I made clear in Chapter 3, success in defending CTA does not necessarily require a CTA analysis that defines what we mean by "action" in event-causal terms. It will be enough to show that, given our concept of action, CTA is an acceptable theory of what *constitutes* an action ontologically – and that requires only an "analysis" of action in terms of necessary and sufficient event-causal conditions. Accordingly, Goldman could agree that having yet-to-be-discovered neurophysiological features is not part of what we mean by a nondeviant, action-realizing, causal chain, and still repeat his point that at a certain stage, a CTA analysis of the event-causal conditions sufficient and necessary for action can leave the task of its own completion to empirical science.

The real difficulty with Goldman's suggestion is, of course, a dialectical one: It simply *assumes* that an (ontological) event-causal CTA analysis is possible. We can leave the details of the natural realization of agency for the scientists to discover only if we are satisfied that the skeptical objections to the very possibility of natural agency have been overcome. And at the moment, we are still wrestling with those objections. We want to establish that basic intentional action (understood as involving the agent's exercise of control) is ontologically constituted by behavior with the right sort of event-causes, and to this end we seek a CTA analysis that provides sufficient and necessary conditions for basic intentional action that *uncontroversially refer only to causal relations of the event-causal kind admitted in our natural ontology.* Our proposed CTA analysis will be utterly unpersuasive if, just at the point where we cannot actually produce an analysis that puts paid to belief in essential agent-causation, we say, in effect, "Look, just believe that it can be done, and leave it to future scientific work to show us how!" Goldman's suggestion, then, amounts simply to an *assertion* that agent-causationists are wrong if they suppose that the possibility of basic deviance indicates that for a basic action to be performed, the relevant bodily movements must be brought about by the agent, and that this bringing about cannot be analyzed, even ontologically, as a matter of ordinary event-causal relations. In seeking to develop our CTA analysis, however, we want *arguments* for this conclusion.

None of this discussion entails, of course, that physical systems that realize basic actions do not, in doing so, exhibit common physical properties. Even granted multiple realizability, it might actually turn out, especially among individuals of the same species, that many basic actions are physically realized in the same way. The point is just that while we are developing a CTA analysis of basic action as an argument against skepticism about natural agency, we need to specify some feature at the level of functional organization that characterizes all and only the genuine nondeviant causal chains from final stage intention to matching behavior, and requires ontologically nothing more than ordinary event-causation. So far we have not found such a feature – but some philosophers would claim to have done so, and so we shall now turn, in the next chapter, to consider their theory.

NOTES

1 Donald Davidson, *Essays on Actions and Events* (Oxford, England: Clarendon Press, 1980), Essay 4, p. 79.
2 Adam Morton, "Because He Thought He Had Insulted Him," *Journal of Philosophy*, **72** (1975), 5–15. Other well-known examples along similar lines are Taylor's case of the shy fidgeter in Richard Taylor, *Action and Purpose* (Englewood Cliffs, N.J.: Prentice-Hall, 1966), p. 248; and Goldman's case of the grimacing diner in Alvin Goldman, *A Theory of Human Action* (Englewood Cliffs, N.J.: Prentice-Hall, 1970), p. 54.
3 Christopher Peacocke, *Holistic Explanation: Action, Space, Interpretation* (Oxford, England: Clarendon Press, 1979), p. 87. In "Is Agent-Causality a Conceptual Primitive?" *Synthèse*, **67** (1986), 225–47, I used the term heteronomous to refer to cases of this type. This terminology, however, may suggest that causal chains that pass through a second agent's action cannot realize the first agent's autonomous action. My new terminology avoids this question-begging connotation; Peacocke's example may indeed be deviant, but it remains an open question whether *all* heteromesial chains must be so.
4 Peacocke, *Holistic Explanation*, p. 55.
5 Quoted by Davidson, *Essays on Actions and Events*, p. 79.
6 Irving Thalberg, "Do Our Intentions Cause Our Intentional Actions?" *American Philosophical Quarterly*, 21 (1984), 249–60, p. 252.
7 I do not suggest that Thalberg is unaware of this presupposition. Indeed, he makes it explicit by restricting his concern from the outset to an examination of a causal theory of *intentional* action that takes the notion of action for granted: "when *somebody's body moves*, we are normally able to decide whether *they moved their body*. The causal analysis that I want to discuss starts with the latter cases only; it is not designed to separate them from the former" (ibid., p. 249; Thalberg's emphasis). My complaint is simply that so restricted a causal theory of intentional action is of little interest, certainly as far as resolving the skeptical problem of action is concerned.
8 Roderick Chisholm, "Freedom and Action," in K. Lehrer, ed., *Freedom and Determinism* (New York: Random House, 1966), 11–44.
9 Frederick Stoutland has recently suggested that the problem of deviant causal chains is "intractable" if Davidson is correct in his view that it is only under their physical descriptions that mental states instantiate causal laws linking them to behavioral outcomes. See "Davidson on Intentional Behavior," in Ernest LePore and Brian McLaughlin, eds., *The Philosophy of Donald Davidson: Perspectives on Essays on Actions and Events* (Oxford, England: Blackwell, 1986), 44–59, p. 53. Stoutland argues that "an agent's reason *cannot* cause his behavior in the right way because it cannot cause it qua reason; it can cause it only qua physical event since it is only in virtue of physical properties that events are causes" (ibid.). But this objection misses an essential feature of Davidson's account: Events do not count as causes only relative to a description, "qua this" or "qua that." On Davidson's Humean account, to be a cause of a behavioral outcome, a mental state need only have *a* description under which it is nomically related to behavior

of the relevant kind (see, for example, Davidson's reply to Holborrow, *Essays on Actions and Events*, pp. 242–3). Deviant cases pose a problem, not because the mental states that constitute the agent's reasons fail to be rational causes of matching behavior, but through some feature of the causal chain that links them to it. It is entirely sensible, then, to seek to extend a CTA analysis so that deviant features of causal chains from mental states to behavior can be identified and excluded.

10 The term *basic action* is due to Arthur Danto, "Basic Actions," *American Philosophical Quarterly*, **2** (1965), 141–8. My definition avoids some of the pitfalls of Danto's original formulation; see, for example, Frederick Stoutland, "Basic Actions and Causality," *Journal of Philosophy*, **65** (1968), 467–75. I agree with Daniel Dennett's recent remark in *Elbow Room: The Varieties of Free Will Worth Wanting* (Oxford, England: Clarendon Press, 1984), p. 111, footnote 11:

> One must be careful to avoid any sort of foundationalism resting on a bed of "basic" actions, for while it is the case that at any time . . . the distinction can be drawn between what the agent can decide to do "directly" and what the agent can decide to (try to) bring about by doing something *else* "directly," the easily shifting membership of the classes makes them poor foundation stones for a foundationalist theory.

11 Goldman, *Theory of Human Action*, p. 59.

12 In "Acting and Trying," *The Nature of Mind* (Ithaca, N.Y.: Cornell University Press, 1981), chap. 5, Armstrong claims that "the pattern of [an agent's] practical reasoning shadows out a pattern of operation of causal factors in [the agent's] mind" (p. 79) and then requires for intentional action that the agent's behavior be produced according to this pattern (see especially pp. 76–9).

13 Chisholm, "Freedom and Action," p. 30.

14 John Searle, "The Intentionality of Intention and Action," *Inquiry*, **22** (1979), 253–80.

15 Searle offers an example of this type (ibid., p. 278). "Suppose Bill's prior intention gives him a stomach-ache and the stomach-ache makes him so angry that he forgets about his original intention to kill his uncle, but because of his anger he [intentionally] kills the first man he sees, whom he recognizes as his uncle."

16 Davidson, *Essays on Actions and Events*, p. 79; Davidson's emphasis.

17 The relationship of "level-generation" between nonbasic actions and the basic acts "by" which they are done has been illuminatingly studied by Goldman, *Theory of Human Action*, chap. 2.

18 Myles Brand thus distinguishes between "antecedential" deviance, which affects stage 1, and "consequential" deviance, which affects stage 2. See *Intending and Acting: Toward a Naturalized Action Theory* (Cambridge, Mass.: M.I.T. Press, 1984), p. 18.

19 David Armstrong puts the suggestion thus (*Nature of Mind*, p. 85):

> We have within ourselves certain "mechanisms" with certain powers, including certain "mechanisms" capable of practical reasoning under the influence of beliefs and desires. In Davidson's case, if the climber's belief and desire work within him in the ordinary way, via the mechanism of practical reasoning, then his will is determined in the ordinary way. He deliberately lets go. But in the case that Davidson describes, the physical event of letting go occurs as a result of beliefs and desires, but not as a result of the operation of the "mechanism" of practical reasoning. The letting-go is therefore not an intentional action by the climber.

20 As Thalberg has observed in "Do Our Intentions Cause Our Intentional Actions?"

p. 254. Thus, Thalberg has a further reason for dismissing Davidson's climber counterexample beyond that already discussed. However, since accepting the existence of irreducible intentions in "Intending" (*Essays on Actions and Events*, Essay 5), Davidson would presumably agree that this variant of the climber case is indeed a possibility. Thus "Davidson's fable" may not be so readily "put aside" as Thalberg supposes.

21 Dorothy Mitchell, "Deviant Causal Chains," *American Philosophical Quarterly*, **19** (1982), 351–3.

22 Ibid., p. 353

23 Mitchell, in private correspondence. One may add that the nature of these causal processes is still largely unknown.

24 I here suppose without argument that we can properly admit as causes states that are simultaneous with their effects.

25 Brand, *Intending and Acting*, p. 20.

26 Ibid.

27 Ibid., p. 21; my emphasis.

28 For example, Hugh McCann, who maintains that "where success in overt action is achieved, volition is the fundamental causal means that leads to it." See "Trying, Paralysis and Volitions," *Review of Metaphysics*, **28** (1974–5), 423–42, p. 437.

29 For example, Wilfrid Sellars, "Volitions Reaffirmed," in Myles Brand and Douglas Walton, eds., *Action Theory* (Dordrecht, Holland: D. Reidel, 1980), 47–66, especially §29, p. 53.

30 David Armstrong argues (*Nature of Mind*, chap. 5, pp. 68–75) that the "argument from unexpected paralysis" warrants the positing of "tryings to φ" as causes of φ-ing. Although the argument may show that "A did P intentionally" entails that A tried to do P (I agree that it is self-contradictory to say, "He did it intentionally, but he did not in any way try to do it"), a further step is required to justify the claim that the entailed sentence refers to a separate event that can be the cause of overt behavior. Anyway, if one does regard this argument as a satisfactory basis for recognizing tryings (or volitions) as separate items, one is caught in the dilemma just mentioned. Armstrong clearly opts for the view that tryings are *not* necessarily actions; many are "mental happenings arising in the soul from unknown causes" (p. 75). Given this view, Armstrong is forced to acknowledge that there is scope for deviance in the causal link between a trying and matching behavior. We have already examined his proposal for dealing with this problem, and found it wanting.

31 Goldman, *Theory of Human Action*, p. 62.

32 Hugh McCann, "Volition and Basic Action," *Philosophical Review*, **83** (1974), 451–73, p. 463.

33 Ibid., p. 462.

34 I have discussed the shortcomings of McCann's argument in more detail in "Is Agent-Causality a Conceptual Primitive?" *Synthèse*, **67** (1986), 225–47.

35 For discussion of functionalist philosophies of mind, see Hilary Putnam, "The Nature of Mental States," in W. H. Capitan and D. D. Merrill, eds., *Art, Mind and Religion* (Pittsburgh: University of Pittsburgh Press, 1967), 37–48; J. A. Fodor, *The Language of Thought* (New York: Crowell, 1975); and William G. Lycan, "Toward a Homuncular Theory of Believing," *Cognition and Brain Theory*, **4** (1981), 139–59.

36 As Andrew Woodfield puts it, "a physiologist surely needs [the] information about [what counts as] the right psychological pathway *before* he can start to pin down its neural basis"; see *Teleology* (Cambridge, England: Cambridge University Press, 1976), p. 174.

147

5

Coping with basic deviance

I. THE PROMISE OF THE SENSITIVITY STRATEGY

The upshot of the previous chapter was this: The defense of CTA turns on finding an event-causal analysis of basic intentional action that excludes cases in which causal deviance affects the link between an agent's basic intentions and the behavior that matches them. In this chapter, I shall consider whether such an analysis can be given. I believe I shall be able to show that it can.

Recently, attempts to exclude basic deviance have been made by exploiting the idea, as Christopher Peacocke puts it, that "intentional behaviour is in some way characteristically *sensitive* to certain facts."[1] Adam Morton illustrates this idea with the case of Leo, whose intention to shoot his insulter causes him to become so excited that he trembles and accidentally fires the gun, with the fortuitous result that his insulter is shot. Morton says this:

> Intentional action is action that is guided by information to which it is responsive. . . . If Leo's information . . . about the location of his . . . insulter had changed at the last moment, his time and direction of firing would still have been as they were. The excitement that led to his pulling the trigger was independent of changes in the information which partially initiated it. If Leo's excitement can be modulated by his beliefs . . . then his shooting is intentional, and his excitement a medium rather than a diversion of his will.[2]

The *sensitivity strategy*, then, suggests that a CTA analysis will exclude basic deviance if it includes the requirement that the caused behavior shows a certain responsiveness or sensitivity to the content of the intention that causes it. I will speak of an analysis incorporating such a requirement as a *sensitivity CTA analysis*.

A striking feature of deviant cases is the sheer fluke by which the

148

intervening condition that deprives the agent of control causally contributes to the very behavior intended. Consider Morton's Leo again. Suppose that Leo's basic intention had been slightly different – that instead of intending to fire at time t_0 in direction d, he had intended to fire at t_1 (a moment later) in direction d'. What would have happened then? Given that his actual intention induced excitement sufficient to block control, an intention only very slightly different would surely have had the same effect. For we may suppose that in the circumstances, Leo is disposed to become excited should he form any intention of a certain type, namely, to take aim and fire at his insulter. But if Leo's counterfactual intention would also have caused him to tremble in excitement, who knows what would have happened? It seems false that, if Leo's intention had been to fire at t_1 in direction d', he would have trembled uncontrollably in just such a way that the gun went off at t_1 while pointing in direction d'.

But could there not have been another fluke? Well, perhaps that possibility cannot altogether be excluded. Let us concede it for the sake of the argument. We may then consider another counterfactual intention: to fire slightly earlier, at t_{-1}, and in direction d''. Now, surely it will be false that, had Leo had that intention, his uncontrolled movements would have fired the gun at t_{-1} in direction d''? If it is insisted that there would have been a coincidental match between outcome and intention here too, then just choose another slightly varied counterfactual intention for which there would not have been a fluke. For, if Leo's trembling does deprive him of control, there will be many such intentions to choose from. Match between intention and outcome will be a rarity indeed.

We are thus able to capture what we mean by Leo's trembling interfering with his control as follows: Over an indefinitely large range of slightly different gun-firing intentions, it is in general false that, had Leo had such an alternative intention, the control-blocking excitement would still have yielded a matching outcome. If we suppose, however, that Leo would have fired as intended, no matter which of a wide range of gun-firing intentions he had had, then his excitement will no longer count as an obstacle to his control but will be, as Morton says, "a medium of his will." Excitement as such need not block control; for some people and tasks it may indeed enhance it.

In basic intentional action, the agent *carries out* a basic intention by making controlled bodily movements to fit its content. According to the sensitivity strategy, this reference to the agent's exercise of control can be analyzed without reference to agent-causation. There is exercise of control if and only if the causal link from basic intention to matching behavior is sensitive, in the sense that *over a sufficiently wide range of differences, had the agent's intention differed in content, the resulting behavior would have differed correspondingly.* The sensitivity condition is thus understood in terms of the existence of a suitable pattern of counterfactual dependence of resulting behavior upon the content of the agent's basic intention. (This suggestion is borrowed from David Lewis's hypothesis for a causal theory of perception that distinguishes genuine perceptions from deviant cases of veridical hallucination.[3]) Adding such a sensitivity condition to the CTA analysis offers a hypothesis for eliminating deviance that has the merit of avoiding Goldman-style appeals to yet-to-be-discovered physiological facts as well as circular references to action or agent-causation.

This counterfactual version of the sensitivity strategy has a rival, however. Peacocke has proposed a "differential explanation" version of the strategy, according to which a causal link is sensitive if and only if it is subsumed by a law of nature that specifies behavioral outcomes as an appropriate kind of (mathematical) function from the domain of possible intentions.[4] Initially, this proposal may seem equivalent to the first: Functional laws of the type envisaged will presumably support patterns of counterfactual dependence. But there are some cases on which the different construals of the sensitivity strategy deliver different verdicts, and it may therefore be necessary to choose between them, or even to consider further interpretations. There is something to be learned by examining the debate between the counterfactual and the differential explanation versions of the sensitivity strategy, although as we shall see, there are limitations to a sensitivity CTA analysis that seem to threaten it on any current interpretation. I explain what I think these limitations are in Section III, whereas Section II concerns the more specialized issue of the choice between alternative versions of a sensitivity CTA analysis.

The Frankfurt Examples Again

Recall Frankfurt's counterfactual intervener examples, discussed in Chapter 1 in connection with the question whether (and in what sense) moral responsibility for behavior requires that the behaver "could have done otherwise." Here matching behavior does not depend counterfactually on the content of the agent's basic intention, for had the agent not had the very intention he did have (to do *a*, say), the intervener would have ensured that the agent produced *a*-ing behavior nonetheless. Thus, the counterfactual version of the sensitivity condition yields the counterintuitive result that agents beset by counterfactual interveners do not perform genuine intentional actions. The differential explanation version seems able to deliver the right result, however. Even if there is no pattern of counterfactual dependence, the law subsuming the causal relation between intention and behavior may still be of the required functional type.

The counterfactual version however, may, be refined so that it survives this objection. Counterfactual intervener cases are to action what the "visual censor" case is to perception.[5] If the analogous counterfactual version of a sensitivity condition is applied in the causal theory of perception, visual censor cases count as veridical hallucination. But as Lewis's familiar, Bruce Le Catt,[6] has observed, this result is counterintuitive – just as it is counterintuitive to maintain that agents subject to a behavioral censor do not really act.

Le Catt offers an amendment (truly feline in its elegance) that saves the genuineness of the visual censor cases. He suggests that Lewis require only *stepwise* counterfactual dependence for genuine seeing. And this suggestion may equally well be exploited in amending the counterfactual version of the sensitivity condition for intentional action so that it counts the behavioral censor cases as genuine. As it applies to the action case, the proposal goes as follows: In a behavioral censor example, it is indeed false that had the agent's intention differed (had it been I_1 instead of I_0), his behavior would have differed correspondingly. For had it been I_1, the intervener would have registered that fact and intercepted the causal processes that would otherwise have produced the corresponding outcome, B_1, in order to ensure that the agent's behavior did not deviate from B_0. However, there would have had to have been a time interval between the agent's forming of intention I_1 and the censor's blocking of the causal processes leading to B_1. Now consider some intermediate point, M_1, on the usual physiological path from I_1 to B_1 that is located *before* the censor's interception. Then it will be true that had the agent's intention been I_1 instead of the actual I_0, physiological stage M_1 would have been reached. Now, Le Catt claims that it is *also* true that if stage M_1 had been reached, then the behavioral outcome would have been B_1 – since, after all, M_1 belongs to a causal process that usually yields outcome B_1. Thus, although it is false that if the agent had had intention I_1, he would have behaved as B_1, it is true that had he had intention I_1, M_1 would have occurred, and true also that had M_1 occurred, the behavioral outcome would have been B_1. So there is a pattern of *stepwise* counterfactual dependence between the agent's intention and his behavior in the censor case, given that the same argument may be repeated for an indefinitely large range of alternatives to the actual intention I_0. Accordingly, to exhibit the censor cases as genuine, we have only to amend the counterfactual version of the sensitivity condition so that merely stepwise counterfactual dependence of matching behavior on intention suffices for genuine intentional action.

The weakness of this suggestion lies in the claim that had intermediate stage M_1 been reached, the outcome would have been that which is normal for the process to which M_1 belongs, namely, B_1. Could it not be counterclaimed that had M_1 been reached, the process would have had to have been initiated by I_1, and there would then have been an intervention from the censor bringing the normal B_1-yielding process to a halt and producing the result B_0 in its stead? Le Catt's answer deploys a thesis argued for by Lewis: This counterclaim asserts a "back-tracking" counterfactual (i.e., of the form "had the present differed, the past would have had to have differed appropriately") – and "back-trackers are banned."[7] Whether back-tracking counterfactuals should be banned altogether is controversial. Lewis's own arguments show only a presumption favoring a ban on back-trackers – a presumption that might justifiably be overridden in contexts like the present one, where a nonstandard resolution of the vagueness that infects counterfactuals may be preferred. But no matter, for we may simply build a ban on back-trackers into our formulation of the

sensitivity condition: Sensitivity is then a matter of stepwise counterfactual dependence under a regime that bans back-trackers.

The Reverse Behavioral Censor

This amendment disposes, then, of the objection that sensitivity on
the counterfactual construal is not necessary for intentional action.
But doubts have also been raised about the condition's *sufficiency*.
Both Christopher Peacocke and Martin Davies[8] have proposed
counterexamples to the parallel counterfactual construal of the
sensitivity condition required for the causal analysis of perception,
and there seems to be no reason why parallel ones should not be
constructed for the action case. There could, for instance, be a
reverse behavioral censor (modeled on Davies's reverse censor),
who does not intervene while an agent's intention to do *a* deviantly
(through nervousness) causes his or her *a*-ing behavior but who,
had the agent's intention been significantly different, would have
ensured that nothing blocked the agent's control. Here, there is
deviance even though the pattern of counterfactual dependence
obtains. The alternative differential explanation version is not in
similar difficulty, for in this reverse censor case, the law subsuming
the actual causal relation between intention and matching behavior
(passing as it does through control-blocking nervousness) will not
be of the right functional type. Of course, it will be acknowledged
that had the intention been different, the law subsuming the causal
relation would have been of the right functional type for nondeviance – but this is irrelevant for determining the status of the actual
course of events. Thus, we have an argument for preferring the
differential explanation version of the sensitivity condition since
this time Le Catt's solution will be to no avail: Where there is a
pattern of counterfactual dependence of behavior on intention, a
fortiori, there is a pattern of stepwise counterfactual dependence.

A Problem for the Differential Explanation Version?

Peacocke's hypothesis for a sensitivity condition avoids these trou-
bles but may still face its own difficulties. Davies has recently
argued that in its application to the causal theory of perception,
Peacocke's condition that the scene before the eyes should strongly
differentially explain the matching visual experience is not necessary for genuine visual perception.[9] He gives an example of an

intuitively genuine perceiver, which he calls "the discrete processor," in which, although there is a systematic dependence of visual experience on the scene before the eyes, none of the causal connections are subsumed by intrinsically functional laws.[10] A parallel example of a discrete processing mechanism from basic intentions to bodily movements is presumably constructible and provides an example in which, although the sensitivity condition on the counterfactual construal is satisfied, the differential explanation condition is not. For, although there is clearly a mathematical functional relationship between input and output in discrete processor examples (the working of the whole system is naturally describable in this way), the laws that subsume the actual causal relations that obtain on each occasion of the mechanism's operation are not themselves mathematically functional laws.

A Teleological Construal of the Sensitivity Condition

It is by no means clear that Davies's discrete processor does present a genuine counterexample to Peacocke's hypothesis for a sensitivity condition.[11] All that matters here is that Davies thinks it does, and this conviction prompts him to propose a third version of the sensitivity condition required for a causal theory of perception. For genuine perception, Davies requires that

the invoked generalization which specifies the required (mathematical) functional connexion between the properties of the scene and the properties of the experience should also express the (teleological) function of the operative perceptual mechanism.[12]

And of course, a parallel requirement could be proposed for the case of action.

Davies's condition is, of course, satisfied by the discrete processor since the entire mechanism has as its function (selected for in evolution) the production of experience to match the scene before the eyes. In sum, Davies argues that the functionality of the subsuming causal laws is not necessary for genuine perception (as he believes the discrete processor case to show) and that mathematical functionality at the level of an overall pattern of counterfactual dependence, though necessary, is not sufficient (as the reverse censor case shows). His solution, then, is to require mathematical functionality that is also teleological – selected for its function either by design or in natural evolution. This gives us a third possibility for a precise understanding of the sensitivity condition as it figures in a CTA analysis: The causal link from basic intention to matching behavior must be part of a mechanism that not only guarantees a systematic functional dependence of behavior on the content of intention but also has as its purpose (designed or natural) that it function in that way.

In what follows, then, we should keep in mind these three different construals of the sensitivity condition: First, there is Lewis's requirement of a pattern of stepwise counterfactual dependence of behavior on intention. Second, there is Peacocke's requirement that the intention should strongly differentially explain the behavior. And, third, there is Davies's requirement that the functional relationship between intention and behavior, though it need not count as a law of nature, should express the teleological function of the operative mechanism, namely, to realize an agent-control system.

III. ASSESSING THE SENSITIVITY STRATEGY

Our question now is whether, as the sensitivity strategy proposes, basic intentional action may be analyzed as matching behavior sensitively caused by a basic intention – on whichever of the three canvassed construals of the sensitivity condition we adopt. I shall argue that this analysis is not adequate as it stands.

Prosthetic Aids to Action

To set the stage, let us briefly consider prosthetic aids. Suppose an agent loses an arm but has it replaced with a prosthetic limb, which permits the performance of basic intentional actions. Now, it may be that the prosthetic arm is more like a sophisticated instrument than a genuine replacement that comes to count as part of the agent's own (remodeled) body. If, for example, the prosthesis can be used only by acquiring the knack of making certain movements with the muscles in the stump of the arm, then it will count as an instrument. But if the prosthetic arm were functionally to replace the neural and muscular components of a real arm, it would count as a part, albeit artificial, of the agent's own body. No doubt such fully integrated prostheses do not yet exist, and serious obstacles may strew the path of their development.[13] Still, their development is a real possibility, and there is certainly nothing conceptually absurd about such effective replacement of damaged body parts. In what follows, I wish to consider a more restricted possibility than a fully integrated entire prosthetic limb, namely, the development of a prosthetic device that replaces the lost function of some relatively small neurophysiological component of normal motor control.

Suppose that some damaged portion of a person's efferent nervous system is replaced with such a prosthetic device. Then, when the agent acts (in a way involving the affected section), the action may be entirely nondeviant, even though the prosthetically mediated causal chain from basic intention to behavior is quite unusual for an agent of the species. The sensitivity strategy can well explain why this should be so, for there may be indefinitely many ways of satisfying the sensitivity condition other than in the "hardware" of normal human physiology. The mere abnormality of a causal chain does not entail its deviance. Still, it might be thought that to realize genuine action, the causal link from intention to behavior must be of a normal type at least relative to the agent. Thus, an agent with a neural prosthesis will then regularly perform the relevant basic actions through its operation, and so the causal chain will be a normal and reliable one *for that agent*. Yet even this suggestion is mistaken: Neither the relative normality nor the reliability of the type that a causal chain instantiates is necessary for nondeviance. A unique causal link may still permit genuine action: We cannot exclude the possibility of a prosthetic device that works successfully only once, or even a purely fortuitous substitute for normal function that operates only on a single occasion.[14] And this possibility, too, is accounted for by the sensitivity strategy: Whether the sensitivity condition is fulfilled on a single occasion has nothing to do with whether it would be fulfilled on any similar occasion.

Heteromesial Causal Chains

One of the strengths of the sensitivity strategy, then, is its conformity with these intuitions about the possibility of prosthetic aids to action. Does the principle that the abnormality of a causal chain does not introduce deviance if the sensitivity condition is met apply quite generally?

Consider a recondite situation in which the agent exhibits the behavior required for his or her intended action only by dint of the intentional action of a second agent. Here we say that the intention-behavior chain is *heteromesial*. What view should we take of a case like Peacocke's, where the "second person [is] a knowledgeable neurophysiologist who decides on a particular occasion to produce in me exactly the motor impulses needed to realize what he knows, from my neurophysiological states, to be my intentions"?[15]

Some philosophers are convinced that heteromesial cases will always be deviant, and they would agree with Myles Brand's intuition that "loosely put, a person must perform his own action."[16] Yet it is clearly not *generally* true that heteromesial chains are deviant, for we often perform our own nonbasic intentional actions by way of the intentional actions of others. (Please read the last sentence again to bring about a case in point!) Brand's claim then must be meant to apply only to heteromesial causal chains from *basic* intentions to matching bodily movements: It is these that he thinks cannot realize genuine intentional basic acts. Should we follow Brand, then, in requiring that basic action-realizing chains should be "continuous," in the sense that they have no "proper part consisting of any other agent's action"?[17]

Should a Sensitivity CTA Analysis Also Exclude Heteromesy?

It may at first be assumed that adding an additional clause excluding heteromesy is unnecessary because the sensitivity condition already excludes such cases. But a little reflection convinces us otherwise. The sensitivity condition may be satisfied in a heteromesial case like Peacocke's neurophysiologist, who may be able to recognize a large range of subtle variations in the agent's intentions and have the capacity to stimulate the agent's nervous system differentially for each recognized variant. This seems to be the case whichever of the three interpretations of the sensitivity condition we adopt. Even Davies's teleologized version of the condition may be satisfied since the setup may have been explicitly designed by the neurophysiologist (or his boss!) as a system whose purpose is to achieve otherwise unobtainable match between the agent's intentions and the agent's behavior. So if we do consider such a heteromesial case deviant, our CTA analysis will have to include a heteromesy-excluding clause in addition to the sensitivity condition. We shall have to require that the causal chain from basic intention to matching behavior "should not run through the intentions of another person," as Peacocke puts it.[18]

Adding such a clause may appear to confound hopes for an event-causal CTA analysis: In requiring that the causal chain not be mediated through another person's *action* are we not introducing a circular reference to the very thing we wish to define? Are we not implicitly claiming that agents must be the initiators of their own actions, and thus implicating agent-causation in the analysis? This anxiety may easily be set to rest, however. For, the required additional clause may be understood as excluding chains that have a proper part consisting in a causal link, itself satisfying the sensitivity condition, between a basic intention and matching behavior.[19]

The heteromesial cases, then, do not seem to pose a problem for a CTA analysis under the sensitivity strategy. In the first place, it is not absolutely clear whether heteromesial cases satisfying the sensitivity condition should be counted as deviant at all. Could it not be argued that Peacocke's knowledgeable neurophysiologist operates as a human prosthetic aid, permitting the agent to perform genuine basic actions? But if we do share Brand's contrary intuition that such cases are deviant, then the sensitivity CTA analysis requires only a small and uncompromising addition to meet this intuition. So whatever our view of the heteromesial cases, an event-causal CTA analysis emerges victorious under the sensitivity strategy.

Heterogeneity Among the Heteromesial Cases

However, this defense of the sensitivity strategy rests on an assumption that is open to question. We have implicitly supposed that all the sensitive and heteromesial causal chains from basic intention to behavior are to be classified together – either all as deviant or all as genuine. I wish to argue that this apparently innocent assumption is mistaken. The sensitive heteromesial cases are heterogeneous. Sometimes heteromesy introduces deviance, sometimes not – depending on the precise nature of the second agent's participation in the causal chain. I shall make quite a fuss about this difference, for it provides the basis for my argument that a sensitivity CTA analysis is not fully adequate, whether or not it is supplemented by a clause excluding chains that have proper parts consisting of another agent's action.

The fact that heteromesy needn't introduce deviance may be appreciated by recognizing that, in theory at least, a prosthetic aid to an agent's action could involve the actions of others. Put aside the knowledgeable neurophysiologist case for a moment and think instead of a person fitted with a successful prosthetic neural replacement, which one day breaks down but is briefly repaired by having a second agent intentionally hold the broken wires together until they can be resoldered. (In this flight of fancy I am supposing that the neural prosthesis has electrical components lodged outside the agent's skull.) Here – in what I shall label *case A* – the sensitivity of the causal links between intention and behavior will be preserved since it is quite irrelevant whether the wires are held or soldered together. So the first agent would continue to perform genuine basic actions, despite the heteromesy of the relevant causal chains, for the second agent functions only as a willing temporary cog in a minor part of the first agent's control mechanisms. In case *A*, the first agent *remains in direct control of* his or her bodily movements, though only by dint of another's action. So the second agent's participation in the causal processes of action introduces no deviance.

However, there are circumstances under which heteromesy does introduce deviance. Sometimes the second agent's involvement in the causal chain *preempts or blocks the agent's exercise of direct control* over his or her bodily movements. Then the second agent is no mere cog in the mechanisms that realize the first agent's direct control. Rather, the second agent is part of a system that provides the first agent with, at best, only *indirect* control over the movements of his or her own body. This is the case with Peacocke's example of the knowledgeable neurophysiologist, if we understand the neurophysiologist to intervene just as soon as he recognizes that the agent has formed an intention to make a bodily movement. I now label this example, *case B*. Here, once the first agent's intention to do *a* is formed, it is entirely up to the second agent to initiate efferent neural stimulation in the first agent's brain in order to produce bodily movements intrinsic to *a*-ing. The first agent exercises no further control once the intention has been formed, and so the *a*-ing behavior cannot count as the first agent's own genuinely *basic* action. Cases of type *B* are thus deviant counterparts to basic bodily action. They are examples of what might be called *preemptive heteromesy,* where the second agent blocks the first's direct control over his or her bodily movements rather than providing a medium for it. Yet as already observed, the sensitivity condition may nevertheless apply.

*Considerations About Responsibility as Reinforcing
the Deviance of Preemptively Heteromesial Cases*

This result may be reinforced by reflecting on how we would assign moral responsibility in the various heteromesial cases. Suppose that I am situated as in case B. While under the power of the neurophysiologist, I form some morally reprehensible bodily intention, under whatever conditions are required for me to be fully responsible for so doing. (That is, I haven't been coerced; I understand perfectly well what it is I am intending to do; etc.) This intention is then fulfilled in my bodily movements through the mechanism involving the neurophysiologist's deliberate actions. What effect does this have on my moral responsibility for my behavior?

The answer will depend on whether or not I am aware of my situation and believe the neurophysiologist to be a reliable transmitter of my intentions to the body I cannot directly control. If I am so aware (label this *case B-1*), the heteromesy does not as such cancel my responsibility for the movements of my body and their consequences. In case *B-1*, my bodily movements do come about through my own action. In fact, I perform an unusual but quite nondeviant *nonbasic* intentional action, in which I directly control the formation of basic intentions in order indirectly to bring about matching bodily movements. (It is interesting to speculate on the phenomenology of an agent situated in case *B-1*: The formation of an intention to make bodily movements will here be an even more final commitment than it usually is. Putting the agent in situation *B-1* would provide the ultimate cure for a chronic case of the kind of final stage akrasia whose possibility was discussed in Chapter 3.)

If, however, I am unaware of the neurophysiologist's interference (label this *case B-2*), then I will not be morally responsible for my bodily movements, even though they are caused by my intention and I am, *ex hypothesi,* fully morally responsible for that intention. (It is true that I will firmly *believe* myself to be so responsible, but that is irrelevant. Irrelevant too is the fact that given my responsibility for the intention to do the naughty deed, I can gain no credit for my character from my lack of responsibility for my body's behavior since it is, after all, behavior of the very sort I intended to perform.) This intuition about case *B-2* rests on recognizing that it is wholly up to the neurophysiologist to decide how my body is to move, and that this fundamental feature of the situation remains even when he adopts a general policy of matching my own intentions. Suppose, for example, that the neurophysiologist takes it into his head to make my body ape the first coherent bodily movements he observes upon randomly switching on the television. Then, certainly, I will not be morally responsible for making the relevant movements. And it will make no difference if the bodily movement thus chosen happens by coincidence to be the very sort I intend to produce at the time. Why, then, should it make any difference if the neurophysiologist decides on a general policy of stimulating my body to respond in just the ways I intend? This policy would restore to me a share of moral responsibility for my bodily movements if, at the same time, I come to know my situation; but that describes case *B-1*, and the whole point of case *B-2* is that I am *not* aware of the truncation of my sphere of direct control.

Granted the intuition that I am not morally responsible for my bodily movements in case *B-2*, and given (as we are supposing) that I am responsible for the intention that (partially) causes them, it follows that my matching bodily movements are not intrinsic to intentional basic actions of mine – that is, that case *B-2* is one of basic deviance. For, if those bodily movements had been intrinsic to my own basic intentional actions, in the circumstances I would certainly have been responsible for them.

By way of contrast, suppose that I form a morally significant intention under case *A* and am fully morally responsible for so doing. In this case, where a willing bystander holds the wires of my broken neural prosthesis together at a crucial moment, my moral responsibility for the behavior thus enabled is preserved, whether or not I am aware of this assistance. Here, the second agent need not even count as my accomplice, and may be so much of a mere cog in the machinery of my bodily control mechanisms that he or she could not know what I was about. But even if the second agent knows what basic intentional action he or she is facilitating, the most that person will enjoy is *shared* responsibility for my bodily movements; the second agent will not have *sole* responsibility, as in case *B-2*. Of course, it is true that in each case, *A*, *B-1*, and *B-2*, bodily movements matching my intention would not have occurred without the action of the second agent. But that in itself is not sufficient to put my body's behavior beyond my responsibility. For, it is possible for my own control to be exercised through the action of another agent, as in cases *A* and *B-1*. But it is also possible for another's participation in the intention–behavior causal chain to block my control over my bodily movements altogether, as in *B-2*, and then, if a match with my intentions is achieved, the case is deviant.[20]

It would be mistaken, then, to regard the difference between cases *A* and *B* simply as a difference in the complexity of the mechanism that realizes the (first) agent's control. There is a difference here between genuine basic action and its deviant semblance. For, in both cases *B-1* and *B-2*, match between the (first) agent's bodily movements and his or her basic intention is not under that agent's *direct* control, although in *B-1*, as we saw, match with the nonbasic intention is under that agent's *indirect* control. However, in case *A*, despite the heteromesy, the (first) agent's direct control over his or her bodily movements is preserved. There is, I think, a further way of distinguishing the different kinds of heteromesial cases in terms of their detailed architecture. For the moment, it is sufficient to acknowledge that some heteromesial cases block control and so are deviant, whereas others give effect to control and thus are nondeviant.

Implications of Preemptively Heteromesial Cases for a CTA Analysis

If the heteromesial cases are heterogeneous in the way we have claimed, then the implications are clear. Basic action will not be analyzable as behavior that matches and is sensitively caused by a basic intention, where the causal chain does not pass through the actions of any other agent. For, this analysis will exclude the case in which a second agent forms part of a successful prosthetic aid to the first agent's action. Yet an analysis of the basic action, *a*-ing, as *a*-ing behavior sensitively caused by the basic intention to *a*, will fail because the analysans admits preemptively heteromesial cases, which *are* deviant. A further necessary condition beyond sensitivity seems to be required for basic intentional action – but it is not the blanket exclusion of heteromesy. What it appears to be is the exclusion of heteromesy (or any other condition) that *blocks the agent's control*. But this condition cannot be added to our event-causal CTA analysis without giving the game away, for our analysis will then be equivalent to the claim that basic action is matching behavior sensitively caused by a basic intention in such a way that it counts as the agent's exercise of control. And appeal to exercises of agent-control is precisely what we need to avoid if we want to use a CTA analysis as an argument for accepting the CTA's core claim that ontological commitment to actions is compatible with naturalism.

So far, then, Davidson's pessimism about the possibility of a CTA analysis seems to be borne out. However, one might feel suspicious that the enterprise should founder on so recondite a counterexample. Given the benefits of a CTA analysis in resolving the problem of natural agency, would it not be more rational to revise our classification of a preemptively heteromesial case like *B-2* as deviant? Arguably, we here face the same kind of choice as we did with the alleged problem of final stage akrasia. Do we reject our CTA analysis on the basis of a tentative intuition about a highly contrived imaginary case, or do we tutor our intuitions to fit the analysis? So put, the decision makes itself, but there is room to doubt whether our intuition about the basic deviance of case *B* is merely tentative. This intuition is certainly as robust as the judgment that the agent in case *B-2* could not rightly be held morally responsible for his or her bodily movements – and that judgment is really quite secure, as we have argued. Our intuition of the deviance of case *B-2* is thus better entrenched than out intuition that final stage akrasia is a possibility. Nevertheless, the sensible course may still be simply to insist on tutoring recalcitrant intuitions; we may appreciate, however, that there is sufficient high-handedness about using this procedure in the present case for the defender of a CTA analysis to find alternative strategies attractive.

One such alternative is to argue that intuitions about case *B* need not trouble us because case *B* does not describe a coherent possibility. For case *B* to be possible, a second agent must be able to "read off" from neurophysiological information the content of a first agent's intentions. However, this would be possible, it might be argued, only if the second agent could employ a well-confirmed psychophysical theory – but there can be no such theories. Hence, the scenario envisaged in case B is incoherent.

Evidently, this argument for dismissing the preemptively heter-omesial cases could be, at best, only as strong as the case for psychophysical anomaly.[21] But in fact, it has a further flaw since the inference here drawn from the presumed truth of psychophysical anomaly is unwarranted. Even if psychophysical theories are impossible, case B remains a coherent if farfetched possibility. In case B, it is not essential that the second agent should *know* that his or her stimulation of the first agent's efferent nervous system is actually giving effect to the first agent's intentions. The second agent need only proceed according to rules that specify a given efferent stimulus for each identified brain state. That the brain states identified realize intentions, and what intentions they realize, need not be known to the second agent. In practice, such rules could not be supplied other than by derivation from a psychophysical theory. But it is not logically impossible that they should arise in some other way, and that is enough for the example to be constructible.

This approach to dismissing case B counterexamples might be smoothed, however, by accepting Davies's teleologized version of the sensitivity condition – assuming, of course, a good case for psychophysical anomaly. For, without a psychophysical theory, how could anyone work out the "rules" for reading intentions from brain states? Without such rules, the setup envisaged in case B could never purposely be designed. Therefore, because it is also impossible that such an arrangement could have evolved purely naturally, its existence as a mechanism functioning to produce match between intention and behavior could only be purely accidental. But in that case, it is no threat to Davies's version of the sensitivity CTA analysis since the teleological component of his sensitivity condition will not be met. The power of this argument depends crucially on just how much Davidson's arguments for psychophysical anomaly can establish. These arguments, I believe, do not exclude the discovery of reliable *correlations* between physical and psychological states; all they rule out (if they succeed at all) is the upgrading of such general correlations into strict laws[22] – in which case, the possibility of providing a set of rules for the second agent to go by in case B examples can be defended even granted the thesis of psychophysical anomaly.

So despite a brave attempt, the strategy of defending a sensitivity CTA analysis by dismissing the case *B* examples as incoherent doesn't quite do the job. It is a more attractive option for the proponent of CTA to insist on revising those intuitions that classify these examples as deviant. Yet as we have already argued, provided the coherence of such cases is granted, the intuition of their deviance is actually quite robust. Furthermore, we must remember that there are other intuitions, apart from those about preemptively heteromesial cases, that we shall need to revise in order to retain a sensitivity CTA analysis. Thus it is not just one recalcitrant intuition that the proponent of CTA has to persuade us to abandon. Indeed, as our discussion has progressed, we have gathered from three sources intuitions that suggest that performing a basic action is not constituted solely by the agent's final stage intention sensitively causing matching bodily movements.

First, we have the intuition that there can be basic action that is not intentional under any description. If such purely voluntary action is possible, an analysis of basic action in general in terms of causation by basic intentions obviously fails. As noted in Chapter 3, however, a successful event-causal analysis of *intentional* action might well sustain a revision of this intuition. But if it should turn out that we cannot provide necessary and sufficient conditions for intentional action without referring to the agent's exercise of control, then it will appear that actions *tout court* are ineliminable constituents of intentional actions. And the intuition that admits purely voluntary exercises of control will thus be reinforced.

Second, we have the intuition that there can be final stage akrasia – that an agent can act (though not, of course, intentionally) contrary to a final stage intention. This intuition mutually reinforces the previous one: Final stage akrasia is possible if and only if nonintentional exercises of control are possible.

Third, we have the intuition that even where an agent's behavior matches his or her final stage intention and is sensitively caused by it, the agent may still fail to perform the relevant basic intentional action. Our having this intuition suggests that once a final stage intention is formed, the associated basic intentional act occurs only if the agent exercises his or her control in carrying out the intention – which brings a reference to voluntary action into our account of what constitutes intentional action. Thus, this third intuition reinforces the first. But it also mutually reinforces the second: We will allow that an agent's opportunity to carry out a final stage intention may be preempted if and only if we are also prepared to allow that *the agent* may fail to take this opportunity. There is, therefore, a consilience of reasons for disquiet about a sensitivity CTA analysis.

These considerations do not amount to a *proof* that the sensitivity CTA analysis must be rejected in favor of the thesis of agent-causationism. For one thing, these weaknesses in the sensitivity CTA analysis may simply indicate its incompleteness, and there is no need to assume a priori that whatever is required for a complete analysis will require essential reference to agent-causation. The potential for further elaborating CTA analyses may not yet have been exhausted. But even if the sensitivity analysis is the best we can do, the option of revising those intuitions that do not meet it still remains. Our discussion has shown only that we may repudiate the suggestion that the problem cases for a sensitivity CTA analysis generate purely marginal intuitions that are readily revisable. They are not mere "spoils to the victor" (to use Lewis's suggestive phrase). For, our intuitions about the problem cases are symptoms of an entrenched intuition that a concept of the agent's exercising control is primitive to the notion of the kind of agency necessary for moral responsibility.

Preemptive heteromesy and final stage akrasia indicate that for basic intentional action, the agent must carry out his or her final stage intention, and this must be an exercise of the agent's control. The possibility of satisfying the sensitivity condition in a case of preemptive heteromesy establishes that "being an exercise of the agent's control" is not equivalent to "being sensitively caused by the agent's own basic intention." And then, insofar as the concept of an exercise of control seems to reemerge within our analysis of intentional action, it becomes correspondingly plausible to endorse the intuition that there are nonintentional voluntary actions, "pure" exercises of control, quite lacking intentional states as causal antecedents. Proponents of a CTA analysis thus face a syndrome of agent-causationist intuitions that are central rather than marginal. *Logically*, of course, it is quite defensible to argue that these intuitions must be rejected in order to set to rest doubts about the natural possibility of action. *Dialectically*, however, such an argument will miss the mark. For, the source of doubt about how action can have a place in the natural event-causal order is precisely the intuition of the primitiveness of the notion of an agent's control. Yet it is this very intuition that we now find expressing itself in three guises – as intuitions about final stage akrasia, preemptive heteromesy, and purely voluntary action. It is thus no accident that skeptics about natural agency have strong intuitions about these cases – intuitions that remain unaccommodated under the sensitivity strategy for a CTA analysis.

IV. SENSITIVE AND SUSTAINED CAUSATION

Sustained Causation

The crucial step now, of course, is to consider developing the sensitivity CTA analysis so that it excludes the preemptively heteromesial cases (which are deviant) while including the cases of heteromesial prosthetic aid (which are not deviant). A recent proposal of Irving Thalberg's is relevant here:

A full-blown causal theory [should] prescribe a tighter hookup [between intention and matching behavior] – what I call "ongoing," "continuous" or "sustained" causation. If someone's behavior is to count as intentional Xing, I believe her or his intention must continuously regulate the Xing.[23]

This suggestion exactly fits the intuitions we have about case B – our example of preemptive heteromesy. The reason why agents situated as in case B don't exercise their own control is precisely that they don't "continuously regulate" their behavior so that it matches their basic intentions. Indeed, given the "disconnection" of their efferent nervous system, this guidance and monitoring of their bodily movements in conformity with their intentions can be done only indirectly by the neurophysiologist. Sustained causation of behavior by intention does seem to be what is missing, and Thalberg is surely right to conclude that it will be "very difficult . . . to invent or find instances of action which are at once sustainingly produced by the agent's intention *and* deviantly produced by [e.g.] his nervousness."[24]

Simply incorporating the requirement of sustained causation into the sensitivity CTA analysis will not do, however. For, sustained causation (as so far understood, anyway) is a matter of *the agents' doing something,* namely, monitoring and regulating their behavior so that it conforms with their intentions. Thus, introducing sustained causation into the analysans of basic intentional action threatens to undermine its whole point. (Thalberg's satisfaction with this suggestion thus indicates once again that he does not share my view of the role of a CTA analysis in addressing the skeptical problem of natural agency.)

Neither is there any virtue in emphasizing that it is the agent's basic intention – rather than the agent as such – that "sustainedly" causes matching behavior. For, unless the concept of a mental state sustainedly causing behavior can be unpacked in clearly event-causal terms, it may fairly be suspected of cloaking agent-causation in a new disguise.[25] Or to put it another way, there may be as much skepticism about how the natural order can be understood to contain episodes of sustained causation as there is about how action can be a natural possibility.

Servosystems and Feedback Loops

It may be possible, however, to explicate the idea of sustained causation so that it does not introduce any suspicion of a reference to agent-causation into our CTA analysis. We know that many natural systems (both designed and evolved) count as control systems. In the very broadest sense, any system whose output is a mathematical function of its input might be described as "controlling" its output. Usually, however, a system requires a greater complexity of function before we think of it as maintaining control. Systems that incorporate negative feedback mechanisms provide the standard example – they maintain control by keeping their output within a restricted range despite a contrary tendency. In cybernetics, these mechanisms are known as *servosystems:* They produce or maintain a given output by means of feedback loops.[26] The language of intention and action can, of course, be used in describing servosystems. For a simple (and standard) example, a heater connected to a thermostat might be described, in virtue of its total functional organization, as "having the intention" to maintain temperature within a set range and "acting to fulfill that intention."

Of course, servosystems are not agents as such – or at least, not in the sense in which agency is necessary for moral responsibility. They do not really act or have intentions. As Woodfield remarks, "when we describe servomechanisms as goal-directed, we are employing a mentalistic analogy."[27] But the very appropriateness of this analogy suggests that the sustained causation of matching behavior by an agent's basic intention may be readily realized in a natural system. Sustained causation, then, need not be some mysterious special form of causation, whose place in the natural order might be suspect. The sustained causation of a particular outcome (e.g., an ambient temperature within a certain range) may be achieved by quite a straightforward event-causal mechanism (e.g., a heater controlled by a thermostat). Perhaps, then, the notion of sustained causation supplies the clue for what needs to be added to a sensitivity CTA analysis to exclude cases of preemptive heteromesy – and, we might hope, to dispose of the other intuitions that form the agent-causationist's syndrome. Indeed, it may even be that here we have something more fundamental to the notion of an agent's exercise of control than is captured in any of the various sensitivity conditions.

The suggestion would be that for an intention to be the sustaining cause of a behavioral sequence is just for it to feature appropriately in a causal mechanism that counts as a servosystem having the production of the intended behavior as its function. This suggested identification may seem to involve a ridiculous conflation of humans (and other agents) with mechanisms as simple as thermostats – but of course, I am not suggesting that *the agent* is a servosystem whose function is to produce a single form of behavior. Rather, the idea is that once the agent forms a basic intention, his or her motor system realizes a *transient* servosystem whose function is to produce or maintain the intended behavioral sequence. An agent's motor system will then be flexible enough to form, as occasion demands, servosystems subserving each of the basic action types in his or her repertoire. The concept of a servosystem is thus being employed here simply to defuse the ontological oddity of unexplicated sustained causation.

Preemptive Heteromesy Again

This approach applies to the case of action Davies's previously mentioned suggestion for a "teleologized" version of the sensitivity condition required for a causal theory of perception. In effect the proposal is that a system counts as performing a basic action only if the causal mechanism linking basic intention with matching behavior has the production of such behavior as its teleological function. But this condition fails to exclude the case of preemptive heteromesy. As noted earlier, the teleologized sensitivity condition may here be satisfied. To take case *B* again: The system that consists of the neurophysiologist's monitoring the agent's brain states and then stimulating his or her efferent nervous system accordingly can count, on each occasion of its operation, as a complex servosystem whose (designed) teleological function is to yield the intended bodily movements. Yet the intuition remains that case *B* is deviant. So although appeal to the idea of a servosystem does provide a way of ontologically defusing the notion of sustained causation, it appears that, if adding a condition of sustained causation is going to do the trick of ruling out preemptive heteromesy, there must be more to it than the requirement that the intention–behavior causal chain must belong to a transient servosystem whose function is to produce the intended behavior.

Appeal to the Detailed Architecture of Feedback Loops

This is a fair objection – but it may be met by further specifying *what kind* of transient servosystem must be realized by the causal mechanism that links intention with matching behavior if genuine basic intentional action is to occur. It we consider case *B* from the cybernetic point of view, we shall note at once that the feedback loops enabling the monitoring of the agent's behavior do not return to the agent's own brain but rather to the console at which the neurophysiologist sits, producing efferent stimulation to match his reading of the agent's intention. Thus, there is a servosystem functioning to match the agent's intention all right; but given its detailed architecture, it can hardly count as realizing *the agent's* controlled regulation of his or her bodily movements since the feedback information about orientation and muscular states does not get carried back to *the agent's* central processing system. It seems, then, that to analyze the notion of sustained causation by a basic intention, we need to require of the transient servosystem realizing this function that it be engineered in such a way that it is the agent's own central mental processes that register and respond to feedback information.

Thus, it may seem that we may analyze basic intentional action as consisting in the sustained causation of matching behavior by the agent's basic intention, where the realizing causal mechanism is a servosystem with the appropriate detailed architecture just specified. This analysis will, no doubt, include the satisfaction of the sensitivity condition, but it will be sustained rather than sensitive causation that will form the nub of agent-control.

Such an analysis, however, offers conditions that are too strong for basic intentional action. There is no conceptual reason why all basic actions should involve feedback to the brain's central processes. In fact, there is evidence to show that some exercises of control take so little time that feedback of this order would be impossible, yet they need not fail to count as basic intentional acts just because of that.[28] In such cases, then, the sensitivity of the causal chain from intention to matching behavior will be enough to guarantee nondeviance. But we cannot analyze nondeviance *in general* simply in terms of sensitivity, as the case of preemptive heteromesy shows.

To get the CTA analysis right, we shall therefore have to retain the sensitivity condition but add to it this conditional requirement: that if the system that functions to produce the behavior does so by means of feedback loops to central mental processes, it is to *the agent's* central processes that those feedback loops return. This condition excludes the case of preemptive heteromesy, allows the possibility of genuine but heteromesial prosthetic aids, but does not exclude those basic intentional actions that operate independently of feedback to the central processes of the agent's brain.

The Final Breakthrough?

I believe that I am now in a position to make a well-founded claim that basic intentional action may be analyzed as matching behavior that is sensitively caused by the agent's basic intention, and in a context where any feedback to central mental processes returns to the agent's, rather than to anyone else's brain. This analysis offers what is needed for a defense of CTA because it provides necessary and sufficient conditions for basic intentional action that make no essential reference to agent-causation. It is true that it has turned out to be necessary to make a reference to the agent in order to exclude the preemptively heteromesial cases of deviance. But this reference is innocuous because identifying the agent's central neural processes as those to which any feedback loops return is simply a matter of distinguishing one central nervous system from another. And of course, we have been assuming that we could do that throughout by requiring for intentional action that the behavior be brought about by *the agent's* relevant intentional states.

The causal analysis of basic intentional action that I want to propose amounts, then, to this:

CTA-BI: M performs the basic intentional action of a-ing if and only if,

> M has a (basic) intention to do a; and,
>
> M's having this basic intention causes M to produce behavior, b, which instantiates the types of state or event intrinsic to the action of a-ing; where
>
> > (i)   the causal mechanism from M's basic intention to b satisfies the sensitivity condition; and
> >
> > (ii) if this causal mechanism involves feedback, then the feedback signal is routed back to M's central mental processes if to anyone's.

I claim that CTA-BI does exclude all cases of basic deviance, including the most recalcitrant cases of preemptive heteromesy. Yet at the same time, because it avoids any reference to agent-causation, it succeeds in coping with the problem of basic deviance in a way that satisfies the requirements of an event-causal CTA analysis. I cannot, of course, offer any final assurance that further deviant counterexamples will not be forthcoming to challenge CTA-BI. I can only plead that I cannot see how to construct any examples that are not caught in the mesh I have been developing in this and the previous chapter. But this plea is not issued without reason, for I believe that the only grounds there are for objecting to a sensitivity CTA analysis stem from our intuitions about deviant heteromesial cases. Thus, if there is a sensitivity CTA analysis that copes with these intuitions, there is a CTA analysis that may be accepted as fully adequate.

I therefore make the (no doubt bold) hypothesis that CTA-BI is the final breakthrough in the defense of the Causal Theory of Action, and therefore in resolving the skeptical problem of natural agency. But even if this hypothesis remains unassailed, there are limits to what would then have been achieved, which in conclusion I shall now review.

NOTES

1 Christopher Peacocke, *Holistic Explanation: Action, Space, Interpretation* (Oxford, England: Clarendon Press, 1979), p. 57; my emphasis.
2 Adam Morton, "Because He Thought He Had Insulted Him," *Journal of Philoso-*

phy, **72** (1975), 5–15, p. 14. Peacocke justifiably complains that Morton's reference to counterfactual changes in Leo's information "at the last moment" introduces ambiguity (*Holistic Explanation*, pp. 58–9). I seek to avoid this difficulty by construing the case in terms of counterfactual changes in the precise content of Leo's basic intention to fire (i.e., to squeeze his trigger finger while aiming the gun in the chosen direction).

3 Lewis first suggested a counterfactual version of a sensitivity condition in "Causation," *Journal of Philosophy*, **70** (1973), 556–67: "Counterfactual dependence between large families of alternatives is characteristic of processes of measurement, perception, or control" (p. 561). In a later paper, "Veridical Hallucination and Prosthetic Vision," *Australasian Journal of Philosophy*, **58** (1980), 239–49, Lewis elaborates on this idea – although only as it applies to a causal analysis of perception.

4 Peacocke, *Holistic Explanation*. The basic account of differential explanation is given on pp. 66–71 and extended (pp. 79–86) to provide the full notion of "strong" differential explanation.

5 Perceivers are subject to a visual censor when, although their experience as of an X, say, both matches and is caused by the scene before their eyes, had the scene been significantly different, the censor would have intervened to ensure that the visual experience as of an X was maintained. See Lewis, "Veridical Hallucination and Prosthetic Vision," p. 248.

6 Bruce Le Catt, "Censored Vision," *Australasian Journal of Philosophy*, **60** (1982), 158–62.

7 David Lewis, "Counterfactual Dependence and Time's Arrow," *Noûs*, **13** (1979), 455–76. Compare Jonathan Bennett's defense of the propriety of backtrackers in "Counterfactuals and Temporal Direction," *Philosophical Review*, **93** (1984), 57–91.

8 Peacocke, *Holistic Explanation*, p. 77; Martin Davies, "Function in Perception," *Australasian Journal of Philosophy*, **61** (1983), 409–26, pp. 412–14.

9 Davies, "Function in Perception," pp. 415–16.

10 Davies (ibid., p. 415) sets out the example as follows:

> Consider a person who inhabits an environment rather simpler than ours . . . [and for whom] the ability to discriminate one million different scenes is adequate. In our person, any retinal image activates just one of a bank of one million pulse generators resulting in a simple pulse being transmitted along one of one million channels to a corresponding one of a bank of one million experience generators which is thereby stimulated and produces a visual experience which matches the scene before the person's eyes. The experience generators are not memory cells. Rather, the entire mechanism, with its one million discrete pulse generator-experience generator pairs, is a natural product of evolution.

11 To succeed, the counterexample would need to be backed by a theory of natural laws that explains why the mathematical function that describes the behavior of the discrete processor considered as a total system cannot itself count as a law of nature. Furthermore, as Davies notes in a footnote (ibid., p. 416, footnote 15), Peacocke believes that the example can be excluded by a minor revision to his condition of strong differential explanation.

12 Ibid., p. 421. Davies explains what he means by a teleological function as follows:

> (i) It is sufficient for a mechanism to have *F*-ing as its function that it was *selected for* its *F*-ing; the selection might be by (a) the natural selection of the evolutionary process or (b) the intentional selection of the design process. (ii) However much the notion of a function may be extended from this notion of design function, it is not a sufficient

173

condition for a mechanism to have F-ing as its function that it happens (to operate as a totality in such a way as) to F (pp. 421–2).

13 Compare, for example, Steven Hardy's recent judgment on the current state of the art of robotics: "Inadequate solutions to deep theoretical problems are deeply embedded in the crude control systems for most commercial robot systems." See "Robot Control Systems," in Tim O'Shea and Marc Eisenstadt, eds., *Artificial Intelligence: Tools, Techniques and Applications* (New York: Harper & Row, 1984), 178–91, p. 189.

14 Peacocke has successfully criticized attempts to use a reliability condition to exclude deviant cases (*Holistic Explanation*, pp. 89–95). For a bizarre example of a "fortuitous substitute for normal function which operates on a single occasion," consider the case, due to David Pears, of a "gunman who intends to fire his gun and whose cortex sends out the initiating event: unknown to the gunman, the nerve to his index finger has been severed, but the intended movement still takes place because the impulse produced by the initiating event attracts some lightning which itself generates the required impulse in the severed section of the nerve" (p. 93). Whatever reservations one may have about the plausibility of the example, Peacocke is correct to claim that if this setup really does permit differential explanation of his finger movement in terms of the gunman's intention, there is genuine action despite the transience of the mechanism that realizes it. There is thus no justification for requiring nondeviant causal links to be nonaccidental, as Robert Audi has recently suggested in "Acting for Reasons," *Philosophical Review*, **95** (1986), 511–46, p. 529.

15 Peacocke, *Holistic Explanation*, p. 87.

16 Myles Brand, *Intending and Acting: Toward a Naturalized Action Theory* (Cambridge, Mass.: M.I.T. Press, 1984), p. 22.

17 Ibid.

18 Peacocke, *Holistic Explanation*, p. 88.

19 This proposal is advanced by James Montmarquet, "Causal Deviancy and Multiple Intentions," *Analysis*, **42** (1982), 106–10, in defending Peacocke against my own earlier charge that his (Peacocke's) concession that heteromesy needs exclusion introduced an ad hoc element into the defense of a CTA analysis; see "Peacocke on Intentional Action," *Analysis*, **41** (1981), 92–8.

20 I am indebted to a conversation with Andy Clarke of the University of Sussex for provoking these remarks on the variation in our moral intuitions over the different types of heteromesial cases.

21 For Donald Davidson's arguments in support of this thesis, see *Essays on Actions and Events* (Oxford, England: Clarendon Press, 1980), Essay 11 (especially pp. 215–23) and Essay 12.

22 Consider, for example, this passage from Essay 13 (ibid., p. 250):

> Why should it not happen that there are inductively established correlations between physical and psychological events? Indeed, do we not already know that there are? We do, if by laws we mean statistical generalizations. . . . But these generalizations, unlike those of physics, cannot be sharpened without limit, cannot be turned into the strict laws of a science closed within its area of application.

23 Irving Thalberg, "Do Our Intentions Cause Our Intentional Actions?" *American Philosophical Quarterly*, **21** (1984), 249–60, p. 257. Compare Kent Bach's remark that a CTA "should say something not only about how an action gets started, but also about how it gets done," in "A Representational Theory of Action," *Philosophical Studies*, **34** (1978), 361–79, p. 363. Thalberg acknowledges Harry

Frankfurt's similar suggestion in Frankfurt's "The Problem of Action," *American Philosophical Quarterly*, **15** (1978), 157–62. The same idea is also found in Andrew Woodfield, *Teleology* (Cambridge, England: Cambridge University Press, 1976), pp. 173–82, in his discussion of the deviant counterexamples, and it continues to attract adherents (cf. Audi, "Acting for Reasons," pp. 524–5).

24 Thalberg, "Do Our Intentions Cause Our Intentional Actions?" p. 259.

25 The same suspicion arises about Tuomela's analysis of intentional action as involving a non-Humean relation of "purposive causation" between a "willing event" and overt behavior; see Raimo Tuomela, *Human Action and Its Explanation* (Dordrecht, Holland: D. Reidel, 1977). An examination of Tuomela's treatment of Davidson's climber counterexample (p. 258) suggests that this appeal to purposive causation combines two approaches to the problem of causal deviance that we have already dismissed as unsatisfactory, namely, requiring that the causal chain pass through a suitable conative event (a trying or a willing) and suggesting that further characterization of causal nondeviance is "up to scientists."

26 For a useful discussion of servomechanisms, see Woodfield, *Teleology*, chap. 11.

27 Ibid., p. 194.

28 As Patricia Smith Churchland, *Neurophilosophy: Toward a Unified Science of the Mind-Brain* (Cambridge, Mass.: M.I.T. Press, 1986), pp. 430–1, notes,

> Often a movement is too fast to exploit feedback, as for example in the case of the finger movements of an accomplished violinist, or in catching an egg after it slips from one's hand. In such cases the conduction velocities of neurons are too slow to permit feedback data to be used to inform the next motor command, and the movement must be composed as a unified sequence without waiting for feedback.

6

Limits for the causal theory of action

I. DEALING WITH THE AGENT-CAUSATIONIST SYNDROME

The Story So Far

In this final chapter, I shall try to put a proper perspective on what has already been achieved. I need to acknowledge some limitations to that achievement and to consider how serious these are. But before I do so, it will be useful to list the essential points of my argument in the preceding chapters. I have argued that

1. There is a significant metaphysical problem about how the presuppositions of our ethical perspective can cohere with the assumption that persons are wholly part of the natural order as understood by contemporary natural science.
2. To resolve this metaphysical problem it is necessary not only to have a solution to the mind/body problem (i.e., to be able to explain the natural possibility of consciousness and intentionality) but also to resolve the problem of natural agency (i.e., to be able to explain how actions are possible in the natural causal order).
3. Skepticism about natural agency is, in fact, what underlies the whole skeptical tradition about how free action can occur – both under determinism and under indeterminism.
4. If the core ontological thesis of the Causal Theory of Action (CTA) is true (i.e., if it is true that actions are constituted by behavior with a certain kind of mental causal history), then the skeptical problem of natural agency is resolved – assuming (as I have, without argument, throughout) that a naturalist theory of mind is possible.
5. Defending CTA is the best way of defeating skepticism about natural agency (in particular, it is superior to the flight into antirealism about actions).
6. To defend CTA's core ontological claim, it is necessary to provide a causal analysis of action (a CTA analysis) – and although this analysis must provide sufficient conditions for action in purely event-causal terms, it need not yield a full definition of *what it means* to perform an action.

7. Developing such a CTA analysis requires meeting a range of agent-causationist intuitions that suggest that an ontology rich enough for the realization of actions must include a special kind of agent-causation not reducible to event-causation.

8. Although there are many different arguments used to back up these agent-causationist intuitions, the most serious concerns the need to deal with the problem of causal deviance.

9. The crucial step in overcoming the problem of causal deviance is to provide an event-causal analysis of basic intentional action that excludes all the deviant and includes all the nondeviant cases.

10. CTA-BI (arrived at through the discussion of Chapters 4 and 5) provides the CTA analysis of basic intentional action that is needed – and hence, allows us to defend the core ontological claim of CTA, to resolve the skeptical problem of natural agency, and (granted a naturalist solution to the mind/body problem) to explain how some purely natural systems can be the responsible authors of some natural events and states of affairs.

The first set of lingering doubts that may need mopping up are those that focus on CTA-BI: Is it really the key to deflating the intuitions of the agent-causationist's syndrome?

In What Sense Is Basic Action Primitive?

Agent-causationists are convinced that the notion of an agent's bringing something about through the exercise of his or her control is essential to the notion of action that features in our ethical perspective. Even if we grant the (charitable!) assumption that CTA-BI is indeed the last word in event-causal analyses of basic intentional action, is its truth enough to persuade a rational agent-causationist to recant? Well, it depends on what is meant by the claim that agent-causation is essential to our concept of action.

If this claim is just about what we *mean* by the concept of a basic intentional action, then CTA-BI does not repudiate it because CTA-BI is clearly not a definition that explicates *what it means* to attribute a basic intentional action to an agent. Indeed, it is highly likely that the concept of a basic action is a "conceptual primitive": What it is for something to be a basic action cannot be explicated by defining *basic action* in other terms. The reason for this may be illustrated by considering just why we are barred from construing CTA-BI (in particular) as explicating what it really means for a basic action to occur: The trouble is that the explicatory relation is the wrong way around. It is our understanding of what basic intentional action is that explains why the conditions stated in the

177

analysans of CTA-BI are necessary and sufficient for it, and not conversely. It is only because we *already* grasp the concept of action that we can judge that it is necessary and sufficient for basic action that the link from intention to matching behavior be sensitive and have the right sort of detailed architecture for any feedback loops involved. And should CTA-BI turn out to be flawed, we will discover the flaw by bringing our prior understanding of what action is to bear on the analysis; and whatever amendments we make will be explicable in terms of that prior understanding – they will not themselves explicate what action really is. So, within the conceptual framework that underpins our ethical evaluations of behavior, basic actions are indeed primitives.

To this extent, then, the possibility of an analysis of action in event-causal terms is limited. Such an analysis, it seems, cannot be a full definition. And if acceptance of this conclusion is all it takes to be an agent-causationist, agent-causationism is entirely sensible. But agent-causationism of this kind need carry no skeptical force with respect to natural agency. All the defender of natural agency needs is to show that actions are *constituted* by conditions of a kind readily accommodated within our natural ontology. And the fact that actions are so constituted might still be shown, even if an explicatory definition of what it is to perform an action cannot be provided in event-causal terms.

However, if agent-causationists go further and claim that agency cannot be realized without an ontology that offends contemporary naturalism by requiring real, irreducible agent-causation, then I maintain that the success of CTA-BI is enough to refute them. Agent-causation may be a conceptual primitive, but the success of CTA-BI shows that it is not reasonable to regard it as an ontological primitive because CTA-BI specifies conditions that are both necessary *and sufficient* for a basic intentional action to occur. And these conditions (granted a naturalist solution to the mind/body problem) are unproblematically realized within the natural order as modern science understands it.

But is this argument really enough to overthrow agent-causationism? Could the skeptic not insist that the conditions specified in the analysans of CTA-BI are merely correlates of basic intentional action and not constitutive of it? Could it not be argued that it *just happens* to be the case, in the actual world, that basic intentional actions are always accompanied by the event-causal conditions described in CTA-BI? I believe that the way in which CTA-BI was arrived at provides an answer here. Perhaps CTA-BI's analysis of basic intentional action does not apply across all possible worlds. If, for example, there are Cartesian dualist worlds, basic actions may well involve ontic agent-causation in those worlds. But the analysis certainly does apply to all possible worlds *that have the same kind of ontology and causal order that science understands the actual world to have.* To decide whether you accept CTA-BI, you have to ask whether, within a natural scientific ontology, you could *conceive* of just those conditions it specifies applying without being prepared to attribute a basic intentional action to the agent, or conversely. And that question is not simply a question about how things are in the actual world; it is a question about how things would be in any world with the same fundamental natural ontology and causal order.

I submit, then, that once we have found event-causal conditions that are uniformly correlated with the performance of a basic intentional action in any world appropriately like our own, it is more reasonable to regard these correlated conditions as stating how such actions are naturally realized than it is to persist in skepticism. For as long as the problem of causal deviance sustains doubt about whether there are uniform natural correlates of basic intentional action, skepticism about natural agency remains reasonable. But once it is accepted that we can state what those natural correlates are (as I boldly claim the truth of CTA-BI plus a natural realist account of intentions allows us to do), it is no longer sensible to doubt whether agency can belong within the natural order. If, in any natural universe of our type, basic intentional actions are constantly correlated with natural conditions of general type, N, then to persist with skepticism would require positing some further *nonnatural* factor that is required for the realization of basic actions and that is itself also constantly correlated with N. Such a factor is evidently otiose, and one could have no reason for positing it beyond a purely dogmatic attachment to anti-naturalism about agency. Postulating that agency involves a nonnatural factor (agent-causation) may be quite sensible while we lack uniform natural correlates for actions; but it becomes plain silly once we can understand how such correlates may be obtained.

The success of CTA-BI shows that Davidson's pessimism about finding an adequate CTA-analysis was misplaced. True, we cannot obtain any definitional reduction of action in causal terms—but then we don't need one. However, Davidson also doubted the possibility of arriving at a statement of conditions that were sufficient as well as necessary for intentional action.[1] And it is this doubt that CTA-BI shows to be groundless, for CTA-BI provides a set of mentalistic event-causal conditions that are severally necessary *and jointly sufficient* for basic intentional action. Therefore, granted a naturalist account of the mental states cited by its analysis, CTA-BI shows how to understand the place of basic intentional action in the natural order. A fortiori, it also establishes the natural possibility of intentional action in general – although the CTA analysis of *nonbasic* intentional action requires a condition of "match with the agent's plan," the details of which we outlined in Chapter 4. Furthermore, once the place of *intentional* action in the natural order is explicable, it follows, again a fortiori, that we have explained how action in general can be a natural possibility.

Other Aspects of the Agent-Causationist Syndrome

But is CTA-BI really such a powerful result? After all, the defender of CTA faces a whole syndrome of agent-causationist intuitions that fuel skepticism about how action may be understood as part of an event-causal network. Overcoming the challenge of causal deviance is not the only hurdle a CTA analysis must surmount. Nevertheless, I believe it is the crucial one; once it is surmounted, the remaining obstacles dwindle by comparison. To remove doubt on this point, I shall review the two other difficulties our discussion has uncovered, to check that they do not obstruct a CTA analysis once a means of excluding the deviant counterexamples has been provided.

1. Merely voluntary action   First, there is the intuition that there can be actions that are merely voluntary, that is, not intentional under any description of them. This intuition undermines CTA from the start: If there can be actions without appropriate mental antecedents, "being caused by suitable mental antecedents" can hardly be sufficient and necessary for action. Had our analysis of intentional action required final recourse to the idea of action *tout court,* the view that merely voluntary action is possible would have been reinforced. But CTA-BI escapes this difficulty: It excludes deviance without essential reference to the agent's exercise of control. The intentional exercise of control has been shown to belong to an event-causal natural order, and so it is inconceivable that there should be "mere" exercises of control that cannot so belong. Accordingly, to the extent of our confidence in CTA-BI, we may justify revising any intuitions that support belief in merely voluntary action.

After all, it is arguable that belief in merely voluntary action was not very well entrenched in the first place: It *is* odd to suppose that an agent can exercise control without having any end in mind whatsoever. The cases of overt behavior that seem to count as purely voluntary – such as idle fidgeting, for which an agent may certainly be held responsible – are capable of reinterpretation as intentional actions. From the fact that the agent was not aware of any intention in idly drumming his or her fingers on a table, for example, it does not follow that there was no such intention, especially if we recognize (as we have) that the intention could be the purely basic one to drum one's fingers for its own sake. This argument will entail accepting the possibility of subconscious intentions, but I see no reason to count that as an objection.[2]

However, the case of idle or habitual bodily exercises of control is not the only apparent basis for belief in merely voluntary actions. This belief may also be sustained by a conviction that an adequate account of "inner," mental, actions will have to acknowledge that some of these are merely voluntary actions. Considerations about mental actions are, indeed, relevant to the CTA analysis since it is intended to apply to action in general. Thus, the claim that all actions are intentional under some description must apply to all mental actions too. But is this plausible? Can it be true that all mental actions are intentional under some description and sensitively caused by a basic intention whose content they match? Or must some mental actions be purely voluntary, not amenable to a CTA analysis?

If we suppose that a basic intention can come about only through the agent's mental action of forming it, a CTA analysis will indeed be in trouble and will succumb to the famous Rylean vicious regress.[3] But the admission of purely voluntary acts of forming intentions is not the only option for stopping the regress. We may simply reject the initial assumption and hold, alternatively, that intentions (including, sometimes, basic ones) can arise passively. To allow this (as I think we must) does not, of course, somehow suggest that agents can be the virtual victims of their own intentions. A passively arisen conative state of an agent can count as an intention only if the agent has the capacity to reassess and abandon it; and it will always be up to the agent actually to carry it out.

Sometimes, of course, agents do actively form their intentions. This happens regularly when a basic intention results from practical reasoning from nonbasic intentions and beliefs. And then, of course, under the CTA analysis, the action of forming an intention will itself have to be intentional under some description and caused (appropriately) by the relevant intention. This may seem a tall order and may prompt renewed calls for the admission of merely voluntary mental acts. But why should the active formation of a basic intention not itself be caused by a higher-order intention to engage in practical reasoning in order to arrive at intentions (perhaps again, not fully conscious) to perform basic actions that are suitable means to a chosen goal? Arriving at the basic intention to do *a*, might not, indeed, be intentional *under that description,* but it may still count as an intentional action under the description "arriving at a basic intention of a type suitable for achieving chosen goal, *g.*" There is a parallel here with belief. If I intentionally look out the window in order to discover whether it is raining, my consequently forming the belief that it is will not be intentional under the description "forming the belief that it is raining," but it will be intentional under the description "forming a belief on the question whether it is raining." The only special feature of a CTA analysis of mental action will be our general inability to give an independent *physical* characterization of the types of events that are intrinsic to mental acts. But that is no difficulty, for all the analysis requires is that there should be such events.[4]

2. Final stage akrasia   We may be reasonably confident, then, that provided we do indeed possess an adequate event-causal analysis of intentional action, the bogey of merely voluntary action cannot disturb us. May we be equally sanguine about the other remaining source of difficulty for CTA? Intuitions about akrasia bothered us on two fronts. To start with, the fact that akratic intentional acts are not reasonable with respect to the agent's judgment of what it is best to do indicated that the complex of belief and desire backing such a judgment could not in general be the rational cause constitutive of intentional action. This problem was surmounted by introducing final stage intentions, intermediate between final evaluative judgments and actions themselves.

But akrasia also pointed up the intuition that once an agent has formed a final evaluative practical judgment, it remains *up to the agent* to give effect to it. And this intuition suggested that even if such a judgment were a necessary condition for intentional action (which is not, in fact, the case), agent-causation of the behavior favored in the judgment might be a further necessary condition. Well, the expedient used to settle the first of these problems seems to help us also with the second. May we not counter that it is a causal link from judgment to behavior that passes through a final stage intention that constitutes this further necessary condition, rather than agent-causation? This suggestion seems helpful until the possibility of final stage akrasia is suggested. Is it not possible that an agent may act contrary to a final stage intention?

If I am right in claiming that success with an event-causal analysis of basic intentional action gives us good reason to insist on rejecting the possibility of merely voluntary action, then it follows almost at once that the possibility of final stage akrasia may also justifiably be rejected. For, final stage akrasia is possible only if merely voluntary action is possible too. If an intention genuinely is "final stage," and is not displaced, it is a conceptual impossibility that the agent should *intentionally* act contrary to it. Action contrary to a maintained final stage intention, therefore, could at most amount to purely voluntary action. If such purely voluntary action is ruled out, so is final stage akrasia. And as already remarked, our intuitions about final stage akrasia are not so robust that they cannot stand revision. It is a plausible hypothesis that what looks like final stage akrasia is either paralysis of some sort or last-minute displacement of one intention by another.

Thus it seems that overcoming the problem of causal deviance is indeed the key to deflating the agent-causationist syndrome. If CTA-BI does provide necessary and sufficient event-causal conditions for nondeviant basic intentional action, the problems of merely voluntary action and final stage akrasia become much more tractable. Some revision of intuitions about such cases may still be needed to maintain a CTA analysis; but once intuitions about deviance are accommodated, the remaining contrary intuitions are far too tentative to block the analysis. The possibility of a CTA analysis is thus vindicated, and the core ontological claim of CTA is shown to be true: Actions can belong to the natural order because actions consist in event-causal sequences of the kind specified by the CTA analysis that is based on CTA-BI.

II. THE PLACE OF THE CAUSAL THEORY OF ACTION IN THE WIDER PROJECT OF RECONCILIATORY NATURALISM

The remaining doubts that I shall consider – and seek to set aside – have to do, not with whether my attempt at a CTA analysis has been successful, but rather with the claims I have made for the significance of such a success. On my view, achieving a satisfactory CTA is of considerable philosophical significance. I find, however, that not everyone shares this view. The project of "reconciliatory naturalism," they would concede, is indeed important. Overcoming philosophical skepticism about how the presuppositions of our ethical beliefs and practices can apply to human agents who belong wholly to the natural causal order would be, they agree, a very great service. If we can possibly avoid it, we do not want to have to choose between a view of ourselves as part of nature and a view of ourselves as morally responsible agents. But why, they ask, is the defense of a Causal Theory of Action so vital to this project? Perhaps I have shown how to develop a CTA analysis that overcomes the agent-causationist syndrome – but so what? All the interesting and difficult work of understanding how responsible agency is possible in the natural order still remains to be done – or so I envisage my unfriendly critic as maintaining.

This kind of objection takes different forms. The first form that I shall consider maintains that successfully defending a CTA analysis does not even address the most fundamental problem in understanding how natural agency is possible.

A Fundamental Problem Ignored?

It is affirmed by CTA-BI that behavior counts as basic action when caused by a basic intention under certain further specified conditions. But of course, it is not claimed that the formation of a basic intention is *by itself* causally sufficient for the behavior intrinsic to the corresponding basic action. Other conditions are causally necessary for this behavior to occur – an admission that gives

184

leverage to the agent-causationist, who will assert that these other conditions must include a reference to agent-causation. But that suggestion has, I maintain, been scotched by CTA-BI, which without appeal to agent-causation excludes all the counterexamples whose deviance is intuitively explicable as a lack of the agents' exercising their own control in carrying out their basic intentions. Even so, it will be urged, a fundamental mystery remains: What more is needed beyond the formation of the basic intention for the action actually to take place? Without an answer to this question, may we really profess to understand how action can be a natural possibility?

Myles Brand has identified this problem as a matter of explaining adequately "the nature of the proximate cause of action."[5] He agrees that the last stage before behavior is a final stage intention – he calls it an immediate intention – and offers a CTA analysis of basic action as matching behavior "proximately" caused by an immediate intention (an analysis whose shortcomings I believe I have already uncovered in Chapter 4.) To get an adequate naturalistic account of action, however, Brand believes more is required. As he puts it,

An adequate account of the proximate cause of action must specify the nature of this type of mental event. It must say what properties mental events of this type have, and which others lack, such that only they initiate action. . . . why does one type of mental event proximately cause action, while others do not, no matter how fully they occupy consciousness? This problem is a fundamental one in action theory.[6]

Brand argues that an orthodox functionalist account of immediate intention cannot address this problem – for in effect, it simply characterizes an intention as that complex mental state, whatever it is, that plays a certain role in initiating action. What has to be done, Brand believes, is to upgrade the commonsense notion of an intention so that it can take its place in a scientific psychology. And he offers some pointers in this direction,[7] which I shall now briefly review.

An intention has both a cognitive and a conative component: It is both a representation of a state of affairs (the intended goal) and a setting-out-to-achieve that state of affairs. (Thus, intentions count as intentional states in a more full-blooded – and etymologically pure – sense than, say, beliefs or desires. To intend is, indeed, to take aim at some inexistent object.) Brand argues that the cognitive

185

component in intention may be scientifically transformed into "the neobehaviorist learning theoretic concept of a response image, and the computational idea of an abstract structural hierarchy of servomechanisms."[8] Whatever the merits of this suggestion, however, Brand's survey of the extant theories of motivation leads him to conclude that the *conative* aspect of intention currently lacks a "scientific transformation": "There is at present no tenable scientific theory into which this folk psychological concept can be transformed."[9]

Thus Brand fails to offer a naturalistic account of what it is about an immediate (final state) intention that initiates action. But he does not retract his suggestion that naturalistic action theory needs for its completion a scientific theory of motivation that will be some kind of upgrading within psychology of the commonsense notion of an intention. I believe Brand is mistaken here on two counts. First, what he takes to be a (or as he originally said "the"[10]) fundamental question for action theory is, in fact, not even part of the problem of natural agency that we have been considering. That is, a successful CTA analysis does suffice to rebut skeptical doubts about how agency can belong in the natural order even if we have no complete account of the natural conditions that are sufficient to initiate motor activity. And second, Brand's assumption that this account will be developed within scientific *psychology* is open to question. The answer may belong rather to neurophysiology.

If we consider commonsense descriptions of actions and their mental antecedents (at the level of folk psychology), we find that having an intention is always regarded as still leaving it "up to the agent" to carry it out. Even final stage basic intentions are not alone causally sufficient as such for matching behavior. As long as it is this folk psychological notion that we are trying to upgrade, this central feature of it will remain. That is, anything in scientific psychology that is a recognizable transformation of the concept *of intention,* will be such that its instantiation in the agent is not causally sufficient for action. Therefore, Brand's fundamental problem of just what it is that gets the system to produce its intended output will remain. Thus I believe that it will be the theoretical investigation of the physiology of action that answers this question for us.

But this does not mean that we have to postpone the metaphysical quest to render natural agency intelligible until physiology

186

comes up with the goods.[11] It is possible to establish that agency is constituted by unproblematic event-causal conditions, even if we have very little empirical knowledge of what those conditions may be. As I have argued, all we need is an acceptable CTA analysis of basic intentional action, which establishes that, whatever more is needed beyond the formation of a basic intention for a basic action actually to occur, it is something realizable in event-causal terms. And CTA-BI, I have claimed, provides just such an analysis. Provided the structural features of the causal chain from basic intention to matching behavior are as CTA-BI specifies, a genuine basic action will occur whatever the further nitty-gritty details of the realizing causal mechanisms may be. Once we have our successful CTA analysis, then, metaphysical doubts about *whether* action is a natural possibility may be set to rest, even though we continue to be puzzled about *how* physical causal mechanisms actually realize agency. The question about what suffices to initiate action, which Brand takes as philosophically fundamental, is therefore not so at all. Not only is it not a philosophical question – it may not even be a question for psychology![12]

CTA-BI Solves the Problem of Natural
Agency Only Given Natural Realism About
Intentional States

The reason why CTA-BI answers the philosophical question about how action is naturally possible without answering the corresponding physical question is clear: CTA-BI offers an account in terms of the functional architecture required for agency. The conditions it states to be necessary and sufficient for action have to do with the kind of functional organization a system needs in order to realize a genuine agent. Intentions are to be conceived as functionally characterized states realized in physical terms; the sensitivity condition requires a systematic dependence of output on intention – and this, in itself, will be a feature of a system at the level of its functional organization. Finally, considerations about how any feedback processes may work are obviously also at the level of the system's functional architecture. Thus, the philosophical problem of natural agency is resolved, provided there are no further philosophical problems about how there can be natural systems with the kind of functional organization required for basic action. The absence of further *philosophical* problems, however, would not entail the absence of problems *tout court*. Many questions may remain about how physical systems can realize natural agents, and Brand's question about how basic intentions have their motive power is one of them.

As I have already emphasized, the use of CTA to resolve the problem of natural agency presupposes a successful natural theory of intentionality – and in particular, one that is "realist" in the sense that it shows how intentional states and events can play a causal role. I have not attempted to address skepticism about the possibility of providing such a natural realist theory of intentional states; so if anyone thinks that showing how intentional states can be real causes is the most important element in the reconciliatory naturalist program, I can only appeal to the fact that many skeptics have actually attacked the program at another point. They have granted that mental states are real and can be causes, but they have doubted whether such mental causation can yield genuine agency under any conditions. As I explained at the outset, I have chosen to concentrate on trying to rebut doubts of this kind and have left aside the (admittedly, logically prior) task of rebutting skepticism about a natural realist account of intentional states.

My concentration on skepticism about natural agency specifically, under the assumption that the problem of natural intentionality has a solution, would be, of course, either frivolous or complacent were it not for the fact that there are good prospects for defending natural realism about intentional states. The CTA analysis I have arrived at is well suited for a natural realism about intentional states that takes them to be types of functional states, token-identical with real physical states (presumably complexes of neural states), which can be causes of overt behavior. A view such as William Lycan's provides a good illustration of the kind of position I have in mind:

> To be in an intentional state is to host a mental representation, a brain state that bears a natural (causal and teleological) relation to the object represented, or in the case of abstract or nonexistent objects, to linguistic events that go proxy for them.[13]

Thus, despite its difficulty, it is not unreasonable to hope for a successful defense of natural realism about intentional states.[14] It is worthwhile, therefore, to concentrate on the project that has engaged my whole attention in this essay: It would be useful to be able to assure the friends of reconciliatory naturalism that skepticism about natural agency cannot be sustained once natural realism about intentionality is established. And if my results in this essay are correct, that is precisely the assurance that can be given.

Even if it is granted, however, that a natural realist account of intentional states is possible, a doubt might yet remain about a naturalistic account *specifically of intentions*. Indeed, it may be suggested that at this stage in the program of reconciliatory naturalism, we shall discover as much ground for skepticism about how intentions are possible in the natural order as there was at the outset over the possibility of natural agency itself. This anxiety arises through the suspicion that agency is somehow conceptually bound up with intention – that when we properly understand what it is for an agent to have an intention, we shall recognize that it necessarily involves him or her in performing an action of some kind. I have already noted that my account must allow that intentions can arise passively – that coming to have an intention need not amount to the agent's *performing the action* of forming that intention. So here is one way in which action turns out *not* to be essential to intention. But there may be other ways in which it seems that it is. Consider how important it is to distinguish intentions from wants. How, though, could this distinction be drawn without appealing to the idea that an agent's intention is not simply a desire for an end but involves *actively setting oneself* to take steps to achieve an end? In which case, how may we avoid the conclusion that taking a certain kind of inner, mental action is essential to intending? And then, am I not in danger of finding that the idea of an intrinsic doing, having been chased finally from the territory of the causal relation between mental states and behavior, now sickeningly reappears in the territory of the kind of mental states that CTA must take to be the essential antecedents of genuine action?

I doubt whether matters are so grim. I shall not bother to quarrel with the suggestion that intentions cannot be *defined* for what they are without ineliminable reference to agency notions. For, to overcome the present doubt, we need only be satisfied that an agent's having an intention can *ontologically be realized* in a state of affairs that involves no agent-causal relations. Under a functionalist account of mental states, intentions can be distinguished from other sorts of mental states (wants, desires, etc.) according to the kind of functional role they play. And we can accommodate the idea that an intention involves the agent's setting himself or herself to achieve a goal simply by identifying intentions as those mental states that play a specially executive role – which are, so to say, "functionally closer" to those event-types that initiate peripheral movement than any other kind of intentional state. (Actually, on my account, there will have to be a hierarchy of closeness to these initiating events – proximate intentions will be closer than non-proximate ones, basic closer than nonbasic, and so on.) Thus, if functionalism is going to work at all as the key to a natural realist account of intentional states, there is no special reason why it should fail for intentions – and in particular, no reason for supposing that ontological commitment to agent-causation comes in tandem with ontological commitment to intentions.

How Much of a Problem of Natural Moral Autonomy Remains Once CTA Resolves the Problem of Natural Agency?

I have suggested that the first incarnation of my unfriendly critic is making the mistake of expecting from a philosophical theory something that can be provided only by whatever natural science it is that will explain the causal mechanisms by which physically realized intentions yield matching behavior. To my critic's second incarnation, I have suggested that he or she is simply expressing a preference for a work on a different part of the reconciliatory naturalist campaign against skepticism, namely, the defense of natural realism about the kinds of intentional states that CTA takes to be essential to the causal antecedents of intentional action. But my unfriendly critic has a third incarnation, which is perhaps the most serious one. In this final guise, my critic complains that the main task of reconciling the ethical with the natural perspective remains even if we have achieved a natural realist theory of intentionality and an adequate CTA analysis. That is, the main task remains because (as I have more than once admitted) the capacity for action is only a necessary condition for moral responsibility. For an agent to be morally responsible for an outcome, it must have come about through an action in which he or she is *significantly morally free* or *autonomous*. Showing how the bare requirements of agency are naturally realizable still leaves plenty of room for doubting whether all that is required for complete moral autonomy can intelligibly be accommodated within a natural causal order.

The lame reply to this complaint is to observe that whatever else may have to be done to establish the possibility of natural moral autonomy, a solution to the limited problem of natural agency will still be required. Thus my defense of CTA is at least a contribution to an essential part of the reconciliatory naturalist program. This is a lame reply, however, because it leaves room for the impression that my discussion has been unbalanced. It may seem that I have advertized myself as seeking a naturalist vindication of our practice of assigning moral responsibility but have actually delivered on only one rather preliminary aspect of the problem, leaving not so much as a sketch of how one might follow through to complete the whole project.

I do, however, have a more robust rebuttal. First, my examination in earlier chapters of philosophical arguments expressing skepticism about how natural systems can be morally responsible does suggest that the source of the problem is a doubt about how agency as such can belong to the event-causal order. Second, and more important, I claim that once we have a natural realist theory of intentional states and a Causal Theory of Action, we already have all the metaphysics we need to resolve the final problem of explaining how full moral autonomy is a natural possibility. I support this claim by observing that all those further necessary conditions beyond agency itself that are required for moral responsibility ascribe nothing more than further psychological states to the agent. To be morally responsible for an outcome, the agent whose action caused it must have known enough about what he or she was doing; must have been capable of recognizing its moral significance; must have had the capacity (even if it were not exercised) to reflect on and, if necessary, reassess the beliefs, desires, and perceptions that gave rise to his or her intentions; and so on.[15] To get moral agency from agency as such, we need only the right kind of psychology; and if we have a philosophical theory that locates psychological states in general firmly within the natural universe, there can be no further reasons for doubting the possibility of natural moral autonomy beyond a doubt about natural agency itself. There is thus every justification for concentrating a reconciliatory naturalist effort on investigating a potential solution to the problem of natural agency.

CTA and the Vindication of Moral Responsibility

I shall conclude by acknowledging that a successful CTA can provide only part of what is needed to vindicate our practice of holding some behavers responsible for some (and only some) of the outcomes of their behavior. Many people are interested in the issues I have treated in this essay because they wonder whether this practice can be justified as fair and rational. Are we justified in discriminating as we do between, say, responsible criminals and the criminally insane? Is it fair to lock some people up for offenses that when committed by others, bring committal for psychiatric treatment? And so on. To set the present inquiry in perspective, it will be useful to finish by considering the extent to which success in defending a Causal Theory of Action helps in securing the rationality and fairness of our assignments of responsibility, praise and blame, punishment and reward.

Given an adequate CTA analysis, we are able to say why it is that some, and only some, sequences of natural events count as actions for which their agents may be held morally responsible (provided the other relevant psychological conditions are also satisfied). There is a genuine distinction in the real order of things that corresponds to the distinction between actions and nonactions. Our use of the concept of action is empirically (or better, "naturally") well founded in any world in which our use of all the relevant psychological concepts is also naturally well founded. But if someone asks whether we are rationally and morally justified in giving this difference the important role it plays in our practice of making ethical judgments of responsibility and of assigning praise and blame and punishments and rewards, then the truth of CTA itself offers no answer at all. CTA supports the rationality of these ethical practices only to this extent: that it undercuts radical doubts about whether, given a naturalist view of the world, there really is such a thing as an agent's exercise of his or her own control in bringing about an outcome. If you accept the arguments for the CTA analysis that I have put together in this essay, then you should accept that the distinction between action and nonaction has a real basis in the natural world. At least our ethical practices are not founded on a purely fanciful distinction. But the fact that they lack this kind of radical irrationality does not, of course, entail that they are fully reasonable or fair. When we differentiate between morally responsible action and behavior that falls short of it, we are referring to a real difference in the natural world; but why it should be reasonable or fair for us to let that difference *matter* in the way it does is a further question.

An analogy will prove illuminating here.[16] Imagine a group of anthropologists investigating a tribe who use a concept of demon-possession. Among this tribe, it can make a considerable difference to the way you are treated whether or not you are regarded as demon-possessed. After considerable "inside" investigation of the way the concept of demon-possession functions for the tribe, the anthropologists ask themselves whether the tribe's practices are reasonable and fair. They realize, of course, that they are asking this question relative to what *they* take the real natural and moral order to be, but this epistemic relativism does not detract from the importance of the question. If they cannot find any natural conditions (relative to their ontology) that are regularly and exclusively correlated with what is recognized as demon-possession, they will be obliged to conclude that the tribe's practice of attributing demon-possession is irrational. Of course, this conclusion may be mistaken because they might have the wrong ontology or might not be looking for natural correlations in the right places; but the point is that they will be justified in accepting the tribe's practice as rational only to the extent that they can see it as based on naturally well-founded distinctions.

Suppose, however, that the anthropologists do find natural correlates for demon-possession. This discovery will show that in their natural worldview at least, there really is something there that the tribe has latched onto in distinguishing demon-possession from its absence. But it will not show that the practices in which the concept of demon-possession fits are therefore fully reasonable, let alone morally justified. The anthropologists might have reason to conclude that although the tribe is right in holding that people are sometimes possessed by demons, its practices of painful exorcism (for instance) are rationally without point and morally repugnant. Alternatively, the anthropologists might have become so assimilated into the life of the tribe that they fully appreciate the great value of its practices relating to demon-possession, and thus greet with great relief the discovery that demon-possession is indeed naturally well founded! The crucial point is just this: Overcoming skepticism about the natural possibility of demon-possession leaves open a whole range of further questions about whether the practices that give demon-possession its significance are either rationally or morally justified.

I hope the analogy is clear. In fact, if we substitute ourselves for the tribe, and for the anthropologists, a group of Martians for whom our ethics is utterly foreign, the analogy is virtually exact. To justify the rationality of our ethical practices in assigning moral responsibility we need to show that the basic concepts we use are naturally well founded. A CTA analysis satisfies this requirement for the concept of action by showing that it is reasonable to take a certain set of conditions as providing the natural correlates of agency. If the Martians share our event-causal ontology, the CTA analysis will assure them that our talk of actions as a real category is not fanciful. However, the Martians might still doubt whether it is reasonable for us to give this distinction the importance it has in our ethical practice – and so, of course might we.

Even granted our moral acculturation, and our practical (if not theoretical) knowledge of what the ethical point of the distinction between action and nonaction is meant to be, there is always room for critical evaluation of the reasonableness and value of continuing to give the distinction this kind of point. A full vindication of our ethical perspective, as I called it at the outset, would need to respond to all the challenges generated by such a critical evaluation. A defense of the Causal Theory of Action, however, does not purport to offer such a full vindication. It addresses itself only to *one kind* of doubt about whether it is reasonable for us to employ our notions of moral responsibility as we do. It seeks to deal with the suspicion that our ethical perspective is irrational *because it is inconsistent with a proper understanding of ourselves as part of the natural causal order.* Indeed, it focuses on one specific form that suspicion may take – namely, skepticism about the accommodation of genuine exercises of an agent's control within the natural causal order. But as I have sought to argue, it is just this kind of skepticism that underlies the most serious metaphysical concerns about the rationality of our ethical perspective. Effectively then, an acceptable Causal Theory of Action (built, as it must be, on a suitably naturalist account of intentionality) provides our practice of assigning moral responsibility with as much *metaphysical* vindication as it could require.

NOTES

1 See my earlier discussion, in Chapter 3.
2 Here compare Myles Brand, *Intending and Acting: Toward a Naturalized Action Theory* (Cambridge, Mass.: M.I.T. Press, 1984), p. 31, who makes the mistake

of supposing that for every action to be intentional, it would be necessary that every action should be planned. The possibility of subconscious intentions is readily admissible now that the doctrine of direct, privileged (and even on some views, infallible) access to the "contents of one's mind" is out of fashion – and for good reason. See, for example, Patricia Smith Churchland, *Neurophilosophy: Toward a Unified Science of the Mind-Brain* (Cambridge, Mass.: M.I.T. Press, 1986), pp. 305–10.

3 Gilbert Ryle, *The Concept of Mind* (London: Hutchinson, 1949), chap. III, §(2).

4 Hugh McCann, "Volition and Basic Action," *Philosophical Review*, **83**, (1974), 451–73, p. 463, has argued that "unlike acts of moving a finger or flexing a muscle, thoughts do not have results," where the notion of the result of an action is used in von Wright's technical sense (see Chapter 3, footnote 20). If McCann's argument were correct, CTA-BI could not apply to basic intentional mental actions since it requires that the appropriate basic intention cause an outcome that instantiates the intrinsic event-type (i.e., result) of the intended action. However, McCann's argument is unconvincing: To take an example that he considers, why can we not say that the event-type intrinsic to the mental action of "my intentionally thinking of the number 1" is "the number 1's occurring to me"? This type of event is surely necessary but not sufficient for my performance of the mental action of thinking of the number 1 in just the same way that my arm's going up is necessary but not sufficient for me to perform the intentional action of raising my arm. Of course, in the case of peripheral bodily intentional actions, the intrinsic event-type is usually readily given a physical description, whereas this is much more difficult with central mental intentional actions. We do not know, in general, what it is in physical terms for the number 1 to occur to me, whereas we do know in these terms what it is for my arm to go up.

5 Brand, *Intending and Acting*, p. 33.

6 Ibid., p. 35.

7 Ibid., chaps. 7–9.

8 Ibid., p. 202.

9 Ibid., p. 237.

10 See Myles Brand, "The Fundamental Question in Action Theory," *Nous*, **13** (1979), 131–51.

11 Here compare my earlier remarks in Chapter 4 about Goldman's proposal for dealing with causal deviance.

12 Here compare Margaret Boden, "The Structure of Intentions," *Minds and Mechanisms: Philosophical Psychology and Computational Models* (Hassocks, England: Harvester Press, 1981), p. 146:

> Psychology can have nothing to say on the question of how intentions are activated. If intentions are to be executed . . . bodily control must be passed to them so that action-plans are realized in effective operations – much as executive control in a computer is continually passed to specific sections of the program. The electronic mechanisms which make this possible in cybernetic systems are known, whereas the neurophysiological processes performing the analogous function in human brains are not. Psychology takes it for granted that this can happen, for an intention is by definition a mental phenomenon which can control behaviour, but psychology as such cannot explain how it comes about.

13 William G. Lycan, *Consciousness* (Cambridge, Mass.: M.I.T. Press, 1987), p. 71.

14 For a useful survey of the prospects for natural realism about intentional states, see J. A. Fodor, "Fodor's Guide to Mental Representation: The Intelligent Auntie's Vade-Mecum," *Mind*, **94** (1985), 76–100. An interesting defense of causal realism with respect to the intentional states of folk psychology is offered

by Terence Horgan and James Woodward, "Folk Psychology Is Here to Stay,"
Philosophical Review, **94** (1985), 197–226.

15 It is, of course, a major project to specify what is required beyond mere agency
for full moral responsibility. For a useful discussion, see Daniel Dennett, "Conditions of Personhood," *Brainstorms: Philosophical Essays on Mind and Psychology*,
(Hassocks, England: Harvester Press, 1979), 267–85.

16 I owe the suggestion for this analogy to Tim Pitt-Payne.

Bibliography

Anscombe, G. E. M. 1957. *Intention.* Oxford, England: Blackwell.
———. 1983. "The Causation of Action." In Carl Ginet and Sydney Shoemaker (eds.), *Knowledge and Mind: Philosophical Essays.* Oxford, England: Oxford University Press 174–90.
Armstrong, David. 1981. *The Nature of Mind.* Ithaca, N.Y.: Cornell University Press.
Audi, Robert. 1986. "Acting for Reasons." *Philosophical Review* 95: 511–46.
Bach, Kent. 1978. "A Representational Theory of Action." *Philosophical Studies* 34: 361–79.
Bennett, Jonathan. 1976. *Linguistic Behavior.* Cambridge, England: Cambridge University Press.
———. 1984. "Counterfactuals and Temporal Direction." *Philosophical Review* 93: 57–91.
Bishop, John. 1980. "More Thought on Thought and Talk." *Mind* 89: 1–16.
———. 1981. "Peacocke on Intentional Action." *Analysis* 41: 92–8.
———. 1983. "Agent-Causation." *Mind* 92: 61–79.
———. 1986. "Is Agent-Causality a Conceptual Primitive?" *Synthèse* 67: 225–47.
———. 1987. "Sensitive and Insensitive Responses to Deviant Action." *Australasian Journal of Philosophy* 65: 452–69.
———. 1987. "Thought, Action and the Natural Order." In D. Perkins, J. Lochhead, and J. Bishop (eds.), *Thinking: The Second International Conference.* Philadelphia: Lawrence Erlbaum 3–18.
Boden, Margaret. 1981. "The Structure of Intentions." In *Minds and Mechanisms: Philosophical Psychology and Computational Models.* Hassocks, England: Harvester Press.
Brand, Myles. 1979. "The Fundamental Question in Action Theory." *Nous* 13: 131–51.
———. 1984. *Intending and Acting: Toward a Naturalized Action Theory.* Cambridge, Mass.: M.I.T. Press.
Bratman, Michael. 1979. "Practical Reasoning and Weakness of Will." *Nous* 13: 153–71.
Broad, C. D. 1952. "Determinism, Indeterminism and Libertarian-

ism." In *Ethics and the History of Philosophy*. London: Routledge & Kegan Paul.

Chisholm, Roderick M. 1966. "Freedom and Action." In Keith Lehrer (ed.), *Freedom and Determinism*. New York: Random House 11–44.

Churchland, Patricia Smith. 1986. *Neurophilosophy: Toward a Unified Science of the Mind-Brain*. Cambridge, Mass.: M.I.T. Press.

Churchland, Paul M. 1981. "Eliminative Materialism and the Propositional Attitudes." *Journal of Philosophy* 78: 67–90.

Danto, Arthur. 1965. "Basic Actions." *American Philosophical Quarterly* 2: 141–8.

Davidson, Donald. 1980. *Essays on Actions and Events*. Oxford, England: Clarendon Press.

————. 1984. *Inquiries into Truth and Interpretation*. Oxford, England: Clarendon Press.

Davies, Martin. 1983. "Function in Perception." *Australasian Journal of Philosophy* 61: 409–26.

Dawkins, Richard. 1982. *The Extended Phenotype*. New York: W. H. Freeman.

Dennett, Daniel C. 1979. *Brainstorms: Philosophical Essays on Mind and Psychology*. Hassocks, England: Harvester Press.

————. 1981. "Three Kinds of Intentional Psychology." In Richard Healey (ed.), *Reduction, Time and Reality*. Cambridge, England: Cambridge University Press 37–61.

————. 1984. *Elbow Room: The Varieties of Free Will Worth Wanting*. Oxford, England: Clarendon Press.

————. 1984. "I Could Not Have Done Otherwise — So What?" *Journal of Philosophy* 81: 553–65.

Fischer, John Martin. 1982. "Responsibility and Control." *Journal of Philosophy* 79: 24–40.

————. 1983. "Incompatibilism." *Philosophical Studies* 43: 127–37.

Flint, Thomas P. 1987. "Compatibilism and the Argument from Unavoidability." *Journal of Philosophy* 84: 423–40.

Fodor, J. A. 1975. *The Language of Thought*. New York: Crowell.

————. 1985. "Fodor's Guide to Mental Representation: The Intelligent Auntie's Vade-Mecum." *Mind* 94: 76–100.

Føllesdal, Dagfinn. 1980. "Explanation of Action." In R. Hilpinen (ed.), *Rationality and Science*. Dordrecht, Holland: D. Reidel 231–47.

Frankfurt, Harry. 1969. "Alternate Possibilities and Moral Responsibility." *Journal of Philosophy* 66: 829–39.

————. 1978. "The Problem of Action." *American Philosophical Quarterly* 15: 157–62.

Gallois, André. 1977. "Van Inwagen on Free Will and Determinism." *Philosophical Studies* 32: 99–105.

Ginet, Carl. 1966. "Might We Have No Choice?" In Keith Lehrer, (ed.), *Freedom and Determinism*. New York: Random House 87–104.

Goldman, Alvin. 1970. *A Theory of Human Action*. Englewood Cliffs, N.J.: Prentice-Hall.

Hardy, Steven. 1984. "Robot Control Systems." In Tim O'Shea and Marc Eisenstadt (eds.), *Artificial Intelligence: Tools, Techniques and Applications*. New York: Harper & Row 178–91.

Heinaman, Robert. 1986. "Incompatibilism Without the Principle of Alternative Possibilities." *Australasian Journal of Philosophy* 64: 266–76.

Hempel, Carl G. 1965. "Aspects of Scientific Explanation." In *Aspects of Scientific Explanation and Other Essays in the Philosophy of Science*. New York: Macmillan 331–496.

Horgan, Terence. 1985. "Compatibilism and the Consequence Argument." *Philosophical Studies* 47: 339–56.

Horgan, Terence, and James Woodward. 1985. "Folk Psychology Is Here to Stay." *Philosophical Review* 94: 197–226.

Lamb, James. 1977. "On a Proof of Incompatibilism," *Philosophical Review* 86: 20–35.

Le Catt, Bruce. 1982. "Censored Vision," *Australasian Journal of Philosophy*. 60: 158–62.

Lehrer, Keith. 1980. "Preferences, Conditionals and Freedom." In Peter van Inwagen (ed.), *Time and Cause*. Dordrecht, Holland: D. Reidel 187–201.

———. 1981. "Self-Profile." In R. J. Bogdan (ed.), *Keith Lehrer* Dordrecht, Holland: D. Reidel 3–104.

Lewis, David. 1973. "Causation." *Journal of Philosophy* 70: 556–67.

———. 1979. "Counterfactual Dependence and Time's Arrow." *Nous* 13: 455–76.

———. 1980. "Veridical Hallucination and Prosthetic Vision." *Australasian Journal of Philosophy* 58: 239–49.

———. 1981. "Are We Free to Break the Laws?" *Theoria* 47: 113–21.

Lycan, William G. 1981. "Toward a Homuncular Theory of Believing." *Cognition and Brain Theory* 4: 139–59.

———. 1987. *Consciousness*. Cambridge, Mass.: M.I.T. Press.

MacKay, D. M. 1978. "Selves and Brains." *Neuroscience* 3: 599–606.

———. 1983. "Seeing the Wood and the Trees." In William Maxwell (ed.), *Thinking: The Expanding Frontier*. Philadelphia: Franklin Institute Press 5–12.

McCall, Storrs. 1984. "Freedom Defined as the Power to Decide." *American Philosophical Quarterly* 21: 329–38.

McCann, Hugh. 1974. "Volition and Basic Action." *Philosophical Review* 83: 451–73.

———. 1974–5. "Trying, Paralysis and Volitions." *Review of Metaphysics* 28: 423–42.

Mitchell, Dorothy. 1982. "Deviant Causal Chains." *American Philosophical Quarterly* 19: 351–3.

Montmarquet, James. 1982. "Causal Deviancy and Multiple Intentions." *Analysis* 42: 106–10.

Moore, G. E. 1912. *Ethics*. Oxford, England: Oxford University Press.

Morton, Adam. 1975. "Because He Thought He Had Insulted Him." *Journal of Philosophy* 72: 5–15.

Nagel, Ernest. 1977. "Teleology Revisited." *Journal of Philosophy* 74: 261–301.

Nagel, Thomas. 1979. *Mortal Questions*. Cambridge, England: Cambridge University Press.

———. 1986. *The View from Nowhere*. Oxford, England: Oxford University Press.

Peacocke, Christopher. 1979. *Holistic Explanation: Action, Space, Interpretation*. Oxford, England: Clarendon Press.

Pettit, Philip. 1986. "Broad-Minded Explanation and Psychology." In P. Pettit and J. McDowell (eds.), *Subject, Thought and Context*. Oxford, England: Clarendon Press 17–58.

Putnam, Hilary. 1967. "The Nature of Mental States." In W. H. Capitan and D. D. Merrill (eds), *Art, Mind and Religion*. Pittsburgh: University of Pittsburgh Press 37–48.

Rorty, Amélie. 1983. "Akratic Believers." *American Philosophical Quarterly* 20: 175–84.

Ryle, Gilbert. 1949. *The Concept of Mind*. London: Hutchinson.

Searle, John. 1979. "The Intentionality of Intention and Action." *Inquiry* 22: 253–80.

Segerberg, Krister. 1982. "Could Have but Did Not," *Pacific Philosophical Quarterly* 64: 230–41.

Sellars, Wilfrid. 1968. *Science and Metaphysics*. London: Routledge & Kegan Paul.

———. 1980. "Volitions Reaffirmed." In Myles Brand and Douglas Walton (eds.), *Action Theory*. Dordrecht, Holland: D. Reidel 47–66.

Slote, Michael. 1982. "Selective Necessity and the Free Will Problem." *Journal of Philosophy* 79: 5–24.

Stoutland, Frederick. 1968. "Basic Actions and Causality." *Journal of Philosophy* 65: 467–75.

————. 1980. "Oblique Causation and Reasons for Action." *Synthèse* 43: 351–67.

————. 1986. "Davidson on Intentional Behavior." In Ernest LePore and Brian McLaughlin (eds.), *The Philosophy of Donald Davidson: Perspectives on Essays on Actions and Events*. Oxford, England: Blackwell 44–59.

Taylor, Richard. 1963. *Metaphysics*. Englewood Cliffs, N.J.: Prentice-Hall.

————. 1966. *Action and Purpose*. Englewood Cliffs, N.J.: Prentice-Hall.

Thalberg, Irving. 1984. "Do Our Intentions Cause Our Intentional Actions?" *American Philosophical Quarterly* 21: 249–60.

Thorp, John. 1980. *Free Will: A Defence against Neurophysiological Determinism*. London: Routledge & Kegan Paul.

Tuomela, Raimo. 1977. *Human Action and Its Explanation*. Dordrecht, Holland: D. Reidel.

————. 1986. "Explanation of Action." In G. Fløistad (ed.), *Contemporary Philosophy: A New Survey,* Vol. 3 The Hague: Martinus Nijhoff 15–43.

Van Inwagen, Peter. 1975. "The Incompatibility of Free Will and Determinism." *Philosophical Studies* 27: 185–99.

————. 1983. *An Essay on Free Will*. Oxford, England: Clarendon Press.

————. 1984. "Reply to Dennett." *Journal of Philosophy* 81: 565–7.

————. 1985. "Compatibilistic Reflections." *Australasian Journal of Philosophy* 63: 349–53.

Vihvelin, Kadri. 1988. "The Modal Argument for Incompatibilism." *Philosophical Studies* 53: 227–44.

Von Wright, G. H. 1971. *Explanation and Understanding*. London: Routledge & Kegan Paul.

Watson, Gary. (ed.). 1982. *Free Will*. Oxford, England: Oxford University Press.

Wiggins, David. 1973. "Towards a Reasonable Libertarianism." In Ted Honderich (ed.), *Essays on Freedom of Action*. London: Routledge & Kegan Paul 31–61.

Wittgenstein, Ludwig. 1972. *Philosophical Investigations,* 3rd ed. (G. E. M. Anscombe, trans.) Oxford, England: Blackwell.

Woodfield, Andrew. 1976. *Teleology*. Cambridge, England: Cambridge University Press.

Index

References to notes are indicated by a number in parentheses preceded by *n* following the page number.